EAR TRAINING FOR
THE BODY

Sean P. Murphy

EAR TRAINING FOR THE BODY

A Dancer's Guide to Music

by
Katherine Teck

A Dance Horizons Book
Princeton Book Company, Publishers
Pennington, NJ

A Dance Horizons Book
Princeton Book Company, Publishers
P.O. Box 57
Pennington, NJ 08534

Cover design by Frank Bridges
Cover art by Jeroen Henneman
Interior design by Donna Wickes

Library of Congress Cataloging-in-Publication Data

Teck, Katherine.
    Ear training for the body : a dancer's guide to music / by
Katherine Teck.
        p.   cm.
    "A Dance Horizons book."
    Includes bibliographical references and index.
    ISBN 0-87127-192-3
    1. Music and dance.   2. Music—Theory.   3. Ear training.
I. Title.
ML3460.T38   1993
781'.0247928—dc20   93-4805

CONTENTS

APPENDIXES   263

PREFACE

Ear Training for the Body: A Dancer's Guide to Music is intended both as a textbook for introductory courses in music offered within college dance departments and as a book that dancers can read on their own. In any case, the goals are to add expressivity and accuracy to dancers' technical work in class, to enhance the artistry of performers onstage, and to enlarge choreographers' palettes of musical possibilities for their new works—whether these are full-scale theatrical productions or more modest projects for a workshop or improvisation class.

By using this book as a guide, dancers can also expect to:

- improve their listening skills;
- expand their knowledge of musical elements, terminology, and procedures;
- explore various methods of combining music and movement for theatrical dance;
- learn the basics of musical notation and how to scan musical scores for information pertinent to dance performance;
- broaden their acquaintance with contemporary styles as well as with music from the past and from other cultures;
- know how to go about finding appropriate existing music for choreographic projects;
- feel more comfortable in communicating their musical needs— to studio instrumentalists, conductors, performing ensembles, and collaborating composers;
- experience deeper aural and visual awareness when attending performances by other dancers;

- develop personal tastes in musical collaboration for theatrical dance;
- consider practical and affordable ways to include the excitement of live music in dance performances;
- enjoy new approaches to experimenting with movement and sound.

This text is not intended for sedentary listeners. Most of all, the book is intended as a guide for exploration. It is expected that readers will experiment physically with various ways of relating movement to musical sounds. The fundamental approaches presented here can be effective for students with varying backgrounds in music and dance, and can be applied to many theatrical styles.

Acknowledgements

Some of the material presented in this book was gathered during personal interviews with outstanding artists in the field of dance, including dancers, choreographers, and educators, as well as collaborative instrumentalists, conductors, and composers. In addition, as documented in the Notes, the author was able to observe many studio classes, rehearsals, and showings not normally open to the public.

The book owes a great deal to encouragement and suggestions from members of the International Guild of Musicians in Dance. Special thanks go to Richard Cameron-Wolfe, who gave a close reading to an early manuscript draft and raised many questions concerning the definitions of terms. Thanks also for general advice from Beth Mehocic, Lisa Mestre, Norma Reynolds Freestone, and Gwendolyn Watson.

Special appreciation is extended to William Moulton for his inspiring vision and efforts as founding president of the guild, and to Elina Lampinen, president of the European branch of the organization. It should be emphasized that dancers are welcome to attend guild workshops and jointly explore various facets of collaboration.

At this writing, I have just returned from a Florida conference during which a particularly pertinent experiment was conducted by William Moulton. Guild members were instructed to lie on the floor, listen to a wide-ranging variety of live improvisations on the piano and cello, and to be aware of where *in their bodies* the participants were having kinesthetic sensations of the sounds. The reported results seemed rather extraordinary, especially coming from experienced musical collaborators for dance. Moulton's point was well made: that good musical collaborators identify deeply, in a physical way, with the movement of dancers.

It is the premise of this book that the reverse is also true: good dancers identify deeply, in a kinesthetic way, with the sounds of music, and can benefit by increasing their knowledge and understanding of this related art.

Ear Training for the Body would not have come into being without the patient guidance of Charles H. Woodford. Many thanks to him, and to Debi Elfenbein, Roxanne Barrett, and David Schechter for editorial suggestions in molding the final version. The musical examples were prepared by Randa Kirshbaum.

The book is dedicated to all students who get up every morning and take a dance class.

part one

MUSICALITY IN THE DANCER'S ART

I think that, with intelligent appreciation, any student can develop certain sensitivities to music that will improve the quality of her dancing immeasurably.

—George Balanchine

chapter 1

PRACTICING MUSICALITY
IN CLASS

E*ach student's progress toward professionalism is*
inextricably related to his or her understanding of music.

—School of American Ballet catalog

The most obvious reason for dancers to develop a keen awareness of specific musical events is so that they can recognize aural cues during onstage performances. To put it bluntly: If performers cannot quickly sense and remember what they should be doing in relation to the music, they will have a tough time making it in the dance world.

For performing dancers, musicality is often the deciding factor in who gets chosen during auditions, and it certainly separates the consummate artist from the multitude.

For students, an increased awareness of how one relates to the music in class helps with the mastery of difficult technical exercises.

For dance educators, musical ingredients often make or break a class.

For choreographers, the choice of musical components contributes strongly to the stamp of an individual style that attracts audiences.

What Is Musicality?

This quality in dance seems to be something that emanates from every muscle of the dancer's body. It is not something that can be measured precisely, like the angle of turnout or the height of a jump. But it is there to various degrees, or else conspicuously lacking, in all dancing. One definition was attempted by the critic George Dorris:

> When a critic calls [anyone] a musical dancer or points out . . . an unmusical choreographer, he is talking about qualities which are not simply matters of opinion, any more than they are just matters of technique or inventiveness, but which can influence one's emotional reaction far more than a wobbly arabesque or awkward transition. Of course sometimes those with limited technical equipment can compensate by musicality, as by strong personal projection, but in a dancer's prime, musicality shouldn't be confused with technical inadequacy. It is, rather, a way of shaping a role or a ballet so that it seems to interact with the music, each supporting the other, until dance, dancer, and music become one.
>
> It is easier to define musicality negatively. The dancer who always comes in on the beat is not necessarily musical, nor even the choreographer who always starts the dance phrase with the musical phrase. The former may be merely correct and the latter merely academic. The truly musical dancer and choreographer can use rhythm and phrasing far more subtly than that. Such musicality is not a simple matter of "feeling the music," either, for no one can know whether someone else is "feeling" or not. . . . The ability to make visible one's understanding of the music is an even rarer quality than having such understanding.[1]

It has been proven countless times by modern dancers that movement can be a complete expressive art in itself. Dance does not require musical companionship in order to present a satisfying whole, and one does not need to imagine music when it is not there. A classic example of the sufficiency of unaccompanied movement is Doris Humphrey's *Water Study*. The choreographer wished to have natural phrases instead of rigorously counted measures, and went on to comment:

> So the original point, that dancing can stand alone, has been proved over and over, but the main virtue of the silent dance is its power to simplify concentration and rest the ear. After a section or a whole dance with no music, sound is new again and fresher than if it had been continuous.[2]

The quality of musicality can be present even when there is an absence of either regular measured pulsation or music itself.

An example of this last point was the 1992 choreographic setting by Eliot Feld of the *Four Last Songs* by Richard Strauss. Feld had long loved this music, and he molded his ballet with specific reference to both the structure and nuances of the composition. Unfortunately, performance rights had not been cleared and the composer's estate refused permission for this choreographic use. Consequently, Feld's *Endsong* was presented in silence. Yet the dance retained its qualities of musicality.

Focusing on Sound

Paying attention to musicality is not something that dancers can afford to put off until rehearsals and performances. Sensitivity to music is an asset for all a dancer's efforts. For example, if students can keep part of their attention focused on the sounds heard during technique classes, they may experience the sensation of riding the music the way a surfer rides ocean waves.

There are many ways in which movement and music can relate. It is not enough for people to say, "Dance with the music," or, "You are not *with* the music." If you are supposed to be with the music, you might ask, "To which aspect am I relating? Is it the timing, the melody, the articulations, the patterns of the underlying accompaniment texture, the structure, the nuances, the expressive nature? And *how* am I to be with it? Or what if my movement is supposed to be a contrast to the music?"

In Ballet Class

Suki Schorer began teaching classes at the School of American Ballet even while she was a principal dancer for New York City Ballet. She has evolved a series of technical exercises that combine different kinds of articulations, movements, and patterns of energy release, all at the fast pace needed to execute the Balanchine choreography, which some of the students will perform if they are chosen as apprentices for the company.[3]

In Schorer's classes, even opening pliés include several changes of pace, and this type of challenge continues right through the morning's final pirouettes and leaps. She underscores the importance of changes of tempo and accent in the students' training: "Mostly what happens in class is learning how to incorporate the tempo or the changes of the rhythm into their bodies. Each step has its own timing and phrasing."

This master teacher cautions her students against anticipating the music: "If the music gets fast, there is a tendency for the dancers to rush. That was my tendency, and Mr. Balanchine worked with me to stay back. Especially if there are a lot of notes involved in the musical piece, it makes the dancer a little nervous."

What Balanchine did to counteract this tendency was to go to the piano himself and play chords interspersed with long counts of silences. "We had to internalize the tempo. You would see if you rushed, whether you could really hold on to the tempo. Each space *in between* chords was to be equal."

Contrasting the more intense musical concentration required in rehearsals, Schorer suggests:

> *When you get a ballet, you listen to the music. If it is Bach, is there a lilt to it? And if so, how are you going to put that in a lilty step? Then you should listen to the music and know that music. This is a different kind of musicality, and you are not really going to work that way in class. A class is to brush your teeth, to clean up and perfect your technique.*

In the SAB students' weekly music classes, they focus on recognizing rhythms and meters. They learn notation, take dictation, and practice basic keyboard skills as an introduction to harmony. Their teacher, Jeffrey Middleton, observes:

> *I am surprised at how it is a different way of thinking for the dance students to do a rhythm really together, what an upbeat feels like, what rhythmic groupings feel like. This study is a different way of experiencing rhythm, and it is a chance for the dance students to understand what it is they do musically in movement. Up until now, all of their experience is purely from the physical point. They learn what rhythm feels like in their bodies; they move with it. Notation is something at first very foreign to them, until they connect it to their ears and then to their bodies. Going through the intellectual reasoning is a different avenue towards the same goal, a way of understanding rhythm in a deeper way.*

Practical Pointers
for Technical Classwork

Musicians who provide supportive and impelling music for technique exercises also learn what separates musically sensitive dancers from students who are less sensitive musically. The following suggestions were gleaned from comments made by dozens of experienced studio pianists and percussionists.[4] For the most part, the principles apply equally well to ballet, modern, and jazz styles.

During demonstrations, establish an accurate sense of the underlying beat. Move your body in some way to gear into this, perhaps with just a small physical pulsation in your knees, shoulders, arms, or toes. The closer this sensation is to your innermost torso, the better. Continue the physical pulsation until you are sure it is steady. Immediately transfer the timing of the beat to an inner pulse, which should continue throughout the exercise. Listen to the music and gear in with the timing of its flow. The exact pace of the pulsations, or beats, is your speedometer. In both music and dance, this is called *tempo*.

Notice the patterns of subdivision of the dancers' counts and the groupings of pulsed beats. There will often be a regularity to the way time is divided between the main counts given by the teacher. Perhaps there will be two less prominent pulsations; perhaps three or four, or five. In any case, especially in initial exercises of a class, the music is most apt to provide a constant flow of energy with some kind of regularity in the way the time between main counts is divided.

Sometimes the dance instructor will give a clue to these subdivisions by verbal singsong or counting. "One-and, two-and" would suggest that there is a subdivision precisely midway in the time allotted between count one and count two. This is called *duple* timing.

Similarly, if the instructor says "One-and-ah, two-and-ah," with each syllable evenly articulated, you may be prepared for triplets, a division of each major count into three equal subdivisions. Additionally, it can be noted that sometimes dance teachers count triplets by inserting a pause after the first sound: "One—and, two—and." This gives a kind of swinging impression, with a temporary sustaining of both energy and movement after each count due to the silent center segment of time.

Occasionally it may help to mimic mentally what you hear as the main points of timing in the music: "YAH-di-dah, YAH-di-dah," "BUM-bum, BUM-bum," "tick-a-tick-a, tick-a-tick-a," or whatever other syllables work for you to keep an awareness of both the main pulsations and the constant flow of the time in between.

Listen carefully to the musical introduction, even if it is only two beats. Some teachers in both ballet and contemporary styles do not make use of a musical introduction. Instead, the pianist may simply play two chords, or the percussionist strike two beats. In such cases, dancers must gear into the two pulses. But a longer introduction may serve as a clue to the expressive aspects of a combination and should establish the exact tempo of the exercise that follows.

Many ballet teachers use the musical introduction to have dancers execute their own opening preparation, particularly for barre and center combinations. The initial movements may include a port de bras, a positioning of the legs, a subtle shift in the angle at which the head is held, or a change in the focus of the eyes. Students can execute even these initial preparatory movements with awareness of the music.

With faster or more virtuosic movements—such as jumps or pirouettes—preparation is particularly crucial. Many performers find that a habit of paying attention to the music also helps form muscular habits so that they conclude a pirouette or jump in syncronization with the music as well.

Particularly in fast traveling movements, the preparations are of primary importance. To present an audience with the impression of being with the beat, dancers may have to focus their own attention upon being slightly *before* the beat. However, as noted by Schorer, the tendency in allegro work is often for dancers to arrive too soon.

In flowing exercises, ration your energy to keep the rate of movement proportional to the sections of the music. Advanced combinations often include many kinds of movements and energy shapes, each with a distinctive flow or thrust. However, at less advanced levels, the flow within many individual exercises is more apt to be consistent. For example, the flow of pliés may be nonstop, with changes of direction intended to coincide with the main counts of the music, and the movement in between unfolding in direct proportion to the timing of the music. In such exercises, try not to arrive at any count too soon (which might necessitate the insertion of a pause or held pose as you wait for the music to catch up). If you find yourself arriving too soon at what sounds like the musical equivalent of punctuation in verbal language, slow the basic speed at which you are doing the exercise. Conversely, if you are arriving at the musical check-points late, speed up your movement flow.

With sharply articulated movements, notice the goal or highlighted moment of a thrust, and the way in which energy is released to arrive at a pose that is to be held for an instant. In contrast to flowing movements, exercises such as frappé in ballet, or any jutting motion in other styles, often have an instant of *accent*, or emphasis upon the arrival at a certain point in the physical exercise. Frappé is a good example, for you can accent the ''out'' (farthest point of extension), or you can accent the ''in'' (arrival next to the standing leg). In either case, there is a quick burst of energy followed by a brief moment of holding a pose.

Acknowledge the punctuation that indicates the conclusion of musical sections called phrases. Sometimes all that is needed is a breath or a change in the focus of the eyes. Sometimes the acknowledgement will be purely mental if the movement combination was devised to go across the end of a musical section.

In introductory and intermediate dance technique classes, how-ever, a closer relationship between the sections of the music and the sections of the movement patterns is more likely. This holds true for much jazz dance, and is particularly clear in classical ballet. The music used for ballet exercises is usually tailored to partner the structure of the dance combination's counts precisely. Traditionally, ballet phrases are in eight counts, and so are the phrases in the music. Phrases are the equivalent of complete statements or sentences in the structure of verbal language. The structural sections of music will be explored in greater depth in Part Two, but for now, it is enough to notice that eight-count phrases are very common in European and American folk and classical music, as well as in American popular songs and show dances.

In contemporary styles of theatrical music and dance, the counts of the phrases are less apt to be so even. If you are taking modern dance technique now, you probably are expected to remember asymmetrical phrase combinations of five, seven, nine, and eleven counts, as well as symmetrical counts.

Hold a pose or delay a movement slightly to add emphasis. This is analogous to what musicians call an *agogic accent,* an emphasis created by timing rather than force. Masterful dance artists are able to create unusual illusions of defying gravity by maintaining a pose at the peak of a leap for even the slightest instant in time. This adds emphasis to that particular energy shape of a movement pattern. Obviously, this is difficult to do in full flight, but is something dancers can practice while more earthbound.

Retaining a pose at the end of a phrase, or particularly at the end of a dance, also emphasizes the conclusion and provides the audience with a brief sensation of after-image. In addition, if dancers have successfully concluded a strenuous and difficult series of leaps and turns, sustaining a final pose is the cue for the audience to burst into thunderous applause! This can be practiced during technique classes. Hold your pose for an instant after each exercise. Finish your phrases with the music.

One final pose that is usually given particular attention during classes is the sustained relevé. This is an opportunity for dancers to concentrate quietly upon regathering their energy. Do not come down from the relevé by crumbling. Your descent can be controlled, and you are not done until your feet are on the floor again. A controlled, definite sense of ending is a great asset to theatrical dancers onstage, and is certainly an important ingredient of musicality.

Recognize whether or not the goal of the moment is synchronization with the entire class. It is both surprising and understandable that among the most unsynchronized-looking classes are those given for some professional ballet companies. These artists are under pressure to produce onstage. Some performers may be recovering from injuries; others may need to conserve energy for days when both rehearsals and performances follow the technique class. Consequently, some of the shining stars onstage may have moments in class when their movements seem to have little or only vague relationships to what most everybody else is doing. And maybe no one's movements have much to do with the music during initial warmup exercises.

However, for the student and the emerging dance artist, value is to be gained by regarding every exercise as a performance. If everybody in the class pays attention to timing, a lineup of young dancers at the barre doing everyday pliés can become a conbination of beauty, interest, and expressivity.

It should be noted that it is not always a good idea to mimic the leader at the end of the barre lineup or in the center of the studio. An entire class may be off the mark in relation to the music. So if you sense a musical relationship strongly, it doesn't hurt to move according to your convictions, in class. Differences in the way the music is experienced by individual dancers can be discussed by the class. In the context of rehearsals and some performances, of course, synchronization of dancers' movements in relation to the music assumes a more critical importance.

Be aware of how the eyes are focused. The expressive focusing of the eyes—or deliberate nonfocusing—is a major element in the creation of a style that means something. For instance, the late choreographer Alwin Nikolais stressed one possible style by discouraging students in his workshops from always allowing their eyes to follow the extended movements of their arms. In classical ballet, it is more usual for the focus of the eyes to coordinate closely with the impetus of the limbs. If you have achieved a perfect développé, for example, the conquest over gravity could be spoiled by looking down instead of boldly facing the audience. Similarly, the extended line of an arabesque can seem to be extended by a gaze that follows the angle of the arms, again coordinated with the music.

Expressive qualities are often a result of physical coordination. Even in everyday tendu combinations, the overall impression of musicality has a tremendous amount to do with the coordination of arms, hands, legs, and head in connection with the focus of the eyes. Ideally all of this has some relation to the phrasing in the music, too.

This is not to suggest that you inject extraneous emotion or dramatic pantomime. On the contrary: If the relationship of the music and the movement (as set by the choreographer) is observed closely, emotional nuance will often follow naturally. The first step consists simply of deciding to become more aware of the nuances in the music. You must turn some attention to listening, and hear what is actually there. Your expressiveness will then come through more easily in a performance.[5]

Explorations and Assignments

1. For class discussion, make a list of your own musical experiences. Include instruments played, any study of rudiments or theory during elementary and high school, musical concerts attended, music that appealed to you in a dance context, your own current tastes in music for theatrical and social dance, and favorite pieces and songs.

2. Who are some professional dancers you personally consider most musical? Why? What would you like to gain from the study of music, in relation to your dancing? What are your goals as a dancer, and what needs do you foresee in relation to your knowledge of music?

3. How do you listen to music when you are dancing? Is this different from the experience of listening in other contexts? How do you experience the music in technique class? Does it help your efforts or confuse things? Explain.

4. In music class, each student could present one basic combination from a daily technique class, along with appropriate music. Discuss the timing of the movements in relation to the timing of the music. Consider the aspects covered in the chapter: focus, using all the time, preparation, synchronization, endings of phrases, points of articulation, differentiation of sharpness and smooth flow, and expressive nuance.

chapter 2

BODY PERCUSSION
AND MOUTH MUSIC

The challenge to the human race is always to see what is.
That is the challenge to our dance today—to challenge all
basic premises and partial intuitions so that we don't limit
ourselves in our own exploration of our human possibilities,
until the day we die.

—Erick Hawkins

In connection with students' efforts to inject musicality into their dancing, it can be helpful to experience various kinds of music making directly.

To dance artists, the instrument of choreographers is the human
body. What most children know, but other people often seem to forget,
is that in addition to our potential instruments for dance, we all carry
our own musical instruments around in the form of our bodies. While
professional percussionists may take hours to set up for a rock concert,
our original trap sets are ready for playing at a moment's notice.

For dancers, making music by means of body percussion has the
added attraction that sounds are produced by physical motions—mostly
of the fingers, hands, and feet. Body percussion music also has the attraction of drawing upon one skill in which every accomplished dancer
must excel, namely the ability to watch a demonstration of movement
and immediately reproduce the same patterns with one's own body.

The idea of using the body as a percussion instrument is an ancient
one that continues to offer rich resources for dancer-musicians. Among
examples from professional modern dance are sections of Jawole Willa

Jo Zollar's *Girl Friends* as performed by the Urban Bush Women, and the section "A Time to Keep Silence and a Time to Speak" from José Limón's *There Is a Time.* Mark Morris's *Grand Duo,* set to a violin and piano piece by Lou Harrison, effectively uses sounds of slapping the torso as well as stomping feet.

One educator who has encouraged her dance students to explore the artistic use of body percussion is Elina Lampinen of Finland. Extending originally simple patterns both choreographically and musically, she has mounted entire performances for her group called Syrjahyppy. Many of the ideas in this chapter were inspired by Lampinen's work.[1]

Improvising with body percussion and actually practicing patterns can help dancers to become more perceptive about the details in the timing of music. Body percussion music also offers first-hand experience in structuring original pieces.

The following suggestions for explorations can be done alone or with a class of dancers. Students may wear tap shoes, sneakers, jazz shoes, ballet slippers, or other footgear. It should be mentioned that the flooring will affect the sounds produced with the feet. Bare feet on rugs can produce interesting sounds; cowboy boots on a large packing case will produce other qualities. In addition, much body percussion music can be made while sitting down.

Making Music: General Pointers

1. Music is a combination of sounds and silences.
2. The distinct patterns that are formed by various proportional lengths of sounds and silences are called *rhythms.*
3. One basic distinction in various rhythms is between *even* and *uneven* combinations. Good examples of the contrasts are the sounds made by the feet when walking or running (even), and when skipping or galloping (uneven).
4. Another basic distinction is between music that is freely timed and that which has some sort of regular pulsation or beat. If the pulsations reoccur in regular groupings, the music is termed *metric;* if pulsation and such groupings are absent, the terms *nonmetric* or *unmetered* could apply. Both methods may be employed in exploring body percussion, particularly because the timing of sound is directly controlled by the movement of the body itself; one does not have to count (although this may be a useful procedure when students teach their own regularly pulsed patterns to each other).

5. Differing tone quality, or *timbre*, can be combined with any rhythms. This is one way of making something that is easy to do seem complex. This is a basic principle of all percussion playing: Make up a simple rhythmic pattern, but divide the individual sounds among instruments of various tone qualities.

6. Much interesting music is the result of various ways of working out some relatively brief initial patterns, or *motifs*. In the case of body percussion, "brief" means only a few seconds.

7. Music is structured basically by these five processes: development, repetition, contrast, variation, and imitation.

Keeping these points in mind, dancers can devise interesting sound patterns with no reference to written notation. Everything should be felt directly in the body. Many sound patterns can be extended choreographically. In some cases, enlarged movements may necessitate slight changes in the sound patterns, or the division of the class into dancers and sound producers.

One word of caution is in order: Good sounds can be produced with a minimum of applied energy, so treat yourself kindly. Tap and slap gently, and if you are working with others, be particularly mindful of the fact that clapping doesn't mean hitting.

Percussionists usually find it helps to start learning patterns in slow motion and gradually work up speed. That's where practice comes in. Also, keep the patterns extremely brief at first, and repeat each one at least several times until it is experienced securely as a kinesthetic sensation.

AVAILABLE SOURCES OF BODY PERCUSSION SOUNDS

Hands and fingers: holding hands with flattened fingers, tap with combined ends of fingers, with the underside of the knuckles, with the palm area, or with the entire underside of the palm and fingers. Tap lightly with individual fingers. Particularly for puffed-out cheeks, it is good to hold the index and middle fingers together as drumsticks. For producing sounds from the front area of the thighs or on the stomach, hands can be cupped slightly to enhance the sounds.

Clapping: fingers on palm; two cupped hands; one hand held in place with the other moving to strike; both hands moving from the wrist and striking together only on the underside of the fingers; arms held straight out so that the shoulder is the fulcrum; both hands moving to meet in front of you, but with the forearms and hands held straight so that the elbow is the fulcrum.

The method with hands slightly cupped may be the most natural and efficient for most body percussion clapping. However, arms extended offer some good possibilities for slower-paced choreographic effects, because this can be done over the head, coming from extreme extension of second position below shoulder level, or in a movement more like a pendulum, with hands meeting to clap at thigh level.

Slaps are done straight on with the flat of the hands.

Swipes create another kind of sound, as when the hand is moved front to back or back to front on the side of the thigh but with the motion carrying through in the air.

Rubbing creates a quieter sound, with the hand not leaving the surface as it changes direction. This can be done in various timed rhythms.

Scratching, by curving the fingers and using the nails, is a good technique to keep in mind for use on textured cloth or plastic dance pants, and later, on headed drums.

Fists can be used for beating upon the chest caveman fashion. The caveat of treating oneself kindly especially applies here.

Finger snapping is a useful skill that can be incorporated into body percussion music as well as dance works.

All the preceding are methods of producing sound, with the hands acting as an equivalent of the drummer's various mallets, sticks, and brushes. The surfaces used to produce sound will be the following: Cupped hands together, puffed-out cheeks, chest, stomach, and thighs (both front and side).

Easy Moves, Nice Sounds

1. Tap the chest gently and evenly, with flat underside of the fingers: left-right, left-right. Keep it up for a few seconds.

   Switch to fist thumping, ever so gently, keeping same left-right, even rhythm.

   Next, alternate a couple of flat-finger taps with a couple of fist thumpings. Then try left hand always a fist and right hand always flat fingers. This changes the timbre to produce a distinct-sounding pattern, a *duple* grouping of two equal beats.

   To immediately create further interesting patterns, mix hand motions with different tone qualities available on other parts of the body, also taking advantage of the sounds made by clothing.

2. Continuing with the even, duple alternation, tap the thighs evenly left-right, left-right, nonstop.

At this point, some common abbreviations used by percussion players can be introduced: L = left hand; R = right hand. Additionally, a slash means that the preceding pattern should be repeated. For example: L R/ means tap left-right, left-right. There is no pause between the original pattern and the repetition; the pulsation is regular in this case. L R/// means tap four sets of left-right, nonstop.

Next, instead of always alternating hands, do this pattern, evenly slapping on the thighs so that every sound is the same length in time. Do it slowly, keeping each sound even regardless of which hand is playing. This is called the *paradiddle* in drummer's parlance: L R L L R L R R.

Next, move the left hand to the chest and play the same pattern. Because of the two tone qualities, the resultant effect is no longer that of an evenly slapped pattern; the ear somehow also becomes aware of the interrupted pattern produced on the thighs, and of that produced on the chest.

Here are the other paradiddle possibilities. Each line is a separate pattern and should be repeated a number of times, using various combinations of hand position on different parts of the body. Start slowly and work up speed:

R L R R L R L L
L R R L R R L R
R L L R L L R L

3. Sticking with even tapping, puff out the cheeks and tap lightly with underside of flat fingers: L R///

Next, insert a two-handed clap (C = clap) between each L R pair: C L R///

Transfer the pattern to a two-handed clap then chest (ch = chest) left-right.

This grouping into three equal beats can be considered in two ways: as a metric grouping of three pulses or beats; or as a *subdivision* of one beat, into a *triplet* figure.

4. For a metric grouping in fours, try:

    clap   chest R   thigh L   chest R

5. Students may want to devise their own shorthand charts for patterns. The use of pictographs could be especially clear. Elina Lampinen employs a musical staff to represent the use of the body. The method used here, however, is this:

```
  C  =  clap
 ch  =  chest
 th  =  front of thigh
sth  =  side of thigh
 pc  =  puffed cheek
  B  =  both hands
 So  =  stomach
  L  =  left hand
  R  =  right hand
```

The striking hand is indicated below the abbreviation for the body part. As an example, here is one metric grouping in fives. Try it very slowly and then speed it up:

```
C    ch   ch   th   th
B    L    R    L    R
```

6. In much traditional and concert music of the Western world, a grouping of six is more usually considered as two groups of three. So the first and fourth beats would have special emphasis, here provided by the use of both hands:

```
C    ch   ch   So   th   th
B    L    R    B    L    R
```

For greater speed, try the two sets of triplets this way:

```
th   th   th   ch   th   th
L    R    R    L    R    R
```

A grouping of six pulses can also be divided into three groups of two:

```
th   th   th   th   th   th
L    R    L    R    L    R
```

Any meter in which a measure can be divided so that a triplet functions as one longer beat is called *compound*. Meters in 6 occur frequently; those in 9 and 12, less often. In the case of sixes and twelves, the possibility of alternating between groupings of two and groupings of three provides added interest.

7. For groupings of sevens, one possibility is this, with sw = swipe:

```
C    ch   ch   sth   sth   sth   sth
B    L    R    swL   swR   swL   swR
```

The first set of thigh swipes is done front-to-back; the second set, back-to-front.

For a grouping of nine, add a pair of chest, L-R, which works nicely to bring the hands back up in position for the next initial clap:

C	ch	ch	sth	sth	sth	sth	ch	ch
B	L	R	swL	swR	swL	swR	L	R

Alternately, nine can be presented as three main beats each subdivided into a triplet:

pc	th	th	ch	th	th	th	th	th
L	R	R	L	R	R	L	R	R

8. All the preceding patterns can be repeated, but with the uneven timing of swing jazz (basically a long-short or "dah-di" sound).

Structuring Pieces

Entire musical-movement pieces can be formed by combining various brief patterns devised by students. A motif can be extended or varied in some small way; it can be introduced in follow-the-leader or *canonic* imitation, contrasted with new material, or repeated.

Musicians use alphabet letters when analyzing sections that make up a piece. The following example has only three distinct materials: **A, B,** and **C.** Remember that a slash means repeat the pattern.

For **A:**

C	ch	ch	/	/
B	L	L		

For **B:** do the following with uneven, jazz timing ("dah-di, dah-di"):

th	th	th	th
L	R	L	R

followed by two long beats:

sth	sth
swL	swR

To go back: Play **A.** Play **B.** Then repeat both **A** and **B,** then just **A.**

To wind up our piece, a *tag* or *coda* (section **C**) will be added. Use your own timing, or play the puffed-cheeks double time of those in **B** (L R twice as fast); the chest taps could be the same length as in **B.** The spacing below is an attempt to suggest the timing.

C:	pc	pc	pc	pc	ch	ch	pc	pc	pc	pc	ch	ch
	L	R	L	R	L	R	L	R	L	R	L	R

Repeat this entire pattern once.

Then, slower: So   step   step   Jump
                          B

     The overall structure of this piece is **ABABAC.**

     The above process illustrates one process of composition. It makes use of long and short sounds, different tone qualities, and distinct motifs. It presents an idea **A,** then repeats it. The **B** section gives us some contrasting sounds. The last **C** section uses some elements from **A** (namely the chest taps), but winds up with some faster-sounding notes and a definite end.

     To extend such a piece, the process of variation could be employed: Keep the same framework, but change some of the aspects—the basic tempo or speed, the tone qualities, the number of times the brief rhythmic motifs are repeated, and the rhythms that would result from changing the proportions of sounds to silences.

Verbal Frameworks and Visual Patterns

As a framework for structuring body percussion pieces, it is sometimes helpful to mimic the rhythm of poetry. Standard poetic analytical symbols of dashes and hooks can be applied, thus effectively translating any words into long and short sounds. Morse code "dahs" and "dits" also work well. Incidentally, 'the Morse code alphabet can also be used to spell different rhythms. You could also take the sound of your own spoken name and use that as the basis of a body percussion piece.

     Another source of rhythmic patterns is visual geometric space. For example, you could clap according to what you see along the wall nearest you. For a long expanse, clap once and move your arms silently until you come to a window (which might suggest four short claps for different panes of glass), and so on.

Wordless Vocalization

Various sounds of vocalization can be effectively juxtaposed with dancers' repertoire of body percussion sounds. José Limón let the dancer's body do the laughing silently in the solo section of *There Is a Time.* But in other pieces, dancers could also provide their own variations of audible giggles. Sighing and other wordless vocalization can become an effective part of both dance performance and technique classes.

     For inspiration in unusual ways of using the voice, Toby Twining's unaccompanied group *Mouth Music* is highly recommended, especially in his appearances with dance artist gus solomons jr. Twining, who is well known in the dance world as a composer and studio accompanist, has developed skills of yodeling, head tones, overtones, undertones, falsetto singing above the normal male range, flutter tonguing, whistling, humming, and more. Dance students investigating vocal possibilities might also want to consult the bibliographical listing in this volume for Cornelius L. Reid's book on vocal terminology. It includes everything from Adam's apple to yawn-sigh and zero audibility.

Dancers who aspire to perform in musical shows would be well advised to take formal singing lessons. Recently some concert dance choreographers have been experimenting with incorporating dancers' dramatic singing into their works. On occasion, other dancers may also be called upon to give renditions of songs with words.

Such formality is not the focus of the vocalization here, however. Instead, the present investigation gives students free rein to rediscover all the kinds of vocal sounds that young children experiment with before settling upon the vocal combinations found in their native languages. Emphasis is on tone color and timing. Within those parameters of attention, students can sustain a tone while alternately pressing and releasing the nostrils, flubber the lips with fingers, pat the mouth while uttering noises, fake a sneeze; whisper repeated syllables of "chi-chi-chi-chi," and anything else that comes to mind. Here are some other suggestions for experiments with wordless vocalization:

Tongue clicks. Some languages make use of the clucking sounds possible with the tongue. The essential differences in timbre available from tongue clicking depend on changing the *resonating* air cavity of the mouth. Experiment with puckering the lips to an "O" and then expanding to "Ah." Lots of possible sounds in between, too.

Rhythmic panting. Without using the vocal chords, simply exhale forcibly, in different timing patterns. The sound can be enlarged by adding a deep-chested effect and using the vocal chords to achieve "Huh—ho—heh—."

Audible inhalation. With either use of vocal chords or simply sucking in air. The sound changes depending on position of teeth and lips.

"Tsk tsk" tonguing. With lips parted, tongue begins in position behind clenched teeth. Draw tongue back; change aperture of mouth opening by alternately puckering lips and smiling.

Flutter tonguing. Exhaling, set tongue fluttering against back of teeth or roof of mouth, producing a motorlike sound. Add a pitched singing tone.

Sustaining tones. Choose any pitch, high or low, but keep it constant. Alter length of sounds by taking breaths, or allow the tone to continue as long as one breath is exhaled.

Vibrato. Slight change in pitch, an alternation back and forth that changes the tone quality. Untrained singers can simulate this by pursing lips into an "Oh" and just barely dilating and closing the aperture of the mouth.

Sigh. Take a large breath first, and support the exhalation with the diaphragm. The natural tendency is for there to be a downward slide in pitch (high to low).

Glissando. Similar to the effect of a sigh, this is a controlled sliding effect, a continuous gradual change in pitch. It can be short, and can start and end at any pitch level you wish, going either higher or lower.

Vocalise (vo-ca-LEEZE). Wordless melody, using one syllable.

Varied articulations and endings. Try combining various consonants and vowels. For example: dah, di, do, doot; ta, too tee tim tin; lov la la loo list; and so on. What happens to the beginnings and endings of sounds?

Hocket effects. A vocal device of thirteenth-century Europe as well as in some traditional African music. For example, a melody is divided between two alternating singers so that when one sings, the other is silent. The alternation could be as frequent as every note.

Scat singing. A jazz style. Rapid nonsense syllables are used instead of words.

Humming. Especially good to change dynamics (loud and soft) and pitches.

Unusual Vocalizing
in Theatrical Dance Works

The French composer Pierre Henry conceived of his taped musique concrète composition *Variations for a Door and a Sigh* as an improvised ballet for seven dancers. It has been used by Maurice Bèjart, and rather stunningly for a duet choreographed by George Balanchine. The sounds heard on tape all emanate from a human sigh, the striking of a musical saw, and the creaking of a door. Despite the unusual source of the sounds, clear, traditional musical procedures are used to develop the material. The twenty-five sections of the musical work are as follows:

> *Slumber; hesitation; song 1; awakening; song 2; stretching; gestures; reckoning; fever 1; yawning; song 3; wrath; hesitation 2; breathing; fever 2; gymnastics; song 4; wailing; wars; song 5; trance; death-rattle; snoring; song 6; death.*

Among contemporary creators, probably nobody has made such stunning use of wordless vocal qualities for theatrical dance purposes as

Meredith Monk. She can express a child's troubled incomprehension of the Holocaust by the way she uses a single syllable such as "yuh" in *Quarry*. She has transformed untrained voices of dancers into angelic choirs, working only by rote practice. In more extended *vocalise*, the central character in *Atlas* effectively communicates the yearnings of youth to explore the world, during a lengthy opera that has no words. Many of Monk's total theater works use the voice in a way that approaches a universality of nuanced expression precisely because it is free of specific language. The meaning and drama are further defined through movement and staging.

Feet Feats

Dancers have always experimented with the sounds made by their feet. Some of the possible percussive sounds available with bare feet are: flex toes and tap; stomp with flat feet; rub back and forth; move straight leg from the hip so flat foot circles on floor; brush back on ball of foot then come down on heel.

Students can also experiment with various dance footwear, including ballet slippers, soft jazz shoes, heeled boots, character shoes, and hard pointe shoes. Even sneakers offer a different tone quality for ball of the foot and heel, as well as sliding or scraping sounds and a good, solid stomp. High-heeled clicks offer another quality of sound.

Many regional styles of traditional dance incorporate the sounds of shoes into the patterns. For example, the Ballet Folklorico of Mexico regularly includes in its repertoire some dances where the performers are barefoot, others where sandals are worn by all, and many extensive forms in which high-heeled boots are worn by both men and women. One of their dances uses brightly colored wooden-box platforms as resonators to increase the sound of the dancers' feet. As an added challenge, a musician has a smaller box and uses two handheld blocks of wood to duplicate the rhythms that the dancers are creating with the sound of their shoes.

Tap

Tap shoes are a good investment, and if students have not previously taken lessons, even a few sessions of professional instruction can be helpful in developing sensitivity to the details of rhythmic patterns produced.

But even without formal lessons, students can try some of the sound-producing motions that constitute the basic vocabulary of tap dancers. These can be done sitting in a chair or standing.

Toe tap (with sole of toe)

Toe (using tip of toe, vertically)

Tap (single sound, with ball of foot)

Heel drop (ball of foot stays on floor)

Heel dig (lift leg with bent knee and tap back edge of heel on floor)

Stomp (entire foot flat with no change of weight)

Stamp (the same, but weight changes from standing leg to the one creating the sound)

Brush front or back (slide on ball of foot)

Shuffle (front and back brush, nonstop)

Step-heel (toe-heel, two sounds)

Flap (brush forward and tap; no weight shift)

Hop (weight stays on same standing leg)

Scuff (with end of heel alone)

In addition to enjoying a revival in show business, tap dancing has received recent attention in the world of concert dance. For example, Brenda Bufalino and her American Tap Dance Orchestra merge music and movement in ways that are at once fresh and full of intricate jazz rhythms. Bufalino points out: "The emphasis is on the musicality of the taps. Our emphasis is on our feet, on the rhythm. The principle is the sound and the time and the phrasing."

Most important in tap, the whole body must feel the details of rhythm accurately, and at high speeds. The sense of beat, of meter, and of changing pulse is evident. Beyond that, the subdivisions of each beat are of immense importance. For instance, at one point in the Tap Orchestra presentations, the entire company enters and keeps up a regular triplet subdivision while turning in various ways. The performers explain later that their exact placement on the stage varies; the sound should not.

Silence is tremendously effective in tap dance. Brief silences delineate the fast rhythmic patterns and contribute to the distinct motifs of sound; sudden, longer pauses serve to arrest the audience's attention, to stop the action momentarily, and to frame the movement patterns that go before and after.

What are some of the different ways in which tap dancers can vary their movements while nevertheless producing the same rhythmic patterns in sound? Performers can turn, cross the legs, mix heel and toe.

They can execute a pattern with one foot or two; they can echo or amplify the patterns of a lead soloist. They can carry their arms at any angle and mimic the sounds directly with the movement of their arms; or they can create a visual rhythm with their arms that is in contrast to the sounds that are heard. The torso and neck in turn can be carried straight, or bent—and again, the movement of these parts of the body can synchronize or contrast with the audible rhythms produced by the feet.

Dynamics—loud, soft, and gradations in between—are also a common denominator with movement. For tap dancers, there is no distinction; movement and music are created simultaneously. And so the same movement can be done gently to create a soft sound, more firmly for an accent, and then if all the dancers hit the boards hard with their toes or heels in unison, the dynamic level is considerably higher.

Also present is timbre—tone quality—in the sound of the taps. Brenda Bufalino generalizes and calls the heel the equivalent of a bass drum; the toe tap is more like a snare drum. But there are many more sounds possible, such as slides on wood, slides on sand, going up and down stairs, stomp, stamp, or shuffle.

Explorations and Assignments

1. Experiment with different sounds that can be produced with body percussion. Devise a brief combination (five to ten seconds) and teach it to the class, using no words and no counting.

2. When the class is secure with a pattern, divide into two groups. One group continues the body percussion, the other improvises choreographically, relating to the sounds in some way. Discuss the results.

3. Devise flash cards or hand signals for vocal improvisation, and lead the group. Use at least six different kinds of vocalization, but exclude words.

4. Devise a dance improvisation exercise for differently shod dancers, making use of a definite pulse and three kinds of locomotor movements. The sound of the specific shoes should be taken into consideration.

5. Improvise a one-minute sequence of movement that makes use of both body percussion and sounds made by the feet. Repeat, adding some sort of vocalization. Repeat your movement sequence, this time eliminating the sounds. Discuss the results.

6. If anyone in the class has taken tap or clog dancing, have them demonstrate some of the basic techniques.

7. Listen to recorded music sung by Bobby McFerrin, Louis Armstrong, Meredith Monk, Paco Peña, and the Swingle Singers. Additionally, listen to *Philomel,* by Milton Babbitt, *Bachianas Brasilieras No. 8,* by Heitor Villa Lobos, or other contemporary works suggested by your instructor.

   With your own voice, imitate some of the vocal techniques and qualities. Experiment with analogous qualities in dance movement. In each case, consider which aspects of the vocalizing you are inclined to relate to as a dancer.

chapter 3

INSTRUMENTAL PERCUSSION PATTERNS

It must be the biggest shock of life, this onslaught of rhythms that want to drag us out onto the floor and make us dance.

—Mickey Hart

The basic processes of making music with body percussion can be transferred to playing percussion instruments. Again, there is a direct and immediate relationship between one's physical movements and the sounds that are produced. Consequently, dance students need not read written notation in order to play dozens of percussion instruments and to improvise whole pieces that have recognizable musical ideas and form.[1]

In bands and orchestras, percussionists must read notation to perform their assigned parts correctly. But most drummers throughout the world are more likely to improvise on the spot, incorporating rhythmic skills and patterns that they devised themselves or learned by rote imitation of physical motions and verbal singsong. Dance students can do this, too.

Categories of Percussion

Drums and other percussion comprise the category of musical instruments most closely linked with dancing throughout the world. Generally speaking, percussion encompasses instruments that can be struck, grated, shaken, or stamped. Scholarly classifiers have come up with names for separate basic categories: *idiophones,* which are instruments made entirely from the same naturally *sonorous* (sound-giving) materials; and *membranophones,* in which some sort of vibrating head is added, as with drums. Some instruments, such as kettledrums and xylophones, give off discernible pitches (high or low sounds). Others, such as snare drums and rattles, produce only indefinite pitches.

An enormous variety of percussion instruments have been used around the world in connection with dance. The uses of percussion within cultural contexts could easily become a major focus for students of dance history, and several sources of information are listed in the bibliography. For now, it will be mentioned simply that idiophones include rattles, scrapers, cymbals, gongs, log drums, bells, and stampers. They come in many sizes and shapes, made of both natural and manufactured materials.

Headed drums (membranophones) are in a class by themselves. A membrane, or drumhead, is the main vibrating source of sound. In the past, the most common membranes used for drumheads were skins from dead animals such as goats, cattle, lizards, and deer. Nowadays, Latin conga and bongo drums are still made of animal hides, as are African and Native American drums. But the drums that urban people are most likely to see in marching bands, rock groups, and orchestras are usually made with plastic heads.

The bodies of drums come in many shapes: tubular, bowl shaped, barrel, conical, double conical, hourglass, goblet, cylindrical but tapered at one end, and square framed. These instruments can be single or double headed, tunable or nontunable. The cavities of most are occupied by air, but some have water inside to affect the quality of sound. Some drums float in water.

Found Percussion

Hands-on experience with percussion instruments is highly recommended for all dance students. An exploration of percussion from around the world offers unusual sound materials for dance work. In addition to playing commercially made instruments, experimenting with homemade versions can be both valuable and enjoyable. A recommended group project is the collection of everyday materials, or found objects, to be incorporated into a large percussion setup for use within a dance project.

In the absence of extensive percussion equipment, dance students initially can tap tabletops, books, pieces of paper, wastebaskets, soda tins, bike helmets, or coffee mugs—using chopsticks, the eraser ends of pencils, or one's fingers.

Such experiments are never ending for musicians in the professional dance world. For example, percussionist/composer David Yoken incorporated a clothesline hung with suitcases into his score *Who Stole August* for former Nikolais artist Carolyn Carlson. Not only were the sounds good; the suitcases (played with timpani mallets) were consistent with the images of travel presented in the choreographed dance. Another drummer/collaborator for dance, Skip LaPlante, has devised many collections of homemade percussion, including an entire wall of old refrigerator drawers and broiling trays carefully arranged according to their pitches and played with timpani mallets. LaPlante has even organized his composer colleagues in a collective called Music for Homemade Instruments. In their concerts these musicians employ intriguing compositional charts and number sequences to produce wonderful musical pieces from such objects as the pieces of broken dishes, all laid out on rugs.

A Quick Primer on Percussion Playing

The following procedures work well for many types of percussion.

1. Let physical motions determine the sound patterns. Observe and listen carefully to the relative duration of sounds and silences depending on how far through space hands and sticks have to move. For example, if fast-paced sounds are desired, it helps to keep the beaters or hands close to the surface being struck. If long periods of silence are desired between sounds, a nice easy flow of motion might allow a greater distance off the surface.

2. Although sometimes a more muffled sound will be desired, in general, brighter qualities can be produced by allowing the sticks or the fingers to bounce off the drummed surface. This can be achieved, in general, by controlling the stick between the thumb and index finger, with the other fingers curved freely around the stick. Hold the stick tightly enough for control, but loosely enough so that it will bounce freely. To find the optimum bounce, experiment with finding a fulcrum spot. Usually about two-thirds of the length from the striking end will work well. Hold sticks the same way in both left and right hands.

3. Basic strokes consist of alternating left and right, or any possible combinations of repeated notes with one stick. In addition, multiple sounds can be achieved for each stroke by allowing the stick to bounce rapidly off the drumhead. To achieve rapid-fire bounces, a pair of commercially manufactured drumsticks is a good investment.

4. The instruments need to be suspended, held, or secured in some way so that the vibrations will continue without interference.

5. The most useful techniques for playing percussion instruments include striking with a stick or beater, hitting objects together, scraping, jiggling, rattling, and thumping on the ground. Sometimes these methods can be combined, as when tapping maracas gently on a drumhead, for example, or by adding jingles to the drumframes.

6. For hand drumming, it may be most comfortable to grip a large instrument between the legs or a smaller one under one arm.

   Keep the wrists loose, and don't exert more energy than is needed for the sound level you want. This prevents injury of the hands and fingers. Basic techniques include using the tips of the fingers, either curved or flat; the combined underside of the flattened fingers; the heel area of the hand, just below the wrist; the flattened palm; alternations between palm and flattened fingers; the side of a single finger; and the slap, which is done by cupping one hand on the drumhead and giving a quick flick with the other hand.

7. It is worthwhile to spend some time with a music student or someone else who can accurately teach the basic underlying rhythmic patterns of current social dances, as well as traditional dances.

8. Play along with recordings or the radio. Put on a waltz, a tango, or some rock music and try to gear in with a short, repeated percussion pattern. All styles and forms of dance music can be experienced and explored this way, and physical drumming may help one become aware of more details in the music.

9. Even if a student's focus is on ballet, it can be instructive to explore some of the current rock drumming beats, because in doing this one learns how to transform a steady pattern into

interesting effects simply by changing the accents or by inserting silences on different pulses or subdivisions of beats.

10. The more instruments, the better. Some especially good instruments to collect for hand drumming are bongos, congas, tablas, and Middle Eastern dumbeks. Native American drums are usually played with beaters, but they also give off good sounds when played with the hands.

11. The best sound is usually produced not in the middle of a drumhead, but about two-thirds of the way to the edge. However, experiment with different places. What does the middle sound like? The very edge when played with the fingers? The sides when played with cupped hands? And what about scratching lightly with fingernails or rubbing instead of striking?

Another interesting effect is achieved by rotating the wrist sideways so that there is a fast alternation between thumb and little finger plus ring fingers, producing an equivalent to a *tremolo* or *trill* on other instruments.

Reminders of Musical Procedures

The same as with body percussion:

1. Rhythm is made up of sounds and silences, arranged proportionately in timing.
2. Keep patterns brief, uninvolved, and clear at first.
3. Let physical motion determine the sound patterns.
4. Experiment with even and uneven patterns.
5. When you have a pattern going comfortably, change one part of it. For instance, transfer one sound to a different instrument for a contrast in timbre or tone quality. Distinctive qualities can also be produced by playing on different parts of the instrument: the side of a drum, for example.
6. With a group of people, a good procedure is to layer short repeating rhythms simultaneously. It helps to stay together if everyone feels and maintains the same pulse, regardless of how individual the relationship of each sound pattern may be to that pulse.
7. Another way to structure group playing is to have everyone drum the same pattern, but in follow-the-leader or canonic imitative manner. One person starts; the next may come in on the third pulse, the next on the fifth pulse, the next on the sixth.

8. Music can have a definite pulsation throughout, or it can be freely *unpulsed*. Experiment with both.

9. Keep patterns going for one to three minutes without changing. When something is changed, let it be just one aspect at a time: add a silence, vary the timbre, speed everything up, make the music softer or louder, put in one accent, alter an even rhythm to an uneven one and vice versa.

10. When learning a new pattern, start slowly and work up speed gradually. Drumming, like dancing, depends a lot on forming habits of physical patterns. The excellent muscle memory that dancers are developing should also serve them well in percussion playing.

Altering the Sounds of Instruments

Sonorous, or self-sounding, idiophones can be made of materials from the natural world, such as wood, rocks, and hard-packed dirt. Manufactured materials can also be struck, scraped, or hit together to make percussion sounds. Metal, plastic, glass, and pottery are some of the materials used to make percussion instruments used in dance performances.

The sounds of all these instruments can be altered in several ways. Beaters can be made of various materials. The sounds that reach our ears also change depending on whether the vibrations are passed through the air or through water. Good examples occur in the dance scores devised by Lou Harrison, John Cage, and other composers on the West Coast, employing such sounds as those of gongs dipped up and down in water.

The quality and loudness of percussion sounds can also be affected by the addition of a soundbox. Obvious examples are drums of all sorts. But one can easily hear the difference by scraping a rasping instrument held in the air, and then laying it over a wood box, tin can, cardboard box, or styrofoam container.

Dance Use of Various Percussion Instruments

Stampers. Closest to the experiences of dancers are tap shoes and other stamping idiophones, which may be as simple as the cane that the teacher strikes on the studio floor during a class in Caribbean dance styles. A length of bamboo of large diameter makes a particularly good stamping stick. Other do-it-yourself versions are old mop handles, canes, heavy cardboard cylinders, and baseball bats. All of these pounding sticks are useful in establishing steady pulsation for dance.

Stamped instruments. Related to stamping poles and shod stamping feet are stamped idiophones, where the main sound emanates from the surface that is stamped upon. Some ritual dancers of the Pacific islands, for example, found that by digging a sizable pit in the ground and covering it with wood, the sound of their feet would be greatly amplified. (This is another example of the principle of soundboxes.)

Claves and other rhythm sticks. While the pounding stick is useful for establishing a foundation pulse for dance, claves or rhythm sticks often serve as another kind of constant, providing for more varied patterns at higher pitches. These are simply two cylinders of hardwood approximately an inch and a half in diameter and six inches long. In Latin American music for social dances, the patterns of the wood sticks are so important that they are even termed claves rhythm. One extraordinary ballet solo set entirely to the sounds of wood sticks is *Clave,* choreographed by Eliot Feld to music of the same title by Steve Reich. The work has proven a virtuoso tour de force for dancer Buffy Miller.

Rattles. Probably universally a child's first musical instrument is a rattle, whether it is a keychain dangled by urban parents, a farmer's hollow gourd with seeds rattling inside, or a manufactured plastic version. Similar instruments have been important to both ritual and secular dance since time immemorial. Rattles can emphasize the movements of dancers who hold them, in addition to simply adding interesting timbres.

Among the beautiful examples of carved rattles are wooden ones made by native peoples of the Canadian Northwest. Another popular rattle from South America is the rain stick.

Sophisticated performance artists also attest to the continued effectiveness of rattles for dance use. For instance, in *Chaconne,* a theater piece by Meredith Monk and Ping Chong, some of the cast are seated on the floor stage right, shaking cans containing rattling objects and providing very adequate sounds for the action center stage.

Drawing from African-related traditions, the musical group Women of the Calabash have developed rattle playing to a virtuoso art. Using gigantic gourds (calabashes) covered with beads, the players toss and rub and shake the instruments to produce rhythms and different tone qualities. They have collaborated effectively with the dance troupe Urban Bush Women.

Jingles. When many small-voiced objects bump together, a resultant jingling sound can be produced. Nuts, seashells, and tiny pellet bells have served these purposes well, whether worn on the body or attached to poles. Jingles are featured in the traditional dances of Native Americans and in those of the Indian subcontinent.

A recent example of jingles in the modern dance vein is the costuming designed by percussionist Gary Sojkowski for Wendy Perron's *Squall Recycled*. The three women dancers in this piece wear jackets and pants adorned variously with rows of keys, coins, wind chimes, and other objects that give off their delicate sounds according to the moves of the dancers.

Scrapers. Both Japanese and Latin American musical styles make effective use of scrapers, or rasps. Depending on the materials used (such as wood, bone, or metal), the tone quality can vary considerably.

Rasping instruments were used by the Japanese musicians onstage in Jerome Robbins's *Windmill,* choreographed to music by Teiji Ito, for New York City Ballet with Edward Villella portraying the lead role. The musicians, who played entirely without written notes, provided an evocative aural backdrop for the slow unfolding of the seasons of a man's life, all with a Japanese flavor. A reminder that the original virtuoso raspers were insects occurs in the final section of Paul Taylor's *Sunset,* with a romantic twilight setting.

Cymbals and other concussion. Strictly speaking, cymbals would be considered concussion instruments only if there is a pair crashed or sliced together in downward motions to produce sound. Often, suspended cymbals are played singly with wood drum sticks or wire brushes. The secrets of good metal alloy cymbals are closely guarded by manufacturers, and a high-quality pair can be extremely expensive. But if the sounds emanating from various instruments are tested and listened to carefully, a discernible difference can be heard.

Pairs of cymbals are perhaps most familiar in this country because of their use in marching bands. But they also serve widely in orchestral ballet scores for dramatic purposes, often as sound effects. One example is in John Lanchbery's orchestration of the ballet score for *La Bayadère* by Ludwig Minkus. Such scenes as the toppling of the temple in the final act call for obvious cymbal participation. Such use needs to be discreet; if overdone, it could become banal.

A variety of suspended cymbals are an indispensable part of every jazz and rock drum set. A pair that is worked by a foot pedal is called the high hat, and this produces a closed kind of metallic sound that is a useful balance to the bass drum, which is also worked by a foot pedal. The suspended cymbal is usually termed the ride cymbal. This is free to vibrate more fully; it is used to provide color and unexpected variety, or to keep up a distinctive pattern that sets the style for a song or jazz set.

Asian dancers will sometimes provide their own miniature cymbal sounds, using instruments that are only three inches in diameter, attached by loops to the thumb and middle finger.

Clappers. Some related miniature instruments, classified as clappers, are castanets made of wood. These are indelibly connected with Spanish flamenco and gypsy dancing. Consisting of two hollowed pieces of wood attached by strings, they are quite difficult to play and require so much practice to master that most orchestral musicians simply use mounted versions that can be tapped with the finger tips. But dancers specializing in flamenco have to master the proper playing of castanets. Ancient Egyptian woodcarvers fashioned clappers to look and operate as substitutes for clapping arms and hands. Finally, there is a clapper instrument that came to have different theatrical associations: the slapstick.

Bells and gongs. These instruments are most often made of metal, but clay and wood can also function as the main bodies. Bells are played either by an interior clapper, or they can be struck; gongs are struck with beaters or hammers. Some gongs have a predominant, definite pitch and are used as melodic instruments, as in the very elaborate ensembles called gamelans, which provide the music for theatrical dance dramas in Indonesia. Other gongs have long-resonating, complex sound waves that lend themselves best to sparing but attention-getting use. They have been widely used in Asia for religious rituals, and this may account for the popular Western connection with theatrical magicians.

The almost trancelike effect of listening to the sound of a single gong was chronicled by the early modern dancer Mary Wigman. The experience was profound as she described it, and it led her to create her theatrical dance work *Monotony.*

Among American composers, Lou Harrison has been the particularly inspired by Indonesian gamelan techniques. He and William Colvig have manufactured entire gamelan sets of gongs, and Harrison has composed original works for West Coast ensembles that collaborate with dancers.

Steel drums. A fairly recent invention in Trinidad, steel drums have become popular throughout the Caribbean and are widely used as accompaniment for social dancing, as well as for purely musical entertainment. To make these, oil drums are used either in their entire lengths, or else cut in varying depths. The end of the barrel is hammered into grooved sections until they arrive at definite pitches. Some have as many as twenty-five available pitches.

Instruments with pitched bars. In this category are xylophones with bars made of wood; metallophones and glockenspiels with suspended tuned bars; and slit drums, with tongues emitting complex overtones. For dance purposes, wood xylophones are often used in African musical accompaniments. The metal-barred instruments have a tradition in Asia and the Pacific, and are noteworthy as used in the dance dramas of Bali and Java.

Many music and dance educators make use of instruments with removable bars, which allow pitch choices to be decided before group improvisations.

Rocks. Among sonorous stones, marble emits particularly fine-pitched tones. These were used by the dance musician Gary Sojkowski in his work with dance educator Bessie Schönberg. He visited a marble quarry in Vermont and collected odd-sized fragments, subsequently arranging them according to pitch for his homemade lithophone. Marble tiles one-quarter-inch thick are a more accessible source for most urban people. But even if one has the patience to saw by hand with a grit blade, or if one has this done professionally with a power wet saw, there is no guarantee of sonorous results. Broken fragments are actually more apt to provide good pitches.

Pots, pans, bowls, and junk. Though children have long found contentment in banging pots and pans with wooden spoons, few adults seem to continue such explorations. Nevertheless, ordinary kitchen containers, discarded automotive parts, and other metal junk have often served the serious theatrical purposes of professional percussionists for dance. For example, the composer Norma Reynolds Dalby carefully chose steel bowls for their specific pitches and had the dancers themselves play the bowls with mallets as part of her score for Kei Takei's *Light 15, The Dreamcatcher's Diary.*

West Coast percussionists who worked with dancers incorporated such leftovers as discarded automobile brake drums into their battery of effects. Out of such experimentation, the composers Henry Cowell, John Cage, Harry Partch, Lou Harrison, and others developed some of the first formal written concert literature for extended percussion ensemble.

The composer-choreographer Alwin Nikolais also used an array of found percussion for some of his early dance scores and classes at the Henry Street Playhouse. He had been greatly influenced by the work of Franziska Boas. More recently, the musicians Skip La Plante and Fred Frith are achieving considerable reputations because of their varied experiments using homemade percussion and found objects for their work with dancers. Jon Scoville's experimentations growing out of his collaborations with choreographer Tandy Beal are also noteworthy.

Experimental percussionists of today are unanimous in praising the discoveries and constructions of the late composer Harry Partch. He devised many unusual percussion instruments for use in dance dramas, and some of these works continue to be revived. The instruments are now owned by Newband, a group led by Dean Drummond and currently in residence at Purchase College, The State University of New York. The sounds of these instruments can also be heard on recordings made during Partch's lifetime, and these are most highly recommended.

Slit drums. The original slit drum was probably a naturally hollowed tree that someone hit with a sturdy branch. By experimenting, many peoples in Africa and South America discovered that serviceable message systems could be established by means of giant log drums. Smaller, sweet-sounding slit drums have also been designed with boxes and various hardwoods. The sounds are not loud, and consequently require amplification if used in an auditorium. But for small dance studios, slit drums can offer a refreshing change from the sounds of other percussion instruments.

Headed drums: Orchestral equipment. Children who attend New York City Ballet's family matinee programs often delight in the timpani (kettledrum) section of *Fanfare.* This is Jerome Robbins's choreographic setting of Benjamin Britten's *The Young Person's Guide to the Orchestra.* In a totally different style, Laura Dean Dancers and Musicians whirl and create high-energy patterns across the floor for the entire duration of *Tympani,* which uses three kettledrums, always in live performance. Dean created both choreography and minimalist musical score.

For classical ballet with its full orchestral partnering, the percussion most apt to be heard in addition to timpani are bass drum, orchestral toms, snare drums, triangles, cymbals, orchestral chimes, and temple blocks.

In the modern dance repertoire, one of the most startling uses of percussion is John Herbert MacDowell's arrangement for Paul Taylor's *Cloven Kingdom.* For this, the composer/conductor skillfully juxtaposed a Baroque orchestral piece by Corelli with modern percussion music by Henry Cowell.

Trap sets. For twentieth-century students, the most familiar arrangement of headed drums is surely the trap set (short for contraption). Such sets are ubiquitous enough to comprise what is by this time a standard combination of drums and cymbals, and the sounds are recognizable to all those who listen to both rock and jazz music. Traps are often used to provide improvised music for tap, jazz dance, and contemporary concert dance technique classes. These drum sets offer the advantage that one player can provide steady music with a variety of tone colors, because the player employs both hands and feet.

A trap set normally consists of the following: a large bass drum played with a foot pedal; a high hat pair of cymbals played with the other foot; two suspended cymbals, one a crash, the other a ride often played with steel brushes; a snare drum; a large field tom; and two or more higher toms. Nowadays, all drumheads are made of plastic because it does not react to variations in temperature and humidity. Tension is provided by strong metal hardware. Finally, the player is sure to have on hand a collection of at least five or six different kinds of sticks and brushes to achieve a wide variety in tone color.

Additional instruments that the drummer might attach to a drum set include a cowbell, scraper, triangle, woodblocks of several sizes, and temple blocks (which are small, hollowed, closed sound boxes of Chinese origin).

Latin drums. In addition to the trap set, pairs of Latin American drums are among the most popular drums for dance purposes. They are useful for accompanying technique classes in ethnic, jazz, and modern dance, as well as for creative choreographic experimentation. At some schools, such as the Alvin Ailey American Dance Center, the sound of Latin drums is a main ingredient of a large percentage of classes. When played by experts, they can provide a compelling impetus for movement.

Most prominent are the large congas, normally played in pairs, with one pitched low and the other slightly higher. Latin musicians have evolved many strokes that take particular advantage of the various hand techniques possible, including use of the palm, flat fingers together, fingertips, and a combination of cupping one hand and striking with the full force of the other. Damped sounds are also effective. Similar techniques are used to play the smaller pairs of bongos, except that more use is made of faster finger technique.

As mentioned before, the claves are often considered the heart of Latin music for social dances. Cowbells are also an important ingredient in the total sound color. And finally, giant, beaded gourd calabash rattles are a favorite addition. For representative examples of Latin percussion, the recordings and live concerts of Tito Puente's musicians are recommended.

Traditional drums of the Middle East, Asia, and North America. A familiar drum during performances of the Inbal dancers from Israel is the Middle Eastern dumbek. Goblet shaped, it is made of either porcelain or metal, and has a drumhead made of goatskin. It gives very effective response to fast finger techniques.

Another drum that has caused the development of an intricate technique of hand drumming is the conical wood tabla from north India. It is an intrinsic part of classical dance styles on the Indian subcontinent, and is usually paired with a lower-pitched, kettle-shaped metal or clay drum called the baya. In recent years, percussionists in North America have been incorporating these instruments into their work with modern dance classes. Seeking a precedent for the use of instruments and styles from other cultures, one could refer to Ruth St. Denis.

An entirely different type of experience is provided by the ritualistic performances by the Kodo drummers of Japan. What makes the group so special is not only the virtuosic synchronized drumming, but also the variety of tone colors coaxed from barrel and frame drums struck by various sticks and clubs. Certainly there is a choreographic element to all the performances.

In North America, the native traditions honor the drum in religious ceremonies. It is a symbol of wholeness, of continuity, of powers beyond the ordinary. Consequently, when an animal's skin is used to make a drum, it is done with respect, for it is the spirit voice of the animal that speaks through the drum. Native American drum types vary widely in size, from a handheld hoop drum played by the dancers themselves, to large, suspended, deep-toned drums that are struck by three players simultaneously. To observe the use of drums by Native Americans, students may want to attend a powwow or other event open to the public. (Consult the guidebook *Indian America* listed in the Bibliography.) Alternatively, the American Indian Dance Theatre presents highly polished programs based on traditions of many tribes.

African drums. Despite the wide variety in drums from the rest of the world, probably no continent excels in both the making and playing of drums as does Africa. As elsewhere, the drum did not develop in isolation from the dance; rather, it has played an important role in rituals and group celebrations that include dance. In Africa, the hides of zebra, antelope, and many other wildlife have been used to make drumheads. The frames and the bodies of the drums are often elaborately carved from wood.

In recent years, some of the professional dance troupes from Africa have been touring in the United States, presenting traditional forms, all with live drumming accompaniment. Especially recommended are the programs of the National Dance Company of Senegal. Additionally, the group assembled in this country by Babatunde Olatunji is considered exceptional and often tours. Finally, the Chuck Davis Dance Company based in Durham, N.C., specializes in African styles. Students deeply interested in exploring such traditions may contact Chuck Davis himself. He has led many annual tours to west Africa, going into the villages to document traditional dance forms, and allowing opportunities for those who travel with him to make and play drums in the traditional African ways.

Percussion and the Tradition of Modern Dance

A major thrust of the pioneer modern dancers in both America and Europe was to depart from the traditions of European classical ballet and find roots for a new kind of expressive theatrical dance. Part of their thrust, therefore, was to remove themselves from the lush sounds of

European orchestral traditions. With percussion as their sole sound source, choreographers and dancers discovered anew the primal attraction of these timbres, influenced particularly by the German expressionist choreographer Mary Wigman, and by the musician Franziska Boas. During her long career in the theater and in teaching, pioneer modern dancer Hanya Holm always valued percussion for its distinct articulations. Doris Humphrey also used a simple frame drum as part of the effective small ensemble that accompanies *The Shakers*. More recently, Laura Dean has included the percussion composition and performance of Steve Reich for a number of her dances. These make powerful theater works.

Eclectic Percussion Experiments for Dance

If percussion often provides the impetus for dancers, creation works the other way round, too. Musicians may be lured to devise new sources or uses of percussion music, growing out of their work with dancers.

Among the most noteworthy of these inventive musicians have been John Cage, in his work with Merce Cunningham, and Lucia Dlugoszewski in her collaborations with Erick Hawkins.

Dlugoszewski has invented numerous percussion instruments, many of them constructed by Hawkins' designer, Ralph Dorazio. For example, *8 Clear Places* uses more than a hundred pieces of equipment. The composer's experiments with bouncing balls, pouring water, and other familiar noises prompted such early pieces as *Moving Space Theater Pieces for Everyday Sounds* and *Transparencies 1-50 for Everyday Sounds*.

Commenting on Dlugoszewski's collaborative output over the years, dance critic Anna Kisselgoff wrote in the *New York Times*:

> *Over the decades, music written expressly for modern dance has almost never achieved the renown common to ballet scores. In part, this is because such music tends to be used as aural decor.*
>
> *But the long-term and fruitful collaboration between Mr. Hawkins and Miss Dlugoszewski comes out of a creative sense, and that is why both music and dance appear perfectly integrated in their joint pieces.*
>
> *It is easy and right to think of modern-dance pioneers like Mr. Hawkins as rebels against tradition, but it is also true that Miss Dlugoszewski comes out of the line of rugged individualists in American music that would include the composer Harry Partch.*
>
> *She, too, knows how to have her musicians . . . rattle a sheet of metal, to play upon instruments of her invention. The music on the program mixed conventional and unconventional instruments and precision was mandatory, no matter how wonderfully spontaneous the exuberant outbursts sounded.*[2]

Dancers today all too often shy away from using live music for their performances, whether because of fears of high costs or other concerns. Percussion instruments can enliven a program that might otherwise include only taped sounds. Often a single drummer can provide effective collaboration. Consequently, dancers are urged to explore such possibilities, especially for their performance projects.

Explorations and Assignments

1. Take a tour of both the dance and music department collections of percussion instruments. Test as many instruments as possible, for quality of sound and for methods of sound production. Study the classifications in the encyclopedia of instruments listed in the bibliography. Make a list of the percussion instruments that appeal to you for use with dance.

2. Start drumming. Borrow an instrument, buy one, make one, or use your bare hands or pencils on tabletops and books. Start collecting objects that offer interesting percussive sounds.

3. As a class project, jointly construct a percussion ensemble for use in dance improvisation sessions.

4. For a brief oral report, choose one percussion instrument used for dance purposes in another culture. Describe the role of the instrument both musically and emotionally. Are there any ritual connotations? Include either a recording or a brief videotape as part of your report.

5. Practice the basic positions of hand drumming, using a commercially made drum. Take one lesson with an experienced student or master drummer who can offer some pointers on the basics.

6. Devise a costume that creates its own percussive sounds as you move. Create a one-minute dance that takes advantage of the sounds resulting from various physical movements.

7. Listen to recorded percussion music of Tito Puente, Steve Reich, and Lou Harrison. How do they compare? What kinds of dances do they suggest in your imagination? In what ways do they make you want to move? What kind of costumes would you want in each case? What kind of lighting and scenery or other visual props would you want?

chapter 4

MUSCLE MEMORY AND MUSIC

Music is the key. It's the music that gives me the memory *of the steps. When I hear the music, I see the ballet and feel the ballet. That's how it works for me. It's the music and its rhythms that make me remember the steps.*

—Rosemary Dunleavy, Ballet Mistress, New York City Ballet

Drawing attention to the everyday verbal connotations of the word "vocabulary," Jennifer Muller choreographed a buoyant dance called *Thesaurus* for her company, The Works.[1] In it, men and women wearing sunny yellow beach outfits offer witty and high-energy interpretations of more than 400 words related to the verb "move," all to the musical partnering of recorded jazz by Buddy Rich and his orchestra.

The dance begins with absolute stillness. A banner unfurls at the back of the stage, providing the audience with the script of words, which begins: "Go . . . Step . . . Alter One's Course . . . Set Back . . . Step Forward." Muller has woven an ingenious playful dance that wends its way through shuffle, slouch, bounce, wriggle, hurl, roll, leap, and other juxtaposed movements, until the company breathlessly skids to "Stand . . . Stop . . . Wait for Applause."

This crowd pleaser of a piece also expands the dancers' vocabulary in movement far beyond what is expected of performers in classical ballet. Contemporary choreographers, including Muller, have extended the styles of music deemed appropriate for theatrical dance, as well as the ways in which music can relate to physical movement.

Typical of small touring troupes in today's economy, Jennifer Muller/The Works always performs to taped music. For dance concerts, their prime concern is that for each location there be a prior check with an expert on sound equipment. Once onstage, there should be no musical surprises for the dancers. It is in rehearsals and listening to take-home tapes that the professional performers must face the music for their dances in an analytical way.

Music in the Life of "The Works"

Muller is outstanding for the high percentage of new music commissioned especially for her choreography, and for the wide-ranging musical styles she chooses to present to audiences.

For members of The Works the day begins, as with professional dancers around the world, in company class with music. Although other modern artists value the independence of dance to the extent of insisting that even daily workouts be in silence, Muller has a different attitude.

> There is no energy in silence. A dance class has many aims, but there are two basic aims. One is to warm up all the systems of the body. That doesn't mean just physically; it includes one's emotional center, physical center, spiritual center. The other thing is that you are constantly improving your technique. A class goes from quiet to most difficult as the body gets warmed up.

Music helps, she emphasizes. Especially percussion.

Regarding timing, Muller hopes that her dancers will be holistic with the music, even in class. It is pertinent to quote Webster's definition of "holistic": "emphasizing the organic or functional relationship between parts and wholes." In that context, Muller describes her own teaching.

> We do a center that involves breathing and warming up the whole body. Then we do a barre based on classical technique, but really my work. Then we move across the floor and work on phrases.
>
> When you move across the floor and are dealing with a metered beat, you cannot give every movement exactly the same energy, or you have no phrasing. My joke is that then you are out in Kansas—telephone pole, telephone pole, telephone pole. There is nothing to keep you awake, and you go to sleep. Similarly, if you are doing move-move-move, step-step-step, you are putting an audience to sleep because you are not drawing focus to any part of the phrase. For any good musician who plays a musical phrase, there has to be a beginning, middle, end, and climaxes. I also explain this in terms of the movement.

I teach a technique that involves a great deal of Eastern thought, plus relaxation in polarity to energy: no tension, but the parts that are going away from the floor need enormous energy. The main purpose of musical accompaniment in class is to give that energy. It supports you.

Muller's advice to dancers is "You have to be *with* the music. Not follow the music, but be with the music, be part of the music. It's a different depth of understanding. Certainly you can dance on top of the music. That's something different. But if you are going to be a part of the music, you have to be inside it, so it's not something that is there just playing in the distance."

Dancers' Counts/Musicians' Counts

"I work very many different ways in relation to the music," explains Muller. "Sometimes I want the movement to relate directly to the rhythm of the music; sometimes I don't. It depends on what the idea of the dance piece is, and what musical relationship best suits the idea."

Many of this choreographer's dances are not counted at all. In others, only sections will be counted precisely in regard to the timing. Using *Thesaurus* as an example, she observes:

There are some sections that are absolutely counted straight out. Then we are counting the music, not the movement. When I say we count, we always count the music. When we don't count, we don't count at all— either movement or music. So any work that is rhythmic (actually to the beat of the music) is counted from the music, in what are called dancers' counts. These are in direct relationship to the measures of music, except that they are usually slower, often half-time to the musicians' counts.

It's too hard to count music quickly. So dancers' counts are basically in phrases. If you are dealing with a musical 4/4, the phrases are usually in eight. If you are dealing with 3/4, it's sometimes phrases of six. But you are always counting what are considered dancers' counts. I wouldn't call these just the pulses, because then you would not be relating to the measures of the music—and this is something that dancers definitely should do. You're just not counting as fast. It's almost an abbreviation.

Distinguishing Meters

When working with musicians, emphasizes Muller, dancers have to be able to count both ways—in musicians' counts and dancers' counts. This is particularly important in The Works because members frequently function as teachers during the troupe's residencies at college campuses.

One of the first things which dancers need to convey when they are teaching is the basic metric grouping.

What is a 4/4? What is 3/4? What is 6/8? 12/8? Clap it, sing it, count it. Ask what are the different properties of it. What is the difference in nature between a 6/8 and a 3/4, between a 2/4 and a 4/4? What are the properties (like colors have properties), and how do you use them? What class exercises are they appropriate for? Why? What effect does meter have on the physical body?

The obvious simplistic difference between a 3/4 and a 4/4 is that the 3/4 has a moment to breathe. So a 3/4 is a rounder, fuller, softer, swinging motion; it is circular. A 4/4 is not circular; it is square. It has greater strength and drive; it gives more energy to the body. You use it for big moves at the barre like battements, for frappés that are fast and clear and spitting. You use it for jumps because it gets you in the air—in contrast to big jumps, which have to have a 6/8 because dancers have to get off the floor for that moment of breath in the air. Meter does have a definite effect, and it does change the physicality and energy of the body.

Timing and Cues in Choreographed Movement

For choreographed performance, Muller feels that the dancers can generate energy themselves. She has various ways of relating to music for theatrical pieces.

When we do rhythmic work, it's directly counted to the music. However, the majority of my dances are not counted at all. Movement is originated first by muscular rhythm: how long it takes to do a specific move. Do you want a slow arabesque or a fast arabesque?

In the beginning years, I always choreographed to silence and added the music later. It was very seldom that I started with the music. I always believed that if a dance couldn't stand on its own in silence, with its own internal phrasing and its own dynamic build, music wasn't going to help it.

I always thought that music was a crutch. Now, I still have certain beliefs in that, but I also have gone in the other direction, where what I call the molecules of music are the inspiration for the dance. But the dance is not just representative of the music, hitting certain beats or certain accents or instrumental riffs with the music. Instead, you are making an evocation of the musical form. You are becoming the music.

When working with muscular rhythm, the choreographer stresses that the clocked timing of dance movement does not change appreciably from performance to performance. Muller says, "One amazing thing about dance and dancers, at least in my experience as a choreographer, is that if you get the movement where you want it to be, you can time a section in silence—say, three minutes, fifty-two seconds. The next day you time it again, and it will also be three minutes, fifty-two seconds."

During creative sessions, a stopwatch is a handy tool. For example, Muller's *Refracted Light* was choreographed in silence. After completing the choreography to her satisfaction, she timed everything with a stopwatch, found some Tibetan music that seemed to complement her movement ideas, then went into the studio and put together an edited four-track sound score that basically has no strongly metered rhythmic element.

In other works, Muller decides upon music at the very beginning of the creative process and plans points of coincidence between movement and music. These will not vary from performance to performance, but the exact relationship of sound and dance may vary in small ways between these points.

Dancers' Awareness

"I believe that when you rehearse a dance well enough, the dancers have a much better sense of tempo than musicians do," says Muller. "When you are doing a physical move with your entire body, you know if it is just that bit faster or not. There is an amazing sense of tempo that performers develop if they are professional dancers."

Beyond tempo, dancers must become aware of the various ways in which their movement can relate to music. For example, some dances in the repertoire of The Works have a mixture of procedures. In *Woman with Visitors at 3 a.m.*, to original music by Keith Jarrett, most of the choreography does not have counts at all. One section has some counts; another was counted note to note and was choreographed specifically to follow the melody line in the music, even though Muller had experienced the music itself as unmetered at that point. At other moments, the dancers have very little to hang onto in the way of musical cues.

How do dancers pace themselves so that they reach a given choreographed movement by a certain sound in the music? According to Muller, "You have to be super aware. You really have to listen to the music, though you are not dancing *to* the music. The music is a companion, but you definitely have to end up in the same place with the music." How do performers get to be that way? "Rehearsal! We ask: Do you hear that? Do you hear that? Do you hear that? You have to do sections over and over again. It really takes repetition if dancers are not trained musically."

None of the dancers in The Works is ever called on to read or play a musical score. Instead, to bring out the bass or various melodies, Muller gets dancers to sing along or feel the rhythm in their bodies in other ways. They may rehearse to a tape, or only to an accompaniment of suggestively singsonged verbal directions such as: Back and back and a-r-c-h—And UP!—and lunge, and ara-BESque. "Awareness is the most important thing, and teaching people how to listen," reiterates Muller, while acknowledging that her eclectic choices of music do not make for easy analysis by ear alone.

Musical Choices

As with a number of successful contemporary choreographers, Jennifer Muller feels that her training in both music and dance at Julliard has influenced her creative approach. "A lot of it is inspired from music *structure*," she says.

When extant music is chosen for any dance work, the totality of the theatrical production is very much in the hands of the choreographer, including all the interrelations of movement and sound. But some of Muller's works have evolved in a different way, with the interrelationships created entirely by a musician. For example, *Lovers* was choreographed in silence, and a videotape was made of the completed dance. Working in the studio, Keith Jarrett sat down at the piano. The video was turned on, and he improvised jazz music to complement what he was seeing fresh for the first time. Twenty-six minutes later he struck the final notes for a tape that seemed so perfect for the dance that it has served as musical companion for *Lovers* ever since. For another commission, which became *Woman with Visitors at 3 a.m.*, Jarrett left more decisions up to the choreographer, giving her two hours of taped improvisations to listen to, sort out, and select from. After the choreographer decided on the musical content, she then set to work on the movement.

Despite these successes, Muller feels that the most satisfying way to work with a collaborating composer is to start the movement creation and the musical creation simultaneously. For example, her commission from David van Tieghem (for *City*) went like this:

> I made copious notes beforehand. I knew the layout of the piece, the sections, the basic overall tempos and tensions of the dance sections. He initially gave me ten or fifteen seconds of maybe nine things, on tape, like little sketches of different musical ideas. After our discussions, I would listen and say, "Well maybe that's appropriate for the second section," or "I don't think this one works for the piece at all." Then he would come

and watch part of the choreography that had been done in silence. He
would get more music to me. So we were really bouncing the ball back
and forth in collaborating.

In cases where the music is scored to complement finished choreography, Muller gives a composer directions on real time sections,
exact tempos indicated by metronome markings, phrase lengths in
counts, comments on the expressive nature of each section, and requests
for basic rhythms that she would like included. The composing process
becomes akin to creating a film score. In both cases, the visual aspects
are already completed.

How Dancers Hear
Music During Performance

After choreographic movement has been set, the musical focus is on the
performance by the dancers themselves. Concerning what happens onstage, Muller says,

> *The beginning of musicality in dancing is awareness: Do you hear the*
> *music? Are you dancing with cognizance of the music, or not?*
>
> *During actual performance, it is not possible to hear every note. The*
> *mind doesn't function that way; it flips very quickly, from second to sec-*
> *ond. The people who are not musical are actually tuning out the music*
> *for longer stretches of time. The dancers who are musical are more cogni-*
> *zant of the music in a second-to-second way. With some pieces (like the*
> *Chapman songs which I set), you can't lose the music at all. You have to*
> *be right there, because there are molecular relations to the music.*
>
> *I think that if dancers are musical, the music becomes a* part *of them.*
> *When I performed, I felt that I wasn't dancing to the music; rather, mu-*
> *sic and I were dancing. It's as if, when the music surges, a surge comes*
> *up in you. It's a physical sensation. Music is not just something there to*
> *accompany you; you are* with *the music. That is what happens with*
> *someone who is musical. You can see it influence dancers in the way that*
> *they are phrasing. When someone is not musical, you can see that they*
> *are not in relationship to the music.*

With such a keen choreographic eye directing them, the dancers
in The Works are expected to do a lot of preparation on their own. All
members take home tapes of the music for upcoming repertoire—and
listen, and listen, and listen.

"Words are helpful too," comments Muller. "But musicality is a
learned awareness, just as dancing is a learned awareness. You don't just

wake up one day and find you are able to dance. You don't wake up one day and know music.''

Twyla Tharp's Ideas on Music

During a captivating evening program of dance, verbal commentary, and volunteer participation in New York's City Center, one dauntless audience member asked choreographer/dancer Twyla Tharp what hope there was for a person who is tone deaf and can't hear the beat. Twyla Tharp first responded that such a person might consider some career other than professional dancing.[2] However, she went on to make a practical suggestion that could be useful to students with varying musical backgrounds: Put a large wooden box over a loudspeaker or radio and turn up its volume, so that the emanating musical vibrations can be physically felt by feet and hands touching the box.

As an opening solo, the choreographer suggested in movement what it is like to begin each day in the studio, and how physical experiments plus emotional input result in some elaborate and speedy patterns. Where do dances come from? Tharp emphasized: "Music is not always the first ingredient for me." Instead, she said she sometimes thinks of music as scenery. Since her dances already have rhythm, phrases, and counterpoint, she can use music as a context rather than parallel its structure or echo it. The choreographer observed that sometimes the mind can become dormant if one just improvises *to* music. Instead, she stressed the need to know which ingredients contribute to her work, and to recognize the impact that one's choice of music can have upon a theatrical dance.

"You read movement according to your ears," observed Tharp. "Usually the music tells you what the sentiment is."

Early in her career, Tharp presented her dances in silence. Subsequently, she has been astute in choosing music that lends interesting twists to many of her dances, drawing upon ragtime, classical symphonies, and recorded songs by Frank Sinatra, as well as commissioning a new score from rock musician David Byrne.

Music and the Job
of Tharp's Ballet Mistress

After dancing many years for Twyla Tharp, Shelley Washington became ballet mistress, working not only with the choreographer's company of select modern dancers but also on special projects with American Ballet Theatre.[3] Speedy and lithe, and giving the impression of a leprechaun who can do anything, Washington still demonstrates dances full out with recorded music in her work as a teacher and rehearsal director. Her energy and recall of details in both movement and music seem nothing short of phenomenal. Yet, she acknowledges, "Sometimes you work so hard you don't even hear the music." This is a state familiar to all dancers, it seems. All the more reason for dancers to mark dance patterns in an abbreviated manner when they are learning new choreography and becoming familiar with the music, she says.

What happens to the reflexlike muscle memory of dancers when they have formed habits of coordinating certain physical movement patterns with particular musical sounds and subsequently different music is used for final performance? According to Shelley Washington, there is no problem. "It works itself out in the first five minutes, though it does depend whether it is fast or slow. If you do something, let's say on classical music and it is slow and mysterious and has a classical feel, then put on a Michael Jackson song or the Beach Boys, it all of a sudden goes ten times faster, and if it has a definite funko groove, in the beginning it's an adjustment. But then it's lots and lots of fun, and just changes the whole quality and style of the movement."

Counting

Often the matter of relating movement to musical checkpoints is cleared up by using dancers' counts, Washington says.

> *Then you just lay the counts on top of the new music. For example, often we can make up dance phrasing in eights and put it to music in sixes, yet we still count the eights. It may be a little difficult and change the impetus of the movement, but three eights are twenty-four, and four sixes are twenty-four, so every three eights comes out on a one of the music. It's much easier to keep the dance that way than to change it all into sixes, because the momentum and the weight fall on the counts originally used for making the dance movement, and we just slip it into other musical counts.*

Should counting be abolished, because it may become a crutch and detract from important artistic aspects of dancing? Shelley Washington disagrees with that idea. "Counts are a quick way for everybody to associate. Obviously in the early days, one didn't have to count. If you could stand next to somebody, you could learn by osmosis. But counts are a way to get sixteen people moving at the same time, in an hour's rehearsal, as opposed to weeks. Often counts are economical. Yet they can be hindersome, because they can take over."

Washington attributes some of her artistic counting skills to her early study of violin and piano. Though she was a dance student at Juilliard from age seventeen, prior to that, at Interlochen Academy of the Arts, she also minored in piano. In her current work as ballet mistress, Washington also finds it helpful to be able to read a score. "If Twyla Tharp has a piece in mind, often she will write in who comes in on what. It is always useful to have a score. So when you are counting out things like some John Adams music—things that just go on and on—it is good to have that."

Because even some professional dancers have difficulty counting meters or phrases, Washington urges students to take up any musical instrument, mainly for what they can learn about timing and rhythms.

> *It's like a clock chiming, and somewhere in my body I just pick up on the rhythm. I will know: "It's the fifth one." I have a rhythm when I walk; I have a rhythm standing next to somebody to improvise or dance with them. It's a kind of inner clock, and I'm sure that it comes from studying music. I'm not going to say that I was great or anything like that; I was not in love with playing the piano or violin; they were not my passion. But I took private lessons and played in recitals. Could I get up and play now? No.*

Her advice for young dance students who aspire to professional careers:

> *They should be able to read music. They should be able to hear notes. They should be able to count. They should be able to interpret the music.*
>
> *I also think if somebody is working with you, they should be able to say, "Take it from the oboes," or, "Where the clarinets come in." So it's great to know what an oboe sounds like, and what a clarinet sounds like. It also helps to know that something is counted in three sixes and an eight every four sets. It's nice to be able to hear something once and know what it is: OK, that's fifteen eights, a 3/4 and a two. Sometimes we see dancers searching and trying to figure it out, but it's really right there in the music.*
>
> *I found it very hard to go into a dance audition. I've always admired the Broadway gypsies who get up on stage and sing their hearts out and act too. I think the more education you can get, the more things you can try when you are young—it has to go for you, it has to work, whether it's writing, music, acting, dancing, or painting. I think all the visual and hearing arts are very important.*

In performances, professional dancers must be prepared for the musical changes that may occur with different conductors, or even on different evenings. "Change is good. It's good to be able to adapt. It gives an extra *something*," remarks the ballet mistress.

Tharp's choreography demands topmost speed from her dancers. This requires intensive practice, and in teaching parts, Washington may spend days concentrating on the movement patterns, without relating them to the music. "Yet there are times when you put the music on right away," she says. "Music is much nicer to listen to than someone's voice counting."

What kind of listening experiences should dance students concentrate on to prepare themselves for professional work? Washington says,

> *All kinds of music. I find it a wonder that you can do the same movement to twenty styles of music. What inspires one dancer doesn't necessarily inspire another. One person could make a solo, and then another person could do it to country and western and it would be just their thing. Somebody else could do it to Bach, and somebody else could do the dance to a Yiddish song, and someone else would find their feeling in Chuck Berry. So that's interesting. And that would be interesting to do with students: to work on dance phrases and try putting them on different music, to see how people move and where they find their rhythm and their natural weight, and how comfortable they are.*

Another Tharp Dancer, on Coordination

Discussing musical aspects of rehearsal, dancer Richard Colton has offered some insights into what it was like to work on a new piece with choreographer Twyla Tharp. As reported in *Ballet Review,* he said:

> *With Twyla we often develop the movement in silence. There's no music. We're simply seeking in the steps' maximum shading, accents, change of dynamics, variation of speed, rhythmic clarity, contrasts in stillness and movements—all elements in making a musical dance phrase. But there's no outside influence while we're working on the movement itself. . . .*
>
> *Later Twyla may introduce music—a constantly changing assortment of phonograph records, for instance—to encourage new directions (in terms of texture, speed, phrasing, weight) in which the dance steps can go. When the music we will perform to is actually set, it becomes a challenge to keep all these initial discoveries within this new time limitation. We are holding the individuality of the dance phrase but at the same time phrasing it to the new music. As you know, the dance phrase has its own logic. To emphasize this logic plus its relationships to the music is what makes a dancer musical. . . .*
>
> *Our work process varies. We can learn a dance phrase outdoors as an adagio to the Pachelbel canon, only to have the phrase end up a ferocious*

pounding movement on a dark stage to music of The Band, as in Chapters and Verses. *Or we can start rehearsing a jumping phrase indoors and end up doing it downhill in Central Park, as in "Aquarius" from* Hair. *We've developed dance phrases to the intricacies of a Bach partita and then performed them to the Mickey Mouse theme song. What I've been describing is, of course, just one process. We don't always work that way. Many times we work directly with the music. And of course we may keep switching the music.*

All the evolutions get us deeper into the movement. The final quartet in Mud *was choreographed to a Mozart piano piece, but we eventually performed it in silence. The Mozart still served the movement in performance, though, in the manner that a clear container holds water. Although the Mozart music was not heard by the audience or the dancers, our muscles remembered it because the dance movement was held together by the Mozart rhythms, since that was ingrained in the movement itself.*[4]

Explorations and Assignments

1. From your own experience and observations, list some common denominators of dance and music. Demonstrate briefly in movement some of the possible relationships of the variables.

2. Choose a short piece of music you particularly like. Improvise three movement studies: following closely what you hear and mimicking the sounds in movement; contrasting your movement to what is heard; focusing on one element of the music (melody, bass line, rhythm, dynamics, articulation, harmonic rhythm, a particular instrument, phrasing) and making the movements related in some way.

3. Devise a brief movement pattern in silence. Repeat it several times, with different styles of music: Baroque concerto grosso, a solo piano etude, a current rock song, a minimalist piece, a contemporary chamber work, or a progressive jazz work. Adjust and change the movement pattern to merge with the flavor of the work. Discuss what happens to the movement when the music is changed.

4. Talk to a professional dancer about how he or she works with music in rehearsals for choreography, and report your findings to the class. What is helpful for aspiring dance students to learn about music and about ways of relating dance movement and music? In performance, what do dancers listen for?

chapter 5

CHOREOGRAPHY: A COLLABORATIVE EFFORT

W hat I appreciate the most is an openness to a real
collaboration. I like to have my input, but I also like to have
my musician's input. I like us to work together so that what
we both feel is that what we have together is better than
what either one of us might have done alone.

—Shirley Ririe

More than sixty years ago, Martha Hill, a young instructor who was to
become one of the guiding lights in the world of dance education (first
at Bennington, then at New York University and The Juilliard School),
wrote some comments that continue to provide a framework for thinking
about the rhythmic relationships possible between dance and music:

> *First, movement may be based upon the underlying or primary rhythm of
> the accompaniment. This is a simple relationship, perhaps best exempli-
> fied in many folk dances. Second, movement may observe only the overly-
> ing rhythm of the accompaniment, its phrases and longer cadences. The
> new dance employs this method particularly when using sustained and
> flowing movement. Third, movement may synchronize with the exact note-
> pattern of the accompaniment. Fourth, movement may be taken against
> the accompaniment; that is, movement may follow a beat or note as if the
> beat or note were the motivating force, or movement may precede the beat
> or note as if the beat or note were initiated by the movement. Fifth, move-
> ment may be planned as a counterpoint to the accompaniment, the move-
> ment and accompaniment together making a contrapuntal form similar*

to the round, canon, or fugue in music. Sixth, combinations of these
principles may be employed in the same composition.[1]

Performing dancers of today may find themselves dealing with many styles of choreography and music even for a single program. In rehearsing various choreographic works, it may be helpful to be aware of the general methods of the choreographer in using music. When students begin to experiment with their own choreographic projects, it may also be helpful to consider various approaches to collaboration with composers and instrumentalists, as well as to consider different ways of relating dance movement to taped music.

Some common denominators of music and dance have been touched upon already with a view to dancers' concerns in performance. Now they will be explored in a different context, by looking in on a music workshop for professional choreographers.

Musical Coaching for Emerging Choreographers

The Carlisle Project is located in an old converted mill in western Pennsylvania. For the choreographers who attend workshops here, the situation is akin to a laboratory.[2] Barbara Weisberger, the founding director, comments: "It might be presumptuous to think you can create choreographers, but you *can* nourish and stimulate them. We are the research and development arm of the field."

Speaking of the place of music in the total thrust of these efforts, she adds: "I can't separate music from the whole concept, just as it's very difficult to separate music from dance; they're together. Interesting choreography creates the need for interesting music."

The people gathered here now are already professional, highly experienced dancers: one is the ballet master of the Metropolitan Opera Ballet, another is associate director of the Denver regional ballet company, another has performed on Broadway, a fourth is a former principal with American Ballet Theatre. Yet because their early training was focused on the technical aspects of performing choreography set by someone else, these artists feel a need to explore collaborative methods with a fresh approach.

Composer Juli Nunlist leads off a workshop with a session in which the choreographers are to listen carefully to a piano piece by the twentieth-century composer Dimitri Kabalevsky. The dancer-choreographers are to walk during phrases, and to pause at cadences. Surprisingly, the participants find they have differing opinions about how many phrases they hear, and about exactly where these phrases come to an end. This points up the difficulty of grasping everything upon one hearing, and suggests some advantages in being able to study a score for changes of harmony, cadences, phrase markings, and so forth. It may save choreographers time if they can gain information about the music both aurally and visually.

Next, Nunlist asks the dancers about how they think people listen to music. In reply, the choreographers conjure up scenes of music being used to accompany a beautician trimming hair or a mechanic fixing a car or a couple dining in a restaurant or a congregation meditating in church, or even some dancers doing whatever they wish onstage.

When music is used as pure background, suggests Nunlist, the level of listening is apt to be relatively inactive, what she calls "enjoying music as a warm bath." If listening stops with such a general impression of atmosphere, style, or texture, then choreographers usually will not have enough information upon which to build their dances. Choreographers need a more detailed grasp of what they are hearing, plus the kind of information that can best be gained through analysis of music rather than through being able to perform it on instruments.

The choreographers gathered at Carlisle continue to answer the question of what they hear in music: sound, texture, pitch, rhythm. Dynamics, accents, meter. Harmony. Structure. Tempo, melody. Phrasing, counterpoint, pauses. Silence. Instrumental orchestration. Different pitch centers or keys. A suggestion of a story or program. The performer's interpretation. Climaxes, consonance, dissonance, resting places. Finally, someone adds: "The intent to communicate, by the composer!"

Next, Nunlist asks the participants which, of all those elements they had named, would they still have if they were to dance in silence. The group responds: rhythm, meter, dynamics, phrasing—and on and on with a fascinating duplication.[3] But then differences are noted when music is added to a dance previously done in silence: "It gives another dimension," someone says. "There is a greater impact."

It is generally agreed that music can give dancers an ongoing background; it can be soundscape against which you can do your own thing. This possibility has been used both by choreographers who don't use music purposely as well as those who do, such as Merce Cunningham. This is a challenge and a statement of the independence of music and dance even while they are going on simultaneously.

Next, the emerging choreographers consider what music can add to their dances: It can establish an environment, motivate the dancers to move, or suggest a mood, story, or theme. It can be a crutch upon which to put dance steps. More creatively, music can contribute a framework, shape, and design for a theatrical dance piece. It can unify the dancers. Even different qualities of instrumental sound alone can suggest different movements or emotional climate.

Nunlist adds her own suggestion: "Music can be an atmosphere *through* which you dance. It can inspire. It involves the audience in the aural as well as the visual sense." Finally, a more practical soul pipes up: "If you didn't have music, the box office would fall off!"

Using What You Hear

Once choreographers understand what is in the music, Juli Nunlist maintains, they can use any element or elements in it for their dance pieces. They can go with the music or in contrast to it. They can focus on the tempo, the meter, the dynamics, the phrasing—any number of aspects at any moment.

All these suggestions are geared to the process of setting choreography to extant music. It must be pointed out that the process of collaborating with a live composer is likely to be different, and that with many choreographers nowadays the movement is apt to be shaped first.

Barbara Weisberger observes: "Choreographers in the ballet have been using music not as a tool, but as a crutch. They don't really hear it. They might be inspired by it, but they don't hear the elements in it."

As an antidote, at the initial Carlisle workshops, choreographers were directed to start from movement itself as the inspiration and then to put music to it. This was frustrating to some artists who previously tended to start with music as their main inspiration. Because most ballet choreographers are likely to continue using music as their impetus, Weisberger suggests that they should at least learn to use music as a real partner. In order to do that, she says, they should first know how to hear it. "We're absolutely not thinking about mirroring the structure of the musical composition," she cautions. Instead, it is hoped that choreographers will seek logical relationships between music and dance movement, and create a fusion that makes artistic sense.

The more a choreographer knows about ingredients and styles of music, the more likely it is that he or she can elicit or choose music that enhances the movement creation. The advice Doris Humphrey gave in her book *The Art of Making Dances* still rings true today:

> The well-trained ear is sensitive to music, hears the beat, the phrase, the harmony, the dynamics and melody plus the over-all "feel" of what the composer is saying. The choreographer is the sensitive and willing listener, but not the slave of the composer.

He should also be musically literate; know how music is organized on pa-
per and be able to read a score with all its signs, marks, time signatures
and note values; be knowledgeable about the history and literature of mu-
sic, so as to have an informed opinion as to what to choose; be able to
talk to any musician in his language, regardless of the fact that the musi-
cian probably knows little or nothing about dance or its vocabulary. In
conferring with a composer, musical knowledge is particularly important
for insuring clarity in the collaboration and for winning and holding the
respect of the musician.[4]

Methods of Collaboration

Collaborating composers and choreographers have these options:

1. The composer creates a musical score after receiving only general directions from the choreographer. The specifications may touch
upon emotional atmosphere, instrumentation available within the company's budget, real clocked time, and other framing aspects. After the
score is completely finished, the choreographer sets the dance and is in
control of the relationships between sound and movement.

2. The choreographer and composer discuss the work, try out
movement and sound together, edit and change as the joint piece
evolves. The composer attends dance rehearsals; the choreographer listens to preliminary renditions (either on a piano, at an instrumental
rehearsal, or through tapes). There is a give-and-take, and the relationship between movement and sound is a result of communication between the two artists. Almost always, however, it is the choreographer
who is responsible for the total work, and the composer may alter the
music to accommodate the needs of the dance. It is understood that the
choreographer is essentially determining relationships between sound
and movement.

3. The choreographer may work out the total movement design
of a piece in silence. The composer then attends a run-through, or more
frequently nowadays, is provided with a videotape of the movement. The
music composed is absolutely tailored to the movement. The choreographer may give some overall suggestions about what general flavor of
timbre is desired, what general character or mood of music, where the
main accents or climaxes are to occur, and so forth. Depending upon
the detail of the requests, the choreographer still retains control of the
essential character and quality of a work, plus major decisions about the
main points of relationship between movement and sound. For instance,
the choreographer can suggest that for certain sections, the music
should metrically agree with what the dancers are doing—or that if the

dancers are in a triple meter, perhaps something contrasting would be appropriate for certain sections. The choreographer can still determine whether there is to be a close linkage of the time elements, the dynamic elements, the general styles, and the emotional evocations in both music and dance. Alternatively, only certain aspects could relate intimately, while others could be charted to provide contrast or be otherwise supportive. All these factors can be discussed between choreographer and composer. The more they know about each other's style of creation, obviously, the more successful the collaboration is apt to be.

4. The choreographer works out the movement in silence, hands the composer a videotape, and leaves to the composer all decisions about style and the relationships between sound and movement. This is somewhat the opposite method of number one, and it confers upon the composer considerable responsibility for the final product. However, particularly when the choreographer knows the composer's style well, the composer may be trusted to produce a suitable musical score or tape.

5. The composer and choreographer work up their joint piece by a combination of methods described above, depending upon what seems appropriate for various sections. They then seek input from a third artist with differing expertise. Especially when electronic scores are involved, collaborators may seek an opinion from a technical sound engineer. In addition, general theatrical directors have sometimes been able to offer suggestions to collaborating choreographers and composers because they are used to considering contexts that also include lighting, the ambiance of the place where the work is to be performed, and costuming.

Workshops in Collaboration

Among the places where professional artistic directors have gathered to focus on the process of choreography have been the annual two-week Craft of Choreography Conferences held in various locations by the National Association for Regional Ballet (now called Regional Dance America). And thanks to a recent pilot program in conjunction with Meet The Composer, these opportunities to learn about collaboration were extended to composers, in the form of residency fellowships.

Considering the effect these conferences have had upon the musical awareness of participating choreographers, former RDA director Doris Hering observed:

> We found in the beginning that the choreographers who came were musically very conservative. Not only conservative, but also they really used music only rhythmically; they didn't use it in terms of its structure, or its relevance to dance structure. That's why we always have a director of mu-

sic who is usually a composer, because we feel that the choreographers have to have their ears opened, and not think of music as something that's only rhythmic. If the director of music finds that a choreographer is using the same kind of music over and over, or is not as comfortable with a particular kind of music, he or she is pushed out of that niche. For example, some have never dared to use electronic music, so they may be pushed into that area. First they may object strenuously, but then they find it interests them.

Our conferences don't stress finished product. In other words, the choreographers are not there to do one piece and polish it to take home at the end. We emphasize process, so that they do several assignments and are pushed more, musically and structurally.

Nevertheless, one can notice an expanded musical awareness simply by looking at the scores that are used for the finished products presented during the regional spring festivals. "There's a lot more musical daring than there used to be," observed Hering. "In the old days, you'd hear Chopin and Tchaikovsky and then Tchaikovsky and Chopin. You don't find that now."[5]

Example of Graham, Horst, and Hawkins

While conservative tastes in music may have narrowed the vision of some ballet choreographers, the same hardly holds true for modern dance artists. Early in the development of contemporary dance styles, Martha Graham and Louis Horst set about revising the traditional relationships between music and dance, as well as reinventing collaboration.[6] Horst was originally a musician for Denishawn. Then later as music director and mentor to Martha Graham, he exerted tremendous influence upon the choreographer's emerging style. Later, when Erick Hawkins entered the company as a dancer, he too was influential in arranging for commissioned scores from some of the leading composers of the time. And in his subsequent long career with his own company, Hawkins always insisted upon having music specially commissioned for his dances, always performed live by a chamber ensemble that tours with the dancers.

But to go back to Graham. The composer Norman Lloyd provided us with a good idea of what the early modern dance collaborations were like:

Graham's approach to composition was a unique one for the composer. In Wallingford Riegger's words, "When I arrived at her studio I found to my surprise her dance group assembled and ready to perform for me the already completed dance." It was necessary for the composer to work to a definite number of counts and reverse the usual process of having music come before the movement. The advantage to the dancer was obvious—it gave complete freedom to the dancer to experiment with "body rhythm" which is not at all identical with what we think of as dance music, that is regular pulsation with regular phrasing. This free rhythmic approach, "I'll dance it and it is up to you to count it" was most instructive to the composer and gave him a new insight into the problem of rhythmic organization. At the same time, it put a strait-jacket on the music and made the composer aware, too often, of the beat rather than the phrase. Also the problem of filling up a precise number of counts became more important at times than the quality of the music. Many composers felt that it was impossible to achieve anything like a unified piece of music by this approach, forgetting that every time Schubert wrote a song he was limited to a certain extent by the rhythm of the words. Eventually Graham decided that she would get better musical results if the composers had more freedom and in all of her later works has worked with the composer by laying out a scenario, possibly suggesting the type of movement or even the quality of the music and then letting the composer go to work.[7]

Insights into Graham's Movement-Music Relationships

Although in her last years Martha Graham came to lament the lack of documentation of her life's work, for a long time she shunned extensive filming for any purpose, preferring the impact of live theatrical performance. However, when films were made, they often became a valuable tool for later restagings even during Graham's lifetime, and they can provide students of today with insights into Graham's choreographic methods.

Bert Terborgh, one of Graham's last rehearsal directors (and formerly a principal dancer with the company), emphasized the importance of such films in the process of mounting revivals.[8] One of his own projects had been to study silent movies of *Every Soul Is a Circus* (to an original score by Paul Nordoff), as performed by Martha Graham, Erick Hawkins, and others of the original cast. Terborgh followed this general process:

What I will do is look at the video from beginning to end so I have a concept of what the dance is about: how many parts there are, what the relationships of the people are, what the set is like. Then I will go back and do it phrase by phrase. I will take it apart physically and write it down, step-by-step. But at the same time, I will say something like this: You are coming right-left-right-left; make one turn. I would straightaway choose the relationship towards the spacing, the relation to the other people, and the direction of focus as well. Phrase by phrase, I look at the dance, write it down, and go back and do it again. It's a long process.

For a twenty-minute piece, it takes at least five hours to do such a pre-liminary study. Terborgh continued:

> *So this is the way I get the whole piece sketched out. Then the next day I start the same thing all over again, phrase by phrase, from the beginning. I look at the video, have my notes, have all my counts, and sketch where the people are. Then I would do the dance as full-out as I could. Then phrase-by-phrase again. Then I would try to get some of the same people who had danced it before, if possible. They can help by showing what they did. Also, you have to be aware of how people looked then, and the general style of the times.*

Because many of the early films of Martha Graham's dances were silent, Terborgh had the additional task of working out the movement counts in relation to musical cues. When he restaged *Every Soul Is a Circus* (originally premiered in 1939), he was able to benefit from comments written into the musical score. He spoke gratefully about conductors who in the past might have made copious and accurate observations about the stage action and marked this information down on the score. However, there have been cases where even the musical scores themselves were lost, adding to the quandaries.

Speaking generally about how Martha Graham's movements co-incided with the musical structures, Terborgh noted that she sometimes would have traditional rhythmic use of music. In such cases, one would simply count pulses, beats, or meter as dancers are accustomed to doing in classical ballet, for example.

But especially in her more dramatic works, Graham was freer in the relationship between movement and sound. Dancers would have leeway, and the middles of phrases would not necessarily be synchro-nized with every aspect of the music's timing. However, there would be certain musical cues, like pillars for an arc: sounds to mark the time for a dancer to start a certain movement pattern, or to end a movement phrase and achieve a pose in a particular place on the set. Between such points, the phrasing of the dance movements and the phrasing and counts of the music would not necessarily coincide, and they could vary with each performance. Perhaps the counts of the dancers would be different from the counts of the music. Or perhaps the dancers would not need to count at all, but rather just listen to the music for their next discernible cue.

Terborgh's concerns were the practical ones of preparing dancers for public performances. "The dance doesn't have to look the way it did fifty years ago," he emphasized. The tempos too may be different. And in regard to these, he was at times able to consult the original conductors from earlier performances, and to gain a sense of the tempos that had been taken. In general, it was the rehearsal director's impression that a number of earlier works had been speeded up in their revived presentations. Partly this was a reflection of the higher level of physical technique among dancers of today. But in addition, Terborgh stressed the need for presenters to see with the eyes of today's audience. "It can never be the same—though with some pieces we can get a *sense* of what was before."

Current Musical Choices for Dance

Nearing the end of the twentieth century, it seems impossible to pick out a single trend in the use of music for theatrical dance in America and elsewhere. Instead, there are many approaches—some new, some drawing on the past:

1. Methods of musical composition are drawn from many traditions around the world, as well as from techniques developed by individuals. This has resulted in styles coexisting: neo-Romantic, neoclassic, contrapuntal, homophonic, minimalist, chance, controlled process, Asian-based, African-based, atonal, tonal, neoprimitive, melodic, nonmelodic, collage, musique concrète, pop rock, hip-hop, rap, soul, progressive jazz, Dixieland and stride revival, big band arrangements, sonic experiments, and more.

2. Efforts are made to understand and perform the music of various cultures in accurate traditional styles.

3. Compact-disc recordings have greatly enhanced the delivery of sound in auditoriums, so that artistic directors of dance feel free to delve into classical European repertoire as well as recordings of regional styles from around the world.

4. Affordable electronic synthesizers have opened the possibilities of commissioning relatively inexpensive new scores, and setting brand-new sounds.

5. There is a renewed perception of the artistic possibilities inherent in the chamber ensemble as an alternative to the full orchestra used for classical ballet and many modern dance works.

6. Choreography often includes musicians in the visual and theatrical aspects, and there is a thrust to view dance as a multimedia dramatic entity even if the music is not live.

7. Mathematical and electronic procedures have influenced the way music is composed. This includes so-called process music, as well as multitrack recording.

8. New sources of funding are encouraging major collaborations.

9. There is increasing awareness that good musical collaboration for the dance is a specialty that deserves both more training and more professional recognition.

International Guild for Collaborative Musicians

Evidence of this last point lies in the existence of the International Guild of Musicians in Dance.[9] Founded in 1991 by William Moulton, the organization promises to serve an important function in fostering better musical collaboration for dance, both onstage and in the studio. Already, through its workshop conferences, journal, newsletters, archival material, and networking, the guild has done much in the way of both investigating and communicating knowledge about the creative processes involved in composing and improvising music for dance. Although the workshops in both the U.S. and Europe have concentrated on the aspects of collaboration that musicians must master, the entire proceedings of these annual gatherings are also pertinent to the efforts of dancers themselves (an address for information is listed in the appendix). Consequently, dancers are also encouraged to become informed.

Funding for Collaboration

A primary thrust in the renewed interest that composers and choreographers have taken in collaboration is due to major new funding geared specifically to the creation of new music for new dance. This has affected both ballet and the world of modern dance. Companies that formerly eschewed all music or used only tapes of existing works are now welcoming funding that allows them to offer live music as part of their dance performances. For instance, the Mary Flagler Cary Charitable Trust awarded a grant to the Trisha Brown Company recently to incorporate a marching band into performances of *Foray Forêt*. Another grant went to David Dorfman Dance for musicians' rehearsal and performance fees for site-specific performances. A third went to Elisa Monte Dance for orchestral performance of *The World Upside Down*, to a commissioned score by Glenn Branca.

Reflecting on the general effect of new music on the box office, Barbara Greenfield, executive director of Liz Lerman and the Dance Exchange, comments:

> *I think new music might make a difference in a very convoluted way. It gives more artistic license for the creative juices, which ultimately may allow the choreographer to develop a more powerful piece. There is more artistic control over what can and can't be done in a piece. Therefore, I think ultimately the audience gets the best from that artist. There need be fewer compromises made at the artistic level. An audience always benefits from that.[10]*

In regard to funding professional companies, nothing yet has matched the Composer/Choreographer Project of Meet the Composer, funded jointly by the Pew Charitable Trusts and the Ford Foundation.[11] Established in 1988 as a three-year project, an impressive listing of new works soon mounted up. The sizable grants covered composers' fees for scores written in many media.

The brainchild of Meet the Composer's president, John Duffy, the project began with an intensive study by the late dance artist Ian Horvath. In his eloquent report, Horvath noted:

> *The single most important need in dance today is the development of a body of work large enough to sustain the repertory demands of our major institutions. Compared to that of our sister disciplines, our standard repertory is miniscule. All companies received the idea of this new program with enthusiasm and were quick to realize the inevitability and righthead-edness of jointly funding new dance and new music.[12]*

Discussing the project in midstream, Meet the Composer's Duffy observed:

> *When you are creating a work, you put the bucket down, and when you pull up, you hope you've got something. So composers and choreographers working together must put the bucket down in the creative juices and come up with things that are going to nurture each other.*
>
> *I tell young people: Look! You have a chance to earn a living, to hone your craft, to collaborate. There's a dance company out there: Go! Open the doors! Open the windows! Let some light in.[13]*

Ella King Torrey of the Pew Charitable Trusts added this perspective: "If we are going to have a vital arts community tomorrow, it's very important that we seed it with the art of today."[14]

Ideally, for both dancers and musicians, the process of learning to collaborate begins at the student level and continues throughout later creative and performance projects.

Cautions on Copyright and Cultural Borrowing

In connection with the exhortation to explore the musical riches of the world, two precautions should be considered by dancers.

First, not all music is free to be used for choreography. If a public performance is planned, dancers would do well to check the copyright status of music they wish to include. Anything in the public domain can be adapted legally for theatrical use. But if a musical work is still in copyright, its use for choreographic purposes comes under the legal heading of grand rights, which means that individual permission and fees must be arranged with the copyright holder (either the composer or the publisher). If there are questions about contemporary works, the Volunteer Lawyers for the Arts may be able to help. The performing rights organizations ASCAP and BMI may also be able to clarify copyright status of particular works by their affiliated composers, though neither organization may enter into any grand-rights arrangements.

A second consideration for dancers is not about a legal matter, but rather a broad question of aesthetics and respect for other creative artists, as well as for entire cultures. Ethically speaking, there is the question of whether anybody has the right to distort someone else's artistic creation in a context quite removed from the original spirit and intent of the piece. Perhaps the use of religious music is the best example. In any case, if words are involved, it is a good idea to check the meaning as well as the connotations within the culture of origin.

Touching upon both copyright and borrowing, Canadian composer Phillip Djwa wrote a thoughtful letter to *Dance Connection* magazine. His concerns stemmed from observations at the Fringe Festival of International Dance Artists held in Toronto. Djwa commented:

> *I noticed that many choreographers in the festival used canned music without obtaining the rights to do so. This is obviously completely illegal, but the question is not that simple. Although this problem exists more in the independent scene than the company scene, it is an issue that all choreographers could think more about.*[15]

The composer went on to note that ignorance is often to blame; choreographers are not sure how to ascertain the copyright holder. In many cases they are afraid that they could not afford the fees that would be involved in commissioning new music from composers in the area, and artistically, dancers may prefer to retain total control of a work by selecting existing music. What most bothered the letter writer is a cavalier attitude toward the use of any music for dance purposes:

> *Music becomes a part of a dance piece without respecting the fact that music is an artistic creation in itself. Often the music has existed as a complete entity before the dance, and the practice of excerpting parts of it to fit the timing of the dance can violate the spirit of the music. There is an attitude that the music can be sliced, diced, extended or changed without compunction.*

Equally distressing to Djwa is what he calls cultural plundering. He suggests:

> *It is not appropriate today, given the dialogue on cultural appropriation, to take traditional Tibetan, African, or native music . . . and use it for a piece without acknowledging its origin or context (in one awful case the choreographer credited herself as the originator—she had "found" the music!).*
>
> *While the issue of cross-cultural exchange is even more complex, there must be more thought and respect paid to the music used. I have seen many examples of dance where a magpie sensibility informs the choice of stringing together the music of three or four completely unrelated cultures, without understanding, that results in a gooey melting pot.*

One alternative to such results, of course, is for dancers to learn how to collaborate with creative musicians who can skillfully produce appropriate and distinctive music to fit the needs of specific theatrical dance works.[16]

Preparing for Creative Collaboration

Students and other emerging choreographers can prepare themselves for collaborative opportunities partly by acquiring a knowledge of the musical terms, materials, and procedures presented in Part Two. All along, there is much to be said for simply listening attentively to a wide variety of musical styles, taking a hint from what are considered classics within each genre.

Obviously not all musical styles will be suitable for any one choreographer's particular purposes. Additionally, it should be noted simply that there is a lot of dull or even bad music around, or good music that is poorly performed. Certainly good and bad are relative, personal evaluations. Nevertheless, despite daunting titles and procedures found in music (particularly in contemporary music), dancers may encounter musical moments when the most truthful response is equivalent to the remark of the little boy who shouted that the emperor had no clothes.

Ultimately, a dancer's own ears and individual emotion and kinesthetic responses will determine decisions concerning music for choreography. However, if dance works are to enjoy repeated success in performance, music that will withstand repeated hearings on the part of both audiences and performers is best chosen. In addition, it helps if the music not only complements a choreographic idea but also encourages the dancers to perform convincingly. The music should add an interesting flavor, but not so interesting that it detracts from the dance onstage.

Another consideration (which may require some research) is whether a particular piece has already been used by a major choreographer. If so, then an emerging dance artist may invite comparisons or at least memories on the part of audiences, and perhaps alternatives should be explored.

Part Two consists of words on paper but is focused on the needs of dancers who must get most of their musical information by listening while they are moving in space. By gaining more knowledge of the basic building blocks of music, a dancer may automatically develop new ways of listening. This may be helpful in grasping the main events, form, and stylistic aspects of many unfamiliar pieces of music encountered during classwork or rehearsals, or during a personal search for music to be used for choreography.

Explorations and Assignments

1. As a group project, use available videos of brief excerpts and compare the way music and movement relate in one classical ballet, one jazz dance from a musical show, one early modern concert dance, and one postmodern dance. Notice the general relationships of the timing as well as the expressive suggestions and style of the movement and music in each case.

2. What sound equipment should the dance presenter of today be familiar with? What sound equipment do you know how to work? Survey your institution's available equipment. Learn how to use a video camera and playback machine. Learn how to operate a tape recorder and CD deck with loudspeakers for theatrical performance.

3. Go to the library and locate its holdings of musical recordings and dance videos. Locate the reference books listed at the beginning of the bibliography. Locate your library's books on music and browse through the general categories of titles. Survey the holdings of musical scores.

4. Start a listening log or file, including your personal impressions of music you hear as part of dance performances as well as pieces heard over the radio, in concert, or via recordings.

5. Discuss the basic considerations of copyright law as it affects dancers who use music in both the studio and for performance.

6. Write a brief essay giving your opinion about the difference it makes if music is live or taped for dance performances.

7. For class discussion: What are some affordable ways to provide live music for some upcoming student performances? What considerations (such as scheduling) must enter into this choice?

8. List some aspects of music you feel it is important to listen for while you are dancing. For class discussion: What are some helpful approaches to grasping unfamiliar music during initial choreographic rehearsals?

part two

A MOVEMENT-ORIENTED APPROACH TO THE FUNDAMENTALS OF MUSIC

T*housands of hours are spent acquiring the physical skills necessary to dance, but very few dancers spend even a dozen hours learning about music. An understanding of music is not obtained by osmosis nor by following the beat of a stick. It is a delicate, difficult and lovely subject, and must be wooed with as much ardor as you would devote to turnout and extensions.*

—Paul Draper

chapter 6

SOUNDS AND SILENCES

T*he stillnesses are important and are to be on a par with the moves—as important as the negative space in paintings, the yin of the yang—as important as, if not more so than, silences in music.*

—Paul Taylor

All music is made up of sounds and silences. Often people tend to focus on the sounds. But the silences are important too, much in the way that slats in a window may frame what is seen and provide their own pattern for human perception.

The importance of silences was demonstrated quite clearly at one of New York's avant-garde university concerts in which the composer simply switched on an electronic device that would emit a pure sine soundwave. After about ten minutes of this, most of the audience had migrated to the theater's lobby for lively discussions of how intolerable uninterrupted sound can be. For music, in contrast, one must have intentional, functional silences.

Musicians use the term *rests* to indicate the brief silent spaces of time that carve sound into distinguishable patterns. Yet this word does not imply dead or empty segments when nothing is happening, anymore than a dancer's holding of an arabesque pose is inconsequential. Time continues to pass during rests, and the attentive listener will continue to sense the underlying flow and emotional essence of the overall musical work.

The crucial element of silence in music for dance was remarked upon by George Balanchine. In connection with his use of works by Igor Stravinsky, the choreographer wrote:

A pause, an interruption, is never empty space between indicated sounds. It is not just nothing. It acts as a carrying agent from the last sound to the next one. Life goes on within each silence.

An interpreter should not fear (unfortunately many do) Stravinsky's calculated, dynamic use of silence. He should give it his trust and, what's more, his undivided attention. In this use of time, in the extreme, never-failing consciousness of it, he will find one of the living secrets of Stravinsky's music.[1]

Similarly, dancers can benefit from regarding the silences in all music with attention.

Unaccompanied Dances

For artistic purposes, one assumes that silence is the relative absence of relevant intentional sound. During dance performances there are always concommitant noises: the rustle of costumes, pointe shoes hitting the stage floor, heavy breathing during exertion, somebody in the audience coughing or unwrapping a piece of candy at just the wrong moment. It could be said that one purpose of accompaniment is simply to cover up such distracting sounds in the theater.

Dance movement performed in relative silence can be self-sufficient and expressive. Yet silent dance may also share some common denominators with music, and may evoke musical ideas or associations in both dancers and audiences.

If you observe people moving in everyday life and singsong some vocal music to mimic the timing of physical movement, you may automatically become more sensitive to the specific timings of dance movement, and to the possible relationships between movement and music. While singsonging, notice where there is a tendency to break up the sounds by injecting silences, and the points at which you want to breathe in relation to the physical movement observed.

Another experiment could involve a majority of silent time segments, broken only occasionally by the injection of short sounds now and then. One is reminded of psychologists' pictures in which one can focus on either black or white portions and discern entirely different images. So too, one could focus alternately on the sounds or the silences in music for different perspectives. The relative sparseness or density of musical sounds refers to its *texture,* which in ensemble music is often a function of the placement of rests in various parts.

In order to grasp the sounds of music used for any dance purposes, the listener must pay close attention to the silences, and to the moments of delineation between sounds and silences. This is the beginning of all formal study of the art of music.

The Physics of Sound

All sound begins with movement. Something has to move back and forth in order for a tone to be produced; physical vibration must occur for silence to be broken with sound.

With state-of-the-art electronic equipment, there are some ingenious experiments being done to prove that molecules exist and constitute all matter. Just assume, for purposes of this explanation, that they do.

When matter is disturbed in various ways, the molecules pass on movement and energy in wave patterns, which move outward from the source of disturbance in ever-widening and constantly weakening form. It is the *energy,* the movement, that gets passed along. The molecules themselves jiggle back and forth in their own immediate space, to a degree that depends upon the vigor of the disturbance as well as upon how tightly the molecules are packed in each substance.

Sound waves move through matter in consistent patterns, which can be ascertained with electronic equipment and charted on paper. Although the study of how sounds are produced and transmitted through various materials does pertain to the art of the dancer, the details must be omitted here. Those interested may consult the excellent textbook on acoustics by Donald E. Hall listed in the bibliography.

However, it should be noted briefly that the concerns dancers may have in connection with the transmission of sound waves can involve the acoustics in theaters and studios. One important aspect of sound is that it can be redirected and changed as it moves outward from the source. It can also be muffled or quieted completely depending on materials it encounters. In dry air at room temperature, sound travels at approximately 1,130 feet per second—perceptually slower than the speed of light, which is more than 186,000 miles per second. Consequently, even in large dance studios (especially reverberant gymnasiums), problems may arise when the dance teacher stands at one end of the space and snaps his or her fingers, supposedly in synchronization with the pianist at the other end of the room. Or in a sizable theater, one may have the impression, as an audience member, of seeing the movement slightly before the sound arrives. That may actually be the case.

Other interesting things happen in connection with the way sound waves travel in theaters. The music gives a different impression during rehearsals in an empty hall than it does when audience members are present, wearing soft clothes that also absorb and modify sound waves. Or because of the construction of orchestral pits, the sound may travel throughout the hall very well, but become practically inaudible to the dancers waiting backstage for their cues. This is dealt with nowadays by having a microphone pick up the sounds from the orchestra pit and transmit them backstage to the waiting dancers.

In small theaters, there may be no place to put the musicians except backstage in the wings. In this case, heavy stage curtains and the angle of reflection of the sound waves may combine to produce an effect of muffled sounds, and the dance director may opt for some kind of electric amplification even when live musicians are playing.

Sometimes in very large theaters the sounds created by live musicians may routinely be amplified electronically. A drawback of this practice may arise if the miking is unbalanced so that one hears a distortion of the intended balance of instrumentation. In such situations, a sound engineer at a control mixer becomes an important member of the dance company's personnel. So dancers have many reasons to be concerned with the pure physics of sound waves.

Basic Variables as Raw Material for Music

In the field of music, among the most exciting discoveries being made are in the study of acoustics, which is offering us scientific explanations for the variety in musical sounds and even among individual performances. This analytic knowledge in turn is being used to electronically synthesize sounds of familiar musical instruments, and to expand the supply of raw sound materials that are available for composing new music.

The basic variables in all musical sound, however, remain the same regardless of whether the sound source is a state-of-the-art electronic synthesizer or a traditional, acoustic instrument. These variables are dynamics, pitch, timbre, and duration.

From the physicist's point of view, pitch (the high and low in music) depends on the frequency of the sound waves. Dynamics (the intensity of loudness) is a result of the amplitude of the sound waves, but is also related to pitch. Timbre (tone color or quality) depends on the proportional presence of natural, pitched overtones that exist in any particular musical sound.

A general formula for creating all music could read like this: Combine sounds and silences, controlling the variables of pitch, timbre, dynamics, and duration. These are basic ingredients that dancers should listen for in all styles of music, whether a piece is something contem-

miliar, or something unfamiliar from another time or an- spects of music flow from these elements, in- rmony, texture, and form. How they are oser's art.

Hear

are experienced in wordless ways. During any r, it can be helpful for dancers to use whatever ir command to describe what it is they hear. Even cabulary can be useful for increasing your awareness of ... exist in a particular piece of music. As this study proceed... n become more specific in the use of descriptive and analytical wo. s. Learning terms commonly used by musicians can save time in rehearsals and classwork, as well as to help clarify how certain effects and various styles of music are created.

Here, by way of preview, is a chart of musical ingredients and aspects that will be considered in detail throughout the following chapters. These basic components interact in various ways in different styles of music. For dancers, the main purpose of studying them is simply to find more effective ways of listening attentively. The goals are both expressive sensitivity and an understanding of the specific content and structure of any particular music used for theatrical dance. Such understanding can help to speed learning of new choreography, make rehearsals go better, and lend artistic power to dancers' performances onstage. The chart can serve as a continuing reference for things to notice when you are either sitting listening to music or working with it as a dancer.

What to Listen for in Music: A Checklist

DYNAMICS, OR DEGREE OF LOUDNESS

- general overall level of loudness within a piece
- changes in loudness: either gradual or sudden
- accent of particular individual sounds
- climaxes; level of loudness at end
- effect on sense of tension and release

ARTICULATION

- manner in which tones are begun and ended; attack and decay
- legato (smooth) or staccato (crisply clipped)

- general ratio of sound to silence *use of space*
- consistent style or many changes

DURATION, OR TIME ELEMENTS

- clocked real time
- basic pulse or beat, or no pulse
- tempo, or speed of recurring beats
- metric organization, or none
- general subdivision of beats
- distinctive rhythmic patterns *(recurring or not)*
- consistency of general motion, or many sudden contrasts and changes (e.g., flurries of activity and then long moments of silence)

PITCH

a) Melodic Interest

- basic choice of scale
- general range (high or low)
- prominent intervals
- melodic contours: smooth? jagged? peaks and valleys? much stepwise motion? or many skips in pitch?

b) Harmonic Organization

- general flavor: tonal? atonal? modal? jazz? pentatonic? whole tone? freely chromatic? ragas? other?
- general cast of harmony: simple, few changes, or complex
- points of cadence
- harmonic rhythm, or pace of chord changes *(or lack thereof)*
- function of consonance and dissonance

TEXTURE

- underlying density of sound
- general organization: single melody? melody plus accompaniment? contrapuntal? heterophonic? sound collage?
- what is in foreground? background?

- distinctive figurative patterns
- spacing of voices or instrumental parts

TIMBRE, OR TONE COLOR

- overall atmospheric impression
- initial choice of instruments
- expressive directions about qualities of sound
- combination of instruments at particular moments
- special effects on particular instruments, with the voice, or electronically
- prominent solos or distinctive entries that could serve as dance cues

MUSICAL PROCEDURES

a) Materials

- distinctive motifs at beginnings of sections
- contrasting material?
- singable melodies?
- clear bass line?
- phrases or other brief musical sections?

b) Methods of Developing Musical Ideas

- sound collage
- exact repetitions?
- variations?
- imitative procedures? (canon, fugue, free counterpoint)
- set forms (sectional songs, sonata, rondo, dance suite, etc.)? any clues in the title?
- phrase structure or none?
- additive styles (for example, in African drumming)
- minimalist and phasing procedures
- serialist methods
- grouping of shorter sections into larger works (symphonies, masses, sonatas, suites)

NUANCE AND EXPRESSION

- abstract music? or a work with extramusical inferences of narrative or meaning? words?
- suggestive title or expression marks and directives
- general emotional aura of entire piece
- mood changes within sections? or from section to section?
- cultural context of composition
- poetic, visual, or choreographic images suggested by listening
- rubato as an expressive effect, for phrasing

STYLE

- do date and origin of work suggest a general common practice?
- is the composer known for certain procedures that the listener may expect?
- cultural context and any special purpose of musical work?

MUSIC IN RELATIONSHIP TO CHOREOGRAPHY

- specially composed to fit the dance? or music from the past used for a new dance?
- live performance that may vary, or constant tape recording?
- hand-in-glove coordination of movement and sound?
- set relationship for each performance, or varying?
- meeting points of movement and music phrases?
- contrasting phrasing?
- music as a sound backdrop?
- relationship of timings: exact or in contrast?
- relationship of density of sound to number of performers?
- expressive merging, or contrast?

Explorations and Assignments

1. Demonstrate either a technical combination or a few seconds from a choreographed dance that you are currently rehearsing with music. Discuss: What is the relationship between stillness and movement, between sound and silence, between movement in dance and sounds in music?

2. Working in groups of drummers and dancers, experiment with possible relationships between movement and sound, stillness and silence. These can be mimicked, or in contrast, or varied with moments of direct synchronization.

3. In daily life, notice things that move: a blade of grass in a slight breeze, machinery. Imitate the movements. Translate the timing and emotional nuance into sounds, using your voice. Notice the impact of silences.

4. Observe the natural movement of people in daily life and select several movement patterns to mimic with vocalization as a demonstration in class. Develop several movement patterns into a brief dance improvisation, including the vocal sounds or music you provide for yourself. If you wish, you can tape record your vocalizations and use these for your movement in class.

5. As a class project, vocalize the timings of movement patterns as one dancer does the following: walk, run, skip. Divide the class to synchronize vocal sounds with different aspects of the movements. One group could vocally mimic the moments of footfalls, another the swinging of the arms, another the motion of the head, another the timing at the knee joint. Using nonsense syllables, emphasize the accents of the movement. Repeat the exercises, with various dancers going across the floor as soloists while those students who are vocalizing create what they are doing to make the most musical group performance possible in an improvised way.

   Repeat the same movements in silence. Discuss: How is time experienced by audiences, and by dancers, if the same movement is done in silence, with sounds, or with music?

6. Use an electronic synthesizer and experiment with controls that change the variables of a sound. Have a specialist explain how these variables can be reproduced and controlled electronically. If the physics department has an oscilloscope, arrange for a demonstration.

chapter 7

DYNAMICS: THE LOUD
AND SOFT OF MUSIC

Human *perception of musical tones is quite a
sophisticated process, one that we do not yet completely
understand.*

—Donald E. Hall

One of the most obvious aspects of music is the degree of its loudness. In the dance studio, convenient directions are apt to consist of "not so loud" or "a little softer, please." Not exactly technical terms, but they do the job.

Musicians use the general term *dynamics* in reference to loudness, because the word also encompasses overall degrees of softness as well, and can imply differences in individual notes or even parts of tones. The derivation is from the Greek word meaning powerful. *Webster's Third New International Dictionary* gives this definition for dynamics: "variation and contrast in force or intensity (as in music, in the use of color, or in the execution of a dance)".[1] Analogies that dancers may consider in connection with musical dynamics are a sense of weight and a general level of energy.

Overall Levels of Intensity

Exact levels of loudness in music can be measured scientifically in decibels, and these levels result mainly from variations in pressure amplitude of a wave form (though other factors such as pitch and the sustaining of tones also have some bearing).[2] For the artistic purposes of music

80

used by dancers, however, what is of most concern is the relative degree of dynamic intensity. The overall level of sound needs to be considered in relation to the place of performance and the stylistic context of each particular work.

Sound waves emanating from vibrating material do not solely determine the levels of intensity that reach our ears. The original waves can also trigger other objects to vibrate in similar patterns, thus enlarging and enhancing the resultant sounds heard. This phenomenon of reinforcement is called *resonance,* and it is the principle behind the building of many instruments with sound boxes, including stringed instruments with enclosed wood frames, drums, and pianos.

Reflection of sound is similar to what happens with light: Waves of motion hit a surface and are redirected. A familiar example is the echo. Reflection becomes a major consideration in large theaters, where sound both bounces off hard surfaces and is absorbed by soft textures of curtains and upholstery, as well as by clothing worn by audiences. The acoustics of each theater therefore becomes a major consideration for dance artists, whether taped or live music is used. It is important to check sound levels for each performing venue. When the overall loudness of sounds is electrically increased, this comes under the heading of *amplification.*

Whether sound is amplified or not, whether live or taped, the dynamic intensity of sound concerns dancers onstage very much. Artistic taste enters into the control of overall dynamic levels during performances. For example, overamplifying the violin and cello duet in *Swan Lake* to seem considerably larger than life could destroy the illusion of intimacy during the love duet danced onstage.

In contrast, the performers want a high intensity level of loudness in some dance pieces. For example, when former Graham dancer Peter Sparling brought his students and colleagues in the Ann Arbor Dance Works to perform at the intimate Merce Cunningham Studio in New York, the performers seemed to draw considerable energy from the high dynamic level used for *Connoisseurs of Chaos* (choreographed by Jessica Fogel to David Borden's *Continuing Story of Counterpoint, Part Six*), as well as for Sparling's own work, *Rondo,* to music by David Gregory.[3] Another example is the "Golden Section" from *The Catherine Wheel,* in which Twyla Tharp's dancers seem to achieve their high level of energy precisely in relation to the level of dynamic support offered in the soundscore by David Byrne.

In addition to considering the effect of dynamic level upon performers onstage, dance artists must consider the ways their audiences experience sound. At one extreme, high levels of loudness are so intense that listeners' hearing may be permanently damaged. I experienced an amusing instance of such concerns during a performance of the Joffrey Ballet's production of *Billboards,* set to stadium-level amplification of taped music by the popular rock singer Prince. The enthusiastic fan sitting next to me was among the many new ballet-goers attracted by the crossover style, yet she had brought several sets of ear plugs and offered some to me.

Artistically, such high amplification was considered to be in keeping with the energy level of the dance and the expectations of rock fans. For other styles, however, if the sound level is not consistent with the energy of the dance itself, the music may distract the audience's attention from the performance onstage. Conversely, if amplification is not adequate for a theater space, a timid level of musical sound could serve to weaken the impact of a dance performance. This becomes a particular concern when instruments with relatively little carrying power are used (such as acoustic guitars, dulcimers, prepared pianos, harpsichords, and delicate percussion).

Relative Terms for Dynamic Levels

Although words in many languages may appear in written musical scores, musicians commonly use the following Italian terms or abbreviations as indications for general dynamic levels:

word	abbreviation	definition
forte	*f*	loud
piano	*p*	soft
mezzoforte	*mf*	moderately loud
mezzopiano	*mp*	moderately soft
fortissimo	*ff*	very loud
pianissimo	*pp*	very soft

This gearing of loud and soft is further extended by some composers and conductors to include *pianississimo (ppp)* and *fortississimo (fff)*.

All these terms are relative and must be considered in the context of both a composer's style and each specific performing space. A Mozart symphony, for example, was composed for a small eighteenth-century ensemble, a size nowadays called a chamber orchestra, while the late nineteenth-century forces available to Tchaikovsky were considerably larger. When a modern orchestra performs, the dynamic levels used for a Tchaikovsky fortissimo would not be appropriate for Mozart.

Another aspect of dynamics that can change according to current practice is consistency in any chosen level throughout a section or piece. A good example is the terracing effect that was common practice in European concert music of the Baroque era (early seventeenth to mid-eighteenth century). In the works of Vivaldi, Telemann, Corelli, and Bach, for example, a lengthy section goes along at the same general dynamic level, and a change in dynamics is introduced to mark a new contrasting section. Perhaps this practice was influenced somewhat by the mechanical abilities of pipe organs and other keyboards such as harpsichords, where couplings and other devices allowed for an overall change in dynamics, but not for nuancing of individual notes. Voices, strings and winds, of course, have always had the capacity for nuances in dynamics, and surely fine performers always injected expressive differentiations even in works with terraced styles. However, much of this dynamic effect was a result of the conventions of orchestration, when many instruments would double various melodic lines (called counterpoint), for example.

Later, in Classical and Romantic music of Europe, composers were more apt to vary the dynamic shadings within each section, and from moment to moment. This went along with a change in the style of composing. Instead of many doublings of simultaneous melodic lines, there would instead be a single predominant melody supported by other instruments harmonically. A concommitant development with this stylistic change in compositional tastes was the invention of a new keyboard instrument—the fortepiano—that (unlike the harpsichord) could play many levels of loud and soft without any mechanical changes in the instrument. With the abbreviated name piano, this instrument has become the favorite of most composers for testing their own creative ideas, and the nuances available are one of the reasons the piano is so popular with dancers.

Dynamic Level in Relation to Dance

Children and novice dancers often associate fast dancing with loud music. As an antidote to this, the chart below suggests ways in which students can explore variety in their own speed, as well as in the expanse of gestures, both in relation to the tempo and dynamics of music. Read combinations across horizontally.

Musical Dynamic	Speed of Music	Movement Speed	Movement Size
soft	fast	fast	large
soft	fast	fast	small
soft	fast	slow	large
soft	fast	slow	small
soft	slow	fast	large
soft	slow	fast	small
soft	slow	slow	large
soft	slow	slow	small
loud	fast	fast	large
loud	fast	fast	small
loud	fast	slow	large
loud	fast	slow	small
loud	slow	fast	large
loud	slow	fast	small
loud	slow	slow	large
loud	slow	slow	small

This chart alone can provide parameters for dance improvisation. To add more variables, one could specify expressive qualities. For example, loud and fast can be done exuberantly and joyfully, or showing intense anger. In either case, the movement could be contained or expansive. One could convey anger by taking many small steps at a fast speed while barely moving through space, fists clenched with tremendous tension. Or one could repeat the quick small steps in place, use a more released type of energy, put a smile on the face, and produce an entirely different expressivity. Dancers could be exuberant with a sparse musical accompaniment of one long sustained tone at a loud dynamic level, or a different impression could be achieved by having fast music at a relatively low dynamic level, for the same movement, perhaps with a neutral expression on the face.

Paul Taylor offers his audiences the intriguing experience of watching the same choreography performed twice, to different music, in *Polaris,* with a score by Donald York. As a classroom exercise, this procedure is something that could become an important aspect of every dancer's experience.

Gradual Changes

Dynamic level can be increased or decreased gradually—either very quickly, or spread out over a considerable amount of time. In either case, these are the terms commonly used:

how is this done? by increased loudness of particular musician or addition of more player players?

word	dynamic marking	definition
crescendo	**cresc.** or $<$	gradually getting louder
diminuendo	**dim.** or $>$	gradually getting softer
decrescendo	**decresc.** or $>$	gradually getting softer

Perhaps the most famous choreographic example of a lengthy musical crescendo is Ravel's *Bolero,* which was composed for Bronislava Nijinska's choreography and premiered in 1928 by Ida Rubenstein. The score has seen multiple settings by other choreographers.

For an extended, choreographed diminuendo, notice the final moments of Todd Bolender's ballet *The Still Point,* set to Debussy's only string quartet. Another beautiful example of relating gentle dynamics in music to lyrical dance movement is Alvin Ailey's setting of *The Lark Ascending* by Ralph Vaughan-Williams.

Attack and Decay

According to the physics of pure sound, one of the features that give instrumental tones distinctive sounds is the *amplitude envelope,* or overall patterns of growth and decay. Every sound has a moment of *attack* during which the waveforms are initiated, a length of time when the peak loudness has been reached and is *sustained,* and the period of time when the sound *decays* and is delineated by silence.

For example, a cello tone will rise quickly to a steady sound, while percussion sounds tend to have an enormous concentration of energy and intensity during the attack, followed by an almost immediate decay. Pianos owe their tones partly to an interesting envelope: the attack is followed by a sustain and the beginnings of a decay, but then the intensity of the tone increases again before a final decay.

All these patterns take place so quickly that listeners may not be aware of them. Nevertheless, a useful exploration for dancers is to use their voices to create various patterns of attack, sustain, and decay. If done with a group, quite satisfying musical pieces can be improvised using only nonsense syllables. Different tone qualities could be allowed, but the main parameter is that once a syllable and a certain tone quality of voice have been chosen, students have to stick with these and let loudness be the only variable for the duration of one breath's worth of sound. Improvising singers can start softly and gradually increase in loudness (crescendo), then grow soft again (diminuendo or decrescendo). Or percussion sounds could be simulated, with a loud attack followed by an immediate decay toward silence. Or singers could start medium-loud, crescendo, and have an abrupt cut-off at maximum intensity. These are some raw materials to experiment with vocally. Analogies in movement should also be explored.

Some Kind Words for Mickey Mouse

It has become a cliché in the modern dance world to use the cartoon character Mickey Mouse as a negative connotation for "movement that goes bop when the music goes bop." Certainly that one-to-one relationship could get boring if that were the only option for theatrical dancing. However, as observed by the composer/collaborator Richard Cameron-Wolfe: "Mimicking is very difficult. It demands that you truly hear what is happening in the music."

In the theater, if there is a close mimicking relationship between sound and movement for even a few moments, this may focus attention even more closely upon what the dancers are doing. In the classroom studio, mimicking may help dancers to become aware of the details in what they are hearing. This procedure may also alert students to details in their own movement or possibilities for dance that might be overlooked in silence.

The power of physical movement in sensitizing listeners' perception was put to work in a pedagogical approach to music education by Émile Jaques-Dalcroze earlier in the century. Called eurhythmics, it is a method still widely used. It employs natural movements to encourage students to sense various aspects of music with their whole bodies. The system is not intended to produce choreographic dance, but rather to aid students' understanding of musical theory. The approach may be helpful to dancers, and several sources of information are listed in the appendixes. However, because dancers have a larger vocabulary of movement than most music students, dance students can create their own extended gestures and movement patterns in relation to the sounds they hear. Particularly for the topics that follow (on articulation, accents, and elements of time), some one-on-one relationships between sound and movement can serve useful purposes. Enter Mickey Mouse, all ears.

String Articulations

For instrumental musicians, the word articulation signals differences in the attack or initiation of a tone, particularly in regard to the various techniques of production. Articulation also has implications for the manner in which tones are ended (the "decay" according to physicists' study).

For purposes of understanding string articulation, some examples of written notation are introduced here. All you have to know is that each solid notehead with attached vertical stem represents a separate tone. The additional markings provide information about the intended articulations, which are produced by either bowing or plucking the strings. In general, it can be observed that notation of articulation may be only a general indication of style, and that the refinements of nuances are left to the artistic discretion of each performer.

To appreciate some of these available effects, it is helpful to have a string player demonstrate. However, you can become more sensitive to different articulations simply by focusing attention on this single aspect as you listen to recordings or the music used for your dance projects and classes.

It can also be helpful to scan printed scores of familiar music, focusing attention only on the aspects that pertain to dynamics and articulation. The ballet scores of Igor Stravinsky are particularly recommended for their attention to string articulations. For dancers, what is most relevant is simply an awareness of the different styles and effects that various articulations can create in music. Concommitantly, the articulation of one's dance movements can be considered. Everyday adjectives can be helpful in this. For example, in both music and dance one could ask whether something is basically smooth and flowing, or sharp and crisp.

For players of bowed orchestral stringed instruments, a *slur* marking (indicated as an arcing curve over or under the written notes) will indicate smooth bowing, resulting in *legato,* or very connected sounds. The direction of the bow is changed with each slur mark, creating distinct articulation for the first note in each slurred group, with no gaps of silences in between tones.

In contrast to legato is *nonlegato,* or *detaché,* indicated simply by an absence of other articulation markings. In this case, each note is produced by a separate bow stroke. Yet depending on the style of the particular musical passage, the overall effect can still be one of connectedness, without noticeable gaps of silence between the tones.

Louré is an interesting combination of legato and nonlegato, resulting in a kind of gentle pushing effect. This is indicated by adding dashes under or above noteheads, along with bowing slur marks.

Staccato increases the amount of silence between notes, resulting in sounds that are both crisply begun and ended. For stringed instruments, there are several refinements produced by varying bowing techniques, but these are not necessarily specified in notation by composers or arrangers. Among these techniques are *spiccato* or *saltato* (in which the bow actually bounces on the strings, producing a light airy effect).

Among the other bowed techniques is *martellato* ("hammered"), which is produced with the bow beginning on the string and results in rather abrupt beginnings and endings of tones. When the directions *col legno* are seen, the bow is turned so that the wood strikes the strings, providing a distinctive articulation.

Another category of articulations involves various degrees of accent. This subject will be dealt with more in connection with brass instruments, but the notation for strings is similar. In printed scores, look for accent marks pointing either vertically or horizontally. These denote accents of enough force to differentiate one particular note from its neighbors. In string parts, a series of strong notes may be indicated simply by specifying repeated downward strokes of the bow.

A more biting accent is indicated *sfz*, and this actually includes a moment of sharply increased loudness after the initial attack, which then subsides quickly. A related dynamic change is the *fortepiano*, indicated *fp*, which calls for an abrupt change from loud to soft after the initial attack.

Pizzicato is a distinctive sound produced by plucking the strings with the fingers. In notation, it is abbreviated *pizz.*, and the return to bowed articulation is indicated *arco*.

Variations in plucked articulations are a feature of guitar playing, of course. An expert guitarist could demonstrate various techniques of plucking, strumming, using the fingernail or the flesh of the finger, using a pick to strike quickly, and so forth. There may also be a distinct difference in the sound of the downstroke and the upstroke of the fingers. All of these choices of articulation, however, are left to the guitarist, and a composer would not be likely to do more than indicate general style.

In focusing attention upon all instrumental articulations, it can be useful to imitate vocally what you hear. For dancers, of course, the more relevant transferral is to imitation in physical movement.

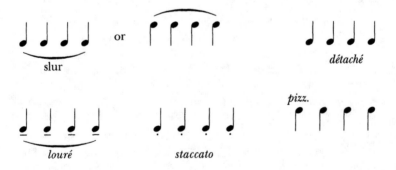

slur   or

détaché

louré   staccato   pizz.

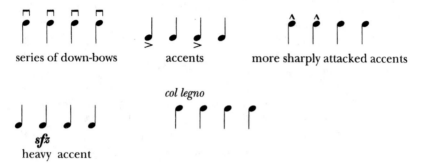

Examples of string articulations.

What analogies to these articulations can be found in dance? Where would flick, fling, punch, press, push, pull, bounce, and a bourrée on pointe fit in?

Brass Articulations and Dynamic Accents

Dancers can experience the various articulations employed by brass players simply by repeating tones at any pitch and using the following syllables.

"Doodoodoodoo" would produce the smoothest legato where the end of one tone merges with the beginning of another. "Tutututu" would be smooth, but a little less so. "Tu tu tu tu" introduces some silence between the end of one note and the attack of the next. "Ta ta ta ta" produces a different quality in the initiation of the sounds as well as their conclusion. "Ti ti ti ti" suggests an even shorter articulation, aiming at staccato.

Most brass players think of a true staccato as being half the length of time the same note would be held without the articulation indication of a dot over the note. Fastest of all possible articulation is the double-tonguing of "tikatikatika" in which the cutoff for alternate notes is actually the initiation of the next note. The articulation for the "ka" sounds are produced at the top of the throat; the "ti" sounds are produced by the backward movement of the tongue away from the teeth.

In experimenting with any of these various articulations, one can sing notes at a fast or slow pace, or vary the amount of silent time between them. The timing could be irregular or even, but it is helpful to focus attention on keeping the articulation constant for the duration of a pattern or brief idea in sound. An analogy should be explored in movement.

Brass articulations cannot be considered apart from *accent,* or particular stress and emphasis of one sound so that it gains prominence. As just outlined, articulation possibilities range from sustained and smooth to slightly detached, through various degrees of staccato or short. Then come varying degrees of accent, and finally the *sfz* or *sforzando* attack, which produces a particularly effective bell-like ringing tone in the brasses. In this, there is a stinging initiation of maximum loudness and concentration of intensity, followed immediately by a sustaining at a moderate level of volume. This is quite different from the *fortepiano* effect, marked *fp,* which indicates an immediate and abrupt change from loud to soft, but without the stinging effect. All these dynamic accents imply different degrees of effort depending upon the stylistic context. For example, in Beethoven, *sfz* could be regarded as just a strong accent; in Tchaikovsky or Stravinsky, however, brass players would exert maximum effort.

Notating Dynamic Accent

Dynamics provide dance students with an easy way to begin learning musical notation. According to the European tradition currently used, musical notes represent individual sounds. In the examples given below, the indication for each tone consists of a note head that is either solid or clear in the middle, plus a vertical stem. (The solid note heads are shortest in timing; the open note heads with stems are of medium length; the plain open note heads are longest in timing.) The marking below each note head indicates articulation. Each note on the chart represents any pitch played on any instrument at any tempo. The variables in this case are dynamics and articulation. These should be demonstrated by a musician, with students immediately experimenting with each effect, using wordless vocalizing. Each accent can be demonstrated alone (solo), followed by group singing, which allows an enlarged level of intensity.

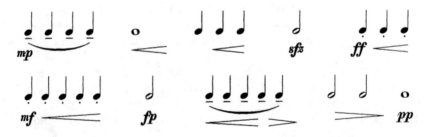

Exercise for dynamics and accent.

What are some analogous articulations in physical dance movement?

Other Types of Emphasis

Dynamic accents are not the only means of focusing attention upon a particular note or group of notes. A similar effect can be achieved simply by introducing a surprising new pitch, or by changing the tone color or introducing another instrument for only one note (as percussion is so often used).

Musicians can also alert listeners to the importance of a particular sound by adding a *grace note* or other quick ornamentation just before the main note. There are several kinds of grace note ornaments, but they tend to be close in pitch to the main note, and they are quick. Percussionists will add a roll of several ultrafast notes before an important longer or accented tone. Additionally, there is the *agogic* accent, in which the note is sustained slightly. In connection with agogic accents, performers may also insert a slight delaying silence just before the note that is to have prominence—the musical equivalent of taking a little breath.

Accent as a Structural Element in Music and Dance

Accents serve not only to call attention to a particular note; they can also delineate groupings of notes so that the listener becomes aware of patterns. For example, a tap or walking footfall in an absolutely undifferentiated steady beat does not make for very interesting music if that is the only sound present. However, what happens if accents are added on certain beats? Here are some experiments:

Walk steadily and lightly, but stomp noticeably for accents. Or tap a tabletop with your fingers and use a different surface for the accents. If you are drumming, exert more force for the accents, use both hands together for just the accented notes, or add a second instrument for the accents.

$\downarrow$ = unaccented $\downarrow$ = accented

The following results in regular groupings of three beats:

The next example will produce regular groupings of four beats, indicated visually here by vertical lines called *bar lines,* which do not affect the continuity of the timing. In this case, the bar lines serve only as a visual aid so that one can quickly grasp the groupings.

Here are groupings of five regularly accented beats:

The next example represents an alternation between four and three beats in a group, with the beat remaining always the same. The only difference is the dynamic level of the attack.

Next is a *decumulative* order of accent, beginning with five beats to a group, then descending consecutively until all are accented, effectively erasing the differentiation.

At this point, you could begin to organize the patterns in *accumulative* order, increasing the notes in each group by one beat as the beats continue steadily.

As explained already, there are degrees of accent. So, for example, you could organize a grouping of six beats, but arrange for a strong accent on every first note of a group, with a lighter accent on every fourth beat:

Or you could make a subgrouping in twos within every six beats:

Accents in *The Rite of Spring*

Perhaps one of the strongest moments in any ballet score is the opening of the "Dance of the Adolescents" from Igor Stravinsky's *Le Sacre du printemps* (The Rite of Spring).[4] The entire string section plays blocked chords—that is, each of the string groups has different pitches, but the instrumentalists all play their notes simultaneously, repeating their respective pitches, ostensibly in a grouping of four notes repeated seven times.

What changes are the accents, and these alone are enough to make the music interesting. In this case, there are dynamic accents when the strings add their own emphasis to certain notes. Further emphasis is added by additional instrumentation and changed tone color (when eight horns enter on just the accented notes). The pattern of accents is as follows, with vertical bar lines indicating where the expected accents of regular groupings in fours would occur. Without the accents or bar lines, one would hear thirty-one identical repetitions of the original string chord.

In much European concert music before *The Rite of Spring*, listeners sensed a regularity of a substantial accent on the first of every *measure* or bar, as the groupings between the vertical lines are called (in this case, occurring every four beats). Traditionally, a stress of some sort would be either present or implied on the first beat of every measure, with a lesser accent on the third beat. In contrast, Stravinsky's use of accents within regular written measures was a departure from common practice.

Devising Charts of Accent Options

Here is a chart of available accent patterns when only four equal beats are considered. Any of these patterns can be used in any order, in any combination, for both musical and movement purposes. Don't put the emphasis on the wrong sy-LA-ble.

By the end of the chart, all the sounds are accented, which in effect deletes all accentual differentiation. Since none of the beats is unevenly stressed, the impression is simply one of increased overall dynamic level.

Accent patterns can be applied to all the body percussion experiments which you devise, as well as to the playing of percussion instruments. The simplest way to experiment is to tap a tabletop with the underside of flat fingers with one hand, and add the second hand only for accented beats.

Accent has been treated in this chapter as an aspect of dynamics because of the physical properties of the sounds that so often produce the effect. But beyond that, accent has many implications for the groupings of sounds to form various distinctive patterns. Consequently, we are led to focus attention on the aspect of music which usually becomes the main musical concern of dancers: timing.

Explorations and Assignments

1. Something to notice in daily technique classes and dance rehearsals is the effect of accent upon movement, and how this is achieved. Some questions to think about are: Where is the feeling of body weight? How is the impression of lightness achieved, and how does this contrast with a feeling of working with gravity? Can an accent be in the air as well as on the ground? How can accents be suggested if dancers are crawling, bending, swaying, sliding, twisting, spinning? What about jumping or leaping? And are there some dance movements that are best done without accent—the equivalent of maintaining an even dynamic level in music? What is the effect of changing direction suddenly, or more slowly? Is there accent in both cases?

   If the dynamic level in music is fairly loud, what is the effect of interjecting an occasional pianissimo note? Where is the effect of accent then? And what if a movement is sustained or a pose held for an instant: are these accents in movement? What happens in regard to the release of energy in each case? Demonstrate.

2. How softly can the class sing? How loudly? As one person conducts, make use of crescendo and diminuendo, as well as sudden changes in dynamics, maintaining everything else (pitch, tone quality, etc.) constant. The ends of sounds can be determined too: gradual dying away, or abrupt cutoff. Dynamic level can also be affected by signaling some parts of the group to be silent, thus cutting down on the total forces at any one moment. Take turns conducting. Discuss: What are the analogous effects in dance? Demonstrate a few in movement.

3. Improvise a movement locomotor pattern and repeat it with music at various dynamic levels. What effects do the different levels of the musical dynamics have upon you as a dancer?

4. With your voice, demonstrate four different articulations. Symbolize these with standard musical notation on flash cards. Use them as the basis for a group vocal improvisation, allowing all other aspects to be freely determined by the singers. Use the same cards as suggestions for articulation in dance movement improvisation. Discuss the results.

5. Select an available orchestral score used for a ballet or modern dance with which you are already familiar. Scan it for words and marks indicating dynamics, articulations, and accents.

6. As a group, view a brief videotaped dance and focus attention on musical dynamics and articulations in relationship to the dance movement. Discuss.

7. Listen to a recording of Ravel's *Bolero*. What dynamic markings would you provide at various points as the work progresses?

8. Establish a grouping of pulses in six, and experiment with changing the placement of a single accent. Then experiment with varying the placement of two accents in every group of six beats, then three accents in every group of six. Make a chart of the possibilities.

9. Using musical note heads to represent beats and added accent marks to indicate dynamic accents, devise several asymmetrical sequences. Play them on a percussion instrument, repeating many times. Mimic the patterns some way in movement.

Next, keep the musical accents the same, but have a contrasting pattern of accents in your movement articulation. How is this effect different, for both viewers and dancers?

chapter 8

DURATION OR TIMING
IN MUSIC

Dance comes from the combination of rhythm and movement; music comes from rhythm and sound. It is natural and important to explore these forms at the same time as they complement, enhance, and reinforce each other.

—Gladys Andrew Fleming

Both the silences and sounds in music share one property that is particularly important to dancers: duration.

The silences in music can be so brief that they are not usually indicated, or they can be longer and symbolized as written rests in the European method. Sounds can be indicated in many ways, including the standard system of notation introduced in this chapter. Both sounds and silences can happen in regular patterns, or irregularly. The relative proportions between silences and sounds can determine an overall quality or style in music, as well as provide raw ingredients for both building-block patterns and lengthy, complex structures. In turn, these patterns of sounds and silences can be used as either a complement or a contrast to the expressive movement of dancers.

Checkpoints in Real Time

Although for both music and dance it is most often a relative sense of timing that is pertinent, nevertheless exact measurement (in real time) is also used. A simple stopwatch often serves as timekeeper. For example, the choreographer/composer Alwin Nikolais used a stopwatch to monitor segments of his choreographic works as the movement ideas evolved.[1] When he was satisfied with the dance in silence, he would go to his electronic music lab and create a soundtrack to fit the timing of his choreography. In turn, when the dancers heard the sound track, they listened for built-in cues that would alert them as to where they should be on the stage, or that would signal the beginning of a new section of the dance. This type of timing relationship is particularly useful in collaborations where the movement and sound come together at specific points and are relatively independent—or at least flexible—in between.

Unpulsed Timing

Within real time segments, the patterns of sound and silences can offer an impression of regular pulsation, or they can be unpulsed, erratic—and in the case of live music, unpredictable and different with each performance.

For instance, a composer could request twelve fast notes (= 12F) followed by three long notes (= 3L) followed by an undetermined length of silence (= S) and then two medium-length notes (= 2M). The cue sheet could read:

12F   3L   S   2M

One could continue on and on with this method, never repeating any part for minutes on end. Or a composer could create a suggestive pictograph:

Unpulsed and irregular timing should be kept in mind as interesting possibilities for theatrical dance—with respect to both the music and the movement. This approach was one of the major thrusts of what is now labeled postmodern dance of the 1960s and 1970s, and it can still be a fruitful way for dancers of today to explore movement as well as music and other soundscapes.

Music with a Regular Pulse

There is, of course, another approach to timing. Commenting about the musical choices of some postmodern dancers in the 1970s, the composer/collaborator Steve Reich made a prediction:

Serious dancers who now perform with pulseless music or with no music at all will be replaced by young musicians and dancers who will re-unite

rhythmic music and dance as a high art form. . . . For a long time dur-
ing the 1960s one would go to the dance concert where no one danced,
followed by the party where everyone danced. This was not a healthy situ-
ation. . . . The real answer is to create a genuinely new dance with roots
that go back thousands of years to the basic impulse at the foundation of
all dance: the human desire for regular rhythmic movement, usually done
to music.[2]

It is safe to say that for dance purposes the world over, music with
some kind of regular pulse or beat is more common historically than
erratically timed music. This holds true particularly when ritual, traditional folk, and social dance are considered along with various styles of
concert and show dance. With regularly pulsing music, the dance movement may coincide with certain pulses or avoid doing so, but it is always
in some kind of relation to that musical equivalent of a heartbeat. A
pulse is always felt as a definite time slot, whether there happens to be
an articulated sound or a silence on any particular beat, and whether a
dancer is in motion or holding a pose. Among other functions, pulsation
in the music can serve to set off moments of unpulsed timing in the
dance movement; in such cases, the very regularity of the music serves
as a foil for contrast in the visual, physical dance.

Setting a Tempo

The rate of the pulses or beats is called the *tempo* in music, and this is
often the single most important consideration that dancers have in connection with the music for their performances and technical exercises
alike.

Most often the tempo will be set in a relative manner, by a sense
of what feels right for the moment, or growing out of a director's experience with class exercises, rehearsals, and performances. When dancers work with musicians, whether in the studio or in the theater, it is
usually sufficiently clear to indicate the desired tempo by means of the
voice. It must be emphasized that the dancer setting the tempo must
first feel the pulse very strongly and regularly. Unless a dancer has
worked with a collaborating musician long enough to develop a tacit
understanding of what is needed, then it is helpful to demonstrate at
least a couple of seconds of a technical exercise or choreographic section
in the exact tempo that dancers are expected to execute the movement
sequence.

In most collaboration, musicians and dancers use everyday language to communicate their ideas about tempo. "A little faster" or "a

lot slower'' may sound inexact, for the terms are only relative; yet when accompanied by a precise verbal or physical indication of the appropriate underlying beat, such words can be helpful for explaining to both musicians and dancers what is needed. For further accuracy and adjustments, people must depend on their nonverbal, directly kinesthetic sense.

Developing a Sense of Steady Pulse

Among the experiences that dancers have found helpful in strengthening their own sense of pulse, drumming is often mentioned. Nevertheless, it is not necessarily easy for anyone to keep a steady beat, even when people are limiting motion to hands and arms instead of dancing with their entire bodies.

Keeping a steady beat becomes even more challenging when attempted with a group of novice drummers, for the common tendency is for everyone to get faster. Consequently, it is helpful to play along with an experienced drummer, or with recorded music, or with the rhythm patterns of an electronic synthesizer, or with the clicks of a *metronome*. (See below for a discussion of the metronome.)

Eventually dancers must be able to feel a pulse securely in their entire bodies. As observed by the composer/collaborator Richard Cameron-Wolfe, dancers should also become sensitive to pulse in music where it is *not* strongly marked. "The overt percussive beat is the enemy of sensitivity," he claims. Nevertheless, drumming and body percussion exercises do seem to help many dance students in their conscious efforts to develop a sense of steady pulsation at different tempos. Although neither the beat of the heart nor the pulse of music and dance is precisely regular, a certain sense of steadiness is a desirable skill to develop.

The Metronome

The metronome is a timekeeping device invented in the early nineteenth century. Useful to both musicians and dancers, it allows one to set a regular rate of beats by means of a clock-like mechanism with a movable weight on a calibrated pendulum. The clicks can occur at various rates between 40 and 208 times a minute. Nowadays, there are also battery-powered metronomes that both emit a click and flash a light.

A metronome set at 60 produces one click per second or 60 beats per minute. Double that, for 120 beats per minute, and you have a brisk marching tempo.

In 1962 the composer Gyorgy Lygeti devised a *Symphonic Poem for 100 Metronomes,* taking into account a slowing as each piece of equipment winds down. In 1991, this concept—including the sounds of 100 metronomes—was adapted for dance purposes by Anne Teresa de Keersmaeker for her work titled *Stella.*

More commonly, the metronome can be a useful reference for establishing a general range of tempo, so that dancers can communicate what they want to conductors and instrumentalists while preparing for performances, or for the purpose of occasionally checking the tempo when movement is rehearsed in silence. Although there may be variations in moments of actual performance, dance artists often attest to the constancy in overall timings for their movement sequences.

Pulse: Not Mechanical

Although a strong sense of a steady beat is important, it must also be emphasized that in the performance of both music and dance, there may be many departures from exact repetitive pulsation. Even what appears to be steady beats drummed in unison by members of the traditional American Indian Dance Theatre might prove complex if analyzed closely. Similarly, in the tradition of modern concert dance, choreographers such as Hanya Holm have also emphasized the need for a sense of breath and flexibility even within the use of a fairly steady pulse. The beat should not be mechanical, in either music or dance.

In connection with this irregularity within steady pulse, it is interesting to notice that with the latest technological developments in electronic drum machines, it is considered a positive asset to program into the patterns some deviations from absolute regularity. So not even the machines are dividing time in a relentlessly rigid fashion. Dancers who try to make their choreography or performances perfectly clocklike in timing, therefore, are attempting to be more mechanistic than our latest music machines. It seems to be more natural and makes for more expressive theatrical performance if music and dance can both have little breaths and slight variations in the pulse.

Terms for Tempo

Even though collaborators often use either exact metronomic rates or everyday words to discuss tempo (the rate of the beats over time), it is useful for dance students to learn the Italian musical terms. These are the words most commonly seen to indicate the overall pace of an entire piece of music or just a section, listed here from slowest to fastest:

grave very slow and serious; heavy

largo extremely broad and slow

larghetto not quite so slow as largo

lento quite slow

adagio slow (literally "at ease")

andante the pace of a slow walk

andantino a little faster than andante

moderato at a moderate tempo

allegretto light and fast

allegro faster still, and more vigorous

presto very fast

prestissimo extremely fast

It should be explained in passing that in European concert music, movements generally refer to the separate sections that could stand alone in a long work such as a symphony, suite, or sonata. These movements are often identified solely by their tempo markings, with no further titles necessary, except perhaps a qualifying adjective. For example, an orchestral symphony might consist of an *allegro* followed by an *andante espressivo* ("with feeling"), then a light *allegretto* or *presto* or *allegro vivace* ("quick and lively").

Changes in Tempo

Gradual changes in tempo are usually indicated by the following terms:

accelerando (abbreviated *accel.* or just *acc.*) increasing in speed little by little

ritardando (abbreviated *rit.*) gradually slowing down

a tempo return to the original speed after any departure from it

fermata (or hold, indicated by this sign over a notehead: ⌒) complete cessation of pulsing (whether for a sustained sound or an extended, unpulsed rest), with the return to tempo chosen by the performer

piu mosso a little faster

meno mosso a little less fast

Phasing

The contemporary composer Steve Reich developed a technique called *phasing*, initially in his compositions for percussion ensemble.[3] The procedure is as follows. The group is divided, with everyone initially playing the same brief patterns that are repeated over and over. After a period of time, one group gradually begins accelerating until the original patterns are out of sync or "out of phase." Because the patterns are short, the group rushing ahead will eventually regain unison with the initial notes of the group that maintained a steady pulse. The stable relationship can be kept for awhile, and new patterns introduced. Then the process of gradual phase shifting and holding of newly arrived stable relationships can be continued.

This process was used by Reich for concert works such as *Piano Phase* for two pianos or two marimbas, and *Drumming*. Both can be heard on recordings. In the last decade, Reich's music and the process of phasing itself has held a particular fascination for many choreographers, including Eliot Feld, Laura Dean, and Lar Lubovitch.

Rubato

A tempo term having to do mostly with expressivity and style is *rubato*. This is basically the practice of treating the pulsation of the music in a rather elastic manner: speeding up slightly or slowing down momentarily, but always in relation to the basic tempo, which is returned to after the deviations. The image of a young sapling swaying in a slight wind is pertinent; it always returns to its original upright position, and doesn't normally sway too far in any direction.

Rubato has probably been present in many styles of music, to varying degrees. It was a particularly noteworthy characteristic in the music of many European Romantic composers in the nineteenth century, but as observed by the late virtuoso pianist Ignacy Jan Paderewski,

> *Tempo Rubato, the irreconcilable foe of the metronome, is one of music's oldest friends. It is older than the romantic school, it is older than Mozart, it is older than Bach. Girolamo Frescobaldi in the beginning of the seventeenth century made ample use of it. . . .*
>
> *It would be wrong to pretend that Tempo Rubato is the exclusive privilege of the higher artistic form in music. . . . Expressed although nameless, it has always been in all national music. . . .*
>
> *Tempo Rubato is a potent factor in musical oratory, and every interpreter should be able to use it skillfully and judiciously, as it emphasizes the*

> *expression, introduces variety, infuses life into mechanical execution. . . .*
> *It gives music, already possessed of the metric and rhythmic accents, a*
> *third accent, emotional, individual. . . .*
>
> *Tempo Rutato appears frequently in popular music especially in dances,*
> *consequently it ought to be used in the works of Chopin, Schubert, Schu-*
> *mann (Papillons, Carnaval), Brahms, Liszt, Grieg, and in all composi-*
> *tions which have folk-music as a foundation. . . .*
>
> *In fact, every composer, when using such words as* espressivo, con
> molto sentimento, con passione, teneramente, *etc., demands from*
> *the exponent . . . a certain amount of emotion, and emotion excludes reg-*
> *ularity. Tempo Rubato then becomes an indispensable assistant, but with*
> *it, unfortunately, appears also the danger of exaggeration. Real knowl-*
> *edge of different styles, a cultured musical taste, and a well-balanced*
> *sense of vivid rhythm should guard the interpreter against any abuse. Ex-*
> *cess of freedom is often more pernicious than the severity of the law.*[4]

For tasteful use of rubato in theatrical dance, one can look to fine performances of Chopin's piano music in the ballet repertoire, for instance in settings by Jerome Robbins for *Dances at a Gathering, Other Dances,* and *The Concert.* In all cases, a sense of the musical rubato element is built into the choreography.

Among the choreographed works of Balanchine are many effective Romantic pieces with rubato, such as the *Liebeslieder Waltzer* of Brahms and the *Davidsbündlertänze* by Schumann. When choreographed and performed to allow for the expressive ebb and flows of the rubato style, such pieces can make for effective theatrical partnering.

In the classroom studio, however, many pianists feel that pieces with a high level of rubato may be inappropriate for the relatively rigid pulsation required during many technical dance exercises. (Hence the unfortunate term "butchering the classics," something to be avoided.) Better to have a studio musician improvise in the style of the Romantic composers, but accommodate the dancers' needs for regularity in timing during technical exercises.

Division of Beats

Every single musical beat can be subdivided in many ways. The basic subdivisions used in music related to European styles are by twos, threes, and fours. But you could also tap main pulses and count "one-two-three-four-five" in between. Or sevens. Or, if you listen to some of the piano nocturnes of Chopin or the *Hungarian Rhapsodies* of Liszt, you may notice fast, filigree-like notes grouped as many as nineteen or more to a beat. In such cases, dancers need relate only to the more prominent main beats.

Duple Divisions

Divisions of beats can be *duple,* that is, in twos or greater multiples divisible by two.

To get parades synchronized, drum majors of marching bands say:

Left—Left—

Left-right-Left—

In doing this, they are dividing a slow march beat equally in two. (Or the reverse could be felt: they are initially grouping two quicker beats into longer, slower ones, half as fast. The same sounds result.)

Another example of dividing beats into two subdivisions is the way brass players double tongue. They alternate a tongued articulation with one made in the throat. You can approximate this by saying: "Ti-ka, ti-ka, ti-ka," etc. (very quickly). Another system adapted from Indian tabla drumming is to say: "ta-ke, ta-ke."

A good example of subdivision of the beat into two equal segments is the regular accompaniment pattern of most ragtime music. Similarly, many of the *petit allegro* sections in ballet are partnered by music that has beats subdivided into either pairs or groups of four notes. During a technique class, dancers are most likely to encounter such duple feeling in music for tendus, small jumps, turns, and evenly paced locomotor patterns such as running.

Triplets

One way to get the feel of dividing a beat into triplets—three equal segments—is simply to walk evenly, and with every single footfall, say "merrily." Some musicians make a mantra: "ga-ma-la." There is a nice rolling or swinging effect to triplets. Each syllable, each subdivision should be exactly equal in length. In the modified tabla system, say "ta-ke-na" for each triplet.

Triplet divisions are often used for dance movements that have a swinging quality, or where a certain smoothness is desired, as with pliés, ronds de jambe, port de bras, and grand adagio combinations in ballet, or for many of the opening floor exercises in a Graham class.

When a silence is introduced on the second note of the triplet, an uneven pattern results, analogous to the physical timing of a skip, gallop, or chassé. This is a useful sound for dance purposes, since the intermediate silence has the effect of drawing extra attention to the third segment of the triplet, which then functions as a strong anticipation going into the next downbeat.

In Fours

Walk again. This time, say "Mississippi" to each footfall, articulating each syllable evenly (and in this case misplacing the accent so it falls on the first syllable). This effectively subdivides each beat into four equal segments.

In the tabla-based system, say "ta-ke-dee-ma" for divisions into four.

A quick articulation in fours can help to underscore such movements as petit battement, or to generate excitement for small turns. Subdivisions in fours can also occur at slower tempos, of course, and serve to fill out the time, for example, between the slower pulses of an expansively timed adagio dance movement.

Notating Beats and Subdivisions

The European system for indicating duration in music is a relative one. Any note can be taken as a basic pulse, and the chosen pulse can go at any tempo. Another important principle to remember is that the system is *proportional.* The relative durations of various notes do not change; the exact durations change together proportionately as the tempo is either speeded up or slowed down. Consequently, the same duration patterns (or rhythms) can be notated in several ways, even though the sounds would be identical.

Notation for musical notes is as follows. Just keep dividing by two to decrease duration proportionately:

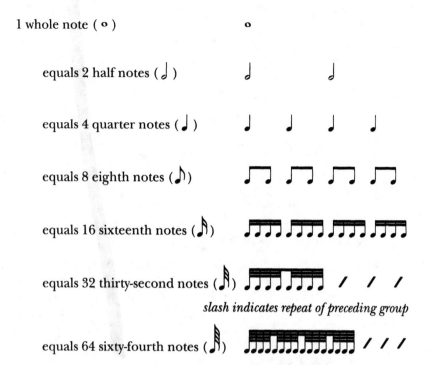

1 whole note (o)

equals 2 half notes (♩)

equals 4 quarter notes (♩)

equals 8 eighth notes (♪)

equals 16 sixteenth notes (♪)

equals 32 thirty-second notes (♪)

slash indicates repeat of preceding group

equals 64 sixty-fourth notes (♪)

Except for whole notes, all the notes are made up of a note head and a stem (which may either rise from the right side of the note head or descend from the left, depending on the vertical placement in regard to pitch). Notice that from eighth notes on, the decreased duration is indicated only by the addition of a flag on the stem. In actual practice of written composition, thirty-second notes and sixty-fourth notes are usually reserved for subdivisions in pieces where the basic beat is extremely slow, or else for very florid, virtuoso sections of fast pieces.

When single notes appear in the subdivisions, the flags are included. When there is a grouping or two or more subdivisions, these are indicated by joining them with an equivalent number of horizontal lines called beams: one beam for eighths, two for sixteenths, three for thirty-seconds, and four for sixty-fourths, as shown above.

Rests

For the important silences in music, rests are used, the equivalent value in time of the notes above:

whole rest	▬
half rest	▬
quarter rest	𝄽
eighth rest	𝄾
sixteenth rest	𝄿
thirty-second rest	𝅀
sixty-fourth rest	𝅁

Extending Duration: Dots and Ties

A further sustaining of any note can be indicated in two ways. A *tie* joining two note heads indicates that the time value of the second note is to
be added to the first. (This is not to be confused with curved bowing
marks or slurs indicating legato—both of which appear well above the
note heads.)   tie: tie: slur:

A dot placed to the right of the note head indicates that the total
duration of the sound is to be equal to the basic note, plus 50 percent
of its time value. So a dotted quarter note is equivalent to three eighth
notes.

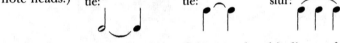

In much of our popular and concert music, the quarter note is
most commonly chosen to represent a beat that is more or less a comfortable walk, though many marches are written with the half note as
the basic beat. The half note will also be found as the basic pulse of
much of English music of Elizabethan times. In contrast, African-based
styles are more apt to feel the equivalent of a fast eighth note as the
basic pulse.

The quarter note is often chosen as the basic pulse for simple or
duple time—when the basic subdivisions of a piece are apt to go along
in subdivisions of two. But when an equal division into threes is desired,
the dotted quarter note itself can be taken as the basic beat or pulse,
and leads to compound timing, which will be discussed soon in connection with meter.

For equivalent silence, dots are placed to the right of the respective rests.

Varying the Subdivisions

A basic choice of subdivisions in three or two does not, of course, prevent the use of other subdivisions within the same piece. If the music is basically in duple timing, a triplet will be indicated in this way:

It will take up the same time that two notes of the same type normally would.

In compound timing (where a triplet subdivision is the norm) a change to subdivisions in two, or duplets, would be indicated:

These would take up the same time slot as the expected triplet.

The introduction of triplets within duple music, or of duplets within basically compound timing, can be very refreshing.

Groups of fives, sevens, nines, and increasing numbers of subdivisions are usually indicated by placing beams equivalent to the closest subdivision in value, plus a numeral alerting the performer as to how many notes are to fall within one beat or other segment of time.

Subdivisions into sixes most often come under the category of compound timing: a pair of two dotted note beats, and a triplet within each of those. Dancers almost invariably count and feel the longer pulsation of the dotted note value.

Sixes can be thought of as two groups of three or three groups of two. Again, switching from one sense to the other adds interest. Such an effect is called *hemiola*. A good example of this is the song "America" in Leonard Bernstein's score for *West Side Story*. Hemiolas appear often in Latin American music, but they are also found in many styles of jazz, and in European music of the Renaissance.

Metrical Grouping of Beats

As discussed in connection with accent, there are many ways to give prominence to particular tones or pulses. If the pulsation seems to fall into regular recurring groups or patterns, the music is considered to be *metrical*. The accent need not always fall on the first beat of each group (which may in fact be silent), yet a sense of the underlying grouping is still the implied framework. Whether a particular beat is articulated, or if a previously articulated note continues to be sustained, or if there is a rest in any particular time slot, and regardless of whether or not a note is accented, the time slots are always sensed within a metrical context as an ongoing way of organizing the time segments. It should be mentioned, however, that no piece of music need retain the same meter throughout. On the contrary; one piece may make use of several meters simultaneously, or could change frequently—even from bar to bar.

Time Signatures, Bar Lines, and Measures

At the beginning of a piece of written metrical music, there will be an indication that looks like a fraction—but isn't—called the *time signature*. The bottom numeral indicates what kind of note is to be felt as the basic beat. The upper numeral indicates how many of those beats are to be grouped together regularly. Each regular grouping is called a *measure* or a *bar*, and is set off by vertical *bar lines*. An extra thick *double bar line* is used to indicate the end of an entire composition or extended movement.

Duple and Quadruple Meters

Among the most frequently used meters nowadays are **4/4** and **2/4**. In both cases, the quarter note gets one beat. According to the top numerals, there will be either four or two beats to a measure. The meter **4/4** is also called *common time,* and indicated by **C**, for historical reasons dating to the Middle Ages. In those times, a circle indicated "perfect" time, then considered a three-unit grouping with symbolism of the Trinity. In contrast, 4/4 time was "imperfect," indicated by a broken circle, which has come down to us as the **C** in common time. Related to this, **2/2** was considered *alla breve* or cut time, indicated with a slash through the original ¢ to indicate a doubling of the timing, with a half note getting one beat.

For music written in cut time, marchers would feel two beats per measure. Although it in effect could sound the same as a 2/4, a 2/2 tends to be less light in articulation, generally speaking. It should be added that over the centuries, the perception of various meters has

changed considerably. However, for dancer
more apt to accompany large movements, w
fast codas where the dancers are doing piqué tu...ns or lots of brilliant
small jumps. Again, this is very generally speaking. One would be more
apt to hear many fast subdivisions in a **2/4**.

There is a considerable difference between **2/4** and **4/4**, having
to do mainly with degree of expected accents. In **2/4**, the strong accent
is most likely to be felt on the first, or downbeat; the second beat will
have a considerably lighter accent. When taken at a fast clip, that regular
alternation of heavy downbeat with a lighter offbeat can provide a reli-
ably steady framework for extremely fast dances such as galops, codas,
and cancans, to the extent that dancers and musicians alike will count
one beat per bar. Some good examples from the ballet repertoire are
the apotheosis and coda of Tchaikovsky's *Nutcracker;* the coda in Glazunov's *Raymonda;* the cancans in *Gaité Parisienne,* to music by Offenbach.

In contrast, the heirarchy in **4/4** goes like this: the downbeat is
strongest, the third beat is next strongest, and the second and fourth
are weakest. Additionally, the fourth beat or some subdivision of it tends
to have emphasis as an *upbeat* going into the next measure.

This sense of upbeat is important for dancers to notice in relation
to their own timing in movement; it is often the moment when dancers
may need to make a preparation for coinciding with the musical downbeat.

When taken slowly, the **4/4** meter is used for many ballet adagios.
At a more moderate tempo, **4/4** lends solid support for movements such
as pirouettes. Generally speaking, the aural impression of a **4/4** is not
as constantly accented and speedy as a **2/4**. Among the preclassic dance
forms cast in **4/4** are straightforward gavottes and bourrées, as well as
flowing allemandes. The rigaudon was written in cut time.

Accenting Fours in Different Ways

Like every other metric grouping, fours can be done fast or slow. This
is the metric grouping most common in current popular and rock music,
as well as in church hymns. Perhaps the emphasis on symmetry in many
cases can be traced to the fact that we have pairs of feet and hands.

As just explained, in European and New World classical concert
music, it is commonly felt that in a metric grouping of four, the downbeat of each measure is potentially the strongest, with a secondary accent
on "three." Beats two and four may be considered *offbeats* in quicker
tempos. In rock music of today, however, a measure in **4/4** characteris-
tically has stronger second and fourth beats than downbeats. So beats

"two" and "four" will often be played on a higher pitched drum, or people will tend to clap on these backbeats. This also happens with gospel singing; the claps are apt to be on offbeats.

Such accenting, however, was *not* the case in classic ragtime and swing jazz, for a steady downbeat was needed as a constant against which to juxtapose different syncopation more clearly. (Syncopation will be discussed soon. For now, it can be defined simply as having a note or an accent in an unexpected place with relation to the normally strong and weak beats of a measure.)

Triple Meters

One example of a metric three with duple subdivisions is **3/4**. The numerals tell us that a quarter note gets a beat, and that there are three beats to a measure. Again, there are different ways to feel and hear this.

Waltzes are usually written in **3/4**—though the so-called Spanish waltz and faster jota dances are notated in **3/8**.

Dancers, however, do not usually feel three beats for the waltz; they feel and count one beat per measure and consider the rest as a triplet subdivision. The familiar caricature of waltz time is "oom-pah-pah," with that first tuba "oom" being a very strong downbeat. However, the downbeat in the music could just as well be silent. The "pahs" are not equal; the first of these is much weaker than the downbeat of the measure; and on some subdivision of the last "pah," one will often hear an emphatic upbeat going into the next downbeat.

Furthermore, many waltzes often have a two-bar grouping, with a dotted quarter note on the second beat of the second measure, followed by a strong eighth note upbeat leading into the next downbeat. This pattern can provide a wonderful lift for dancers. A good example of accenting the second beat in a strong **3/4** waltz pattern is Alexander Borodin's *Polovtsian Dances* from the opera *Prince Igor*.

In contrast, the menuet is also written in **3/4**. This was a European court dance that had six definite steps, done at a much slower tempo than the waltzes that came later. The timing and formality of the menuet stems very much from the clothing worn, and from the sociopolitical implications of showing oneself to good advantage in court. Consequently, when historical dance experts such as Catherine Turocy (of the New York Baroque Dance Company) teach the menuet, each of those six beats is clearly defined. Musically, this means that one must be aware of a grouping of two measures of **3/4**. Unlike the waltz, the menuet should not be felt in a fast one.

Another **3/4** dance, the polonaise, is a processional played at a broad tempo: for example, the one in the last act of Tchaikovsky's *Sleeping Beauty*. It has distinctive inner patterns of the subdivisions, but, the basic meter is a strong **3/4**. Sarabandes are also in a metric three but are very broad and lyrical, with typical expected rhythmic patterns. The mazurka, too, is written in **3/4**, with the strong accent or sustained note often falling on the second beat.

Compound Meters

Compound meters regular groupings in which a dotted note is felt as the basic beat, with the consequent expectation of regular subdivision of each beat into triplets. For dance purposes, **6/8** is one of the most frequently used meters. Although the numerals ostensibly indicate that an eighth note gets one beat and that there are six beats to a measure, nevertheless, particularly in first tempos, musicians and dancers alike almost always count two beats to a measure: two dotted quarter notes, with the meter sometimes indicated like this: **2**

$$\textstyle{\bf 2} \atop {\unicode{x2669}\!\cdot}$$

The **6/8** or **12/8** choice of meter occurs again and again in adagio ballet sections. The broad, slower beats are useful for coinciding with moments of sustained pose in the dance, and the rounded inner groups of three eighths (often subdivided still further into thirty-second notes) serve to provide a graceful flow of energy. In the literature of ballet, the famous "Rose Adagio" from *Sleeping Beauty* is in **12/8**.

In faster tempos, the **6/8** meter can provide a wonderful lift for jumps, skips, and any movement that needs a thrust of preparation going into a burst of energy on the downbeat. The second note of each triplet can be either sustained or silent (resulting in an uneven sense of timing). Consequently, **6/8** meter is found in gigues or jigs, as well as for men's variations in ballets. During technique class, dancers would be apt to hear **6/8** used for glissades, skips, chassés, and jumps.

An even faster **6/8** is the Italian tarantella, where the second beat goes by rather lightly, and the general impression is one of ceaseless frenzy. In Balanchine's setting of Gottschalk's tarantella, for example, there is also no rest for the dancers.

Another compound meter that occurs with varying frequency is **9/8**, which is felt as three longer beats and could be indicated: **3**

$$\textstyle{\bf 3} \atop {\unicode{x2669}\!\cdot}$$

There are quite a few examples of such compound meters in the keyboard suites of Handel, which have various preclassic dance forms as their inspiration.

When west African music has been transcribed into European notation, the favored meter is usually **12/8**. There are many interesting possibilities for grouping the beats within each basic twelve, and in performance practice, the downbeats of each particular ensemble player will fall at different moments.

Fives

In European music and its derivatives in the New World, the most frequent metric groupings are by twos, threes, fours, and sixes. But in some folk traditions (Hungarian, for example), as well as in some newly composed twentieth-century music, a metric grouping of fives is not unusual.

Perhaps because modern dance places such value upon asymmetry, choreographers often make a point of using a five-beat meter. Notice, however, that even within that parameter, there are different groupings possible: 2 + 3; 3 + 2; 4 + 1; or 1 + 4.

Each metric five can have interior groupings that result from sustaining various beats for different effects, too. For example, consider the chart below. The first beat in a bracket is sounded; the subsequent bracketed beats can sustain the original tone or be silent.

```
1 ⌐2 3⌐ ⌐4 5⌐          ⌐1 2 3⌐ ⌐4 5⌐

1 ⌐2 3 4 5⌐            ⌐1 2⌐ 3 4 5

⌐1⌐ ⌐2⌐ ⌐3 4 5⌐        ⌐1 2 3 4⌐ 5

1 2 3 ⌐4 5⌐            ⌐1 2 3 4 5⌐

⌐1 2⌐ ⌐3 4 5⌐          ⌐1 2 3⌐ 4 5

⌐1 2⌐ ⌐3 4⌐ 5          1 ⌐2 3⌐ 4 5

⌐1 2⌐ 3 ⌐4 5⌐
```

In the concert repertoire of music, one of the most famous examples of quintuple meter is the second movement from Tchaikovsky's *Pathétique* symphony.

Mixed Metric Groupings

While music for classical ballet generally was cast in regular meters and phrases (most often eight measures in length), musical scores for modern choreography are more likely to allow the metric structure to flow out of the movement design itself. So one may have a measure of five beats, or seven, before having a recurring strong accent. Or the framework may be a *mixed meter*. In this case, a measure of five beats might be followed by one of four on a continuing, alternating basis. This would be indicated in the time signature as follows: $\frac{5}{4}$ $\frac{4}{4}$

Alternatively, there might be a different time signature in various instrumental parts. In that case, the music is said to be *polymetric*—having several meters simultaneously.

In some collaborative works, the metric organization of both music and dance movement may become quite intricate, with constantly changing groupings of beats and subdivisions and with dance and music either totally different in timing or coinciding in ways that create a new, resultant sense of groupings and accents in time.

Composers and choreographers also make use of accumulative meters (where the groupings add one or more beats as a piece progresses), or decumulative processes (where the opposite happens). These procedures were touched upon in the discussion of accents, and the general idea is the same where metric organization is concerned.

These facts should alert dancers that especially with contemporary styles, it is not enough simply to count to four or eight and keep repeating the same groupings of beats. With classical ballet, that may often be the case: once the meter is established, it is likely to remain consistent at least until the end of a section. But if twentieth-century compositions are used, ballet dancers must also be alert for metrical diversity. The extensive works by Stravinsky and Balanchine provide many examples.

Musicians' Counts
Compared to Dancers' Counts

It is crucial to remember that the basic musical beat can go along at any tempo. Subdividing a beat in any way does not alter the basic pulse or basic tempo chosen, nor does changing the metric grouping alter the basic pulse unless otherwise indicated.

Because we are talking about proportions of time, both the metric groupings and the subdivisions of a beat are directly related. You can play any metric grouping at any speed; you can establish a regular beat to suit your own tastes. There needs to be a differentiation between the overall speed or tempo at which a piece is proceeding and the exactly proportional divisions or groupings of beats into metric measures.

Remember that tempo is the rate of speed for the steady pulsation. Meter is the regular grouping of beats, usually with accents either present or implied.

For all metric grouping, musicians and dancers alike could count each group (bar or measure) as the music progresses. In a basic meter of **2/4**, a musician might say "one-two, two-two, three-two, four-two" and so on until the end of a section to keep track of how many measures have been played.

To simplify matters, the second beat of the bar is not called out at all with numbers. Instead the counting simply focuses on the downbeats of the beginnings of each measure: "One—two—three—four." The timing and the sounds are identical, of course, regardless of which way the measures are counted.

Dancers frequently prefer to feel the larger groupings, and so most likely count according to the second example given. As already mentioned, most certainly this is the case in **3/4** waltzes: one count per bar. In **4/4**, dancers are most apt to count two beats to the measure: the first and third of the musician's score.

Counts Vary; Pulses Don't

On occasion, students may hear dance teachers count steps within a movement combination. Take for example the case of a polka. Written in a light **2/4**, the music may have this melodic pattern:

against a steady bass and offbeat accompaniment. The dance movement, however, has a pattern of "short-short-long—and." Some musicians may be confused by this method of counting, but students still may hear: "One-two-three—and." That sustained "three" takes up the equivalent of three sixteenths in time; there is another fourth eighth note pulse that goes on after the teacher has said "three." The "and" is the upbeat, or last subdivision of the fourth beat if one is pulsing eighth notes.

It cannot be emphasized too much that in music with regular pulsation, the beat does not stop, nor does the musicians' counting cease simply because there is no movement on a certain pulse. The same reminder has to be made for silent beats in music: the pulse and the meter continue whether sounds are articulated during a particular segment of the grouping or not.

George Balanchine emphasized that for him one of the great attractions of Igor Stravinsky's music was precisely the sense of continuity in pulsation. The choreographer noted: "In Stravinsky's music, the dance element of most force is the pulse. It is steady, insistent yet healthy, always reassuring. You feel it even in the rests." This could well hold true for a considerable portion of music used by dancers.

In any meter (not just waltzes in threes) there can be sounds or silences on any beats, and any of the beats can be accented without disturbing the underlying organization by regular groupings of beats. As noted already, the metric organization is also unaffected by the tempo. There are slow waltzes and fast waltzes. Consequently it is never sufficient for a dance instructor or choreographer to request a collaborating studio musician to "play a waltz." How fast? With what kind of accentuation? With what nuance or expressive quality? With what flow of subdivisions?

Dancers can communicate all these things best to their collaborating musicians simply by singsonging a couple of seconds, or by demonstrating the kind of movement that characterizes the combination to follow. One musical colleague who works in dance studios is considering selling T-shirts with the motto: Help Banish Counting. Certainly, the ideal collaboration between musicians and dancers is so kinesthetically based, and so direct, that counting becomes an unnecessary distraction. Yet many choreographers and dance educators continue to find counting a necessary tool in the classroom studio and theater rehearsal. Consequently, it is important for dance students to understand the basis of choreographic counts and to relate them to the musical sounds.

Syncopation

An effective propellant for both music and dance is the placing of accents where they are not normally expected, or alternatively, an absence of accents where they normally are expected.

This effect is called *syncopation,* and it is found in Renaissance music, in compositions of Mozart and Brahms, and in many styles of jazz music.

Along with the unexpected placement of accents, there can be unexpected silences or the sustaining of offbeats over the pulse of the expected accented beat. This is particularly clear in the piano music of the turn-of-century ragtime composers. There, a steady "oom-pah, oom-pah" duple meter is established with regular bass notes and offbeats. These provide a constant against which the right-hand melodies can provide interesting syncopation. This more properly comes under the heading of rhythmic devices, but it does have a bearing on metric feel-ing, because for its effect, syncopation depends upon a steady pulse and sense of regular grouping of beats. So one has to feel what is regular in order to appreciate a departure from metric regularity.

The fact that a steady beat sets off syncopation is highlighted in Scott Joplin's piano rag *Stoptime,* in which the composer even indicated the word "stamp" with every single beat in the composition, in contrast to the syncopation and rests in the piano part and moments of total silence. "Stoptime" has become an important feature in tap dancing: a sudden arrest of both sound and movement.

Conducting Metric Groupings

Although the physical permutations of metric patterns are endless for dancers, it may be helpful to be acquainted with the basic arm patterns used by band and orchestral conductors to indicate meters.

Duple (**2/4** or **2/2** (cut time) or **6/8** when felt in two beats):

a simple down-up, but notice the curved path to facilitate a natural and continuing motion.

Triple (**3/4 or 3/8**):

Down, then to the conductor's right, then up, in a triangle—but again, with curves to facilitate the motion.

It should be noted that often, fast waltzes are conducted the same way that dancers feel the music: in one.

Common or **4/4** time: Down; to conductor's left, then

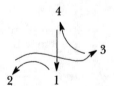

traversing more space across the body to the right, then up.

When the basic beat is slow, each count will be subdivided with an extra pulse.

Five: Jaques-Dalcroze had an interesting pattern for this in his eurhythmics classes: Down, left, right, out towards the front, then up.[5] Other possibilities are:

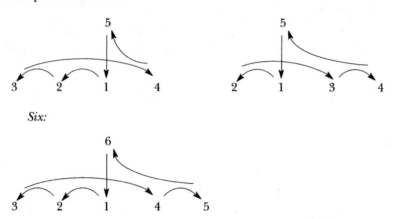

Six:

Again it must be emphasized that when one has chosen the meter or the subdivision, that still says nothing about the tempo. How fast is that "two" or that "three?"

Summing Up

To review, these are three elements of time that are found in music with proportional organization: the pulse rate, called musical tempo; the metric grouping of beats; and the inner flow, which is determined by the general choice of subdivisions within basic beats.

Returning to locomotor movement, here is a brief excerpt for students to consider while walking between classes. It is from *The Listening Book: Discovering Your Own Music,* by W. A. Mathieu, the section titled "In Meter."

> *Walking meter naturally groups into two complementary beats: left, right; or boom, chick. That is duple meter. Now try triple meter—waltz time: boom, chick, chick, boom, chick, chick (evenly spaced). Improvise music inside of that house. Virtually all of music everywhere is some combination of, or alteration between, duple and triple meter. It is another case— an astounding one—of complex results from simple structures.*
>
> *Meter is so compelling that even the best musicians have to remind themselves, when locked in the swing and sway of it, to remember the other dimensions: loud and soft, staccato and legato, rough, smooth, cajoling, majestic, peaceful.*

> *When you feel comfortable playing in duple and triple meters, try deliber-*
> *ately playing without any underlying pulse—outside the house, where*
> *time is wind. Then play in meter again and know the difference between*
> *the measured and unmeasured realms. Now without it again, and savor*
> *that difference.*[6]

That was a musician speaking. In contrast, dancer/musician Martha Partridge observes: "It is difficult to be 'on the beat' when you are
off center with your whole body."[7] Or upside down, or in the air, one
might add. Yet dancers who develop a reliable sense of basic pulse and
meter seem to find this a valuable asset, not only for their own choreographic work, but also when they perform works set by other artists.

Explorations and Assignments

1. With physical dance movement, demonstrate the difference
   between pulsation and nonpulsed timing. Sing or drum some
   examples in music.

2. Experiment in combining regularly pulsating music with
   pulsed movement. Then try nonpulsing, more freely timed
   music with freely timed movement. Then mix the possibilities.

3. Demonstrate a barre exercise to some Romantic music that
   has a great deal of rubato, paying particular attention to
   breathing and expressive nuances of movement. In this case,
   mimic the timing of the music.

4. Using both note heads and rests, notate the pulses in two measures each for the following meters, and indicate the typical
   points of accent.

$$\frac{4}{4}, \quad \mathbb{C}, \quad \frac{2}{4}, \quad \frac{3}{4}, \quad \frac{6}{8}, \quad \frac{5}{4}, \text{ and } \frac{2}{4}\frac{3}{4}.$$

5. Tap or drum the examples in exercise four, first andante, then
   allegro, and at other tempos, specifying which before you begin. Choose one of your metrical examples and demonstrate
   a movement pattern that could be performed at different tempos yet still retain a strong sense of the meter.

6. While listening to music on your own, tap the basic pulse and
   determine the meter. Bring three recorded examples to class:
   one in duple meter, one in triple meter, and one in compound
   meter. Demonstrate how you would conduct each.

7. Making use of available scores and videotapes, explore the classical ballet or modern dance repertoire and find one example of a slow **6/8** dance, a fast **6/8**, a broad **4/4**, and a fast **2/4**.

8. Start a notebook listing metrical types encountered in your dance and listening experiences.

9. Listen to a minuet, a waltz, a polonaise, a mazurka, and a sarabande. Compare the metric organization, tempo, and general feel of the timing in each case. How can you tell these forms apart? If possible, look at the scores to the pieces that you heard.

10. What is your understanding of the words *beat, pulse,* and *tempo?* In class, while examples of many different tempos are played, physically move to the musical pulse: walk, run, skip, jump, leap. What happens to the size of each movement, and to your energy output, if the tempo is increased? What happens if a definite amount of space is to be traversed in each case?

11. What is your understanding of "dancers' counts" and "musicians' counts"? Discuss. Demonstrate one example using a duple meter and one using a compound meter, indicating both musical counts and dancers' counts.

12. In class, establish a pulsed locomotor movement, and keep it constant regardless of what music is played at different tempos. Is this difficult? What happens if, in silence, each individual dancer establishes and maintains a separate tempo, even if the movement pattern is identical?

chapter 9

RHYTHMIC PATTERNS

*M*usical rhythm does/should not manipulate dancers; they
have their own internal and silent rhythmic motivation.

—Richard Cameron-Wolfe

The Harvard Dictionary of Music says: "It would be a hopeless task to search
for a definition of rhythm which would prove acceptable even to a small
minority of musicians and writers on music."[1] Indeed, in the broadest
sense, the word *rhythm* can be taken to refer to all aspects of the passage
of time: for instance, we speak of the rhythm of the seasons. Some educators refer to all time elements in music as its rhythm.

For immediate purposes here, the definition of rhythm will be limited to what some people would label a rhythmic pattern—that is, any
distinctive pattern that results from arranging sounds and silences in
relatively proportional lengths in time. The same rhythm could be
played at many tempos and still retain its recognizable character and
proportions in timing as an organized pattern. It could also be notated
in various ways. It is important to state that in European-based music,
the existence of distinctive rhythms presupposes a system related to regular beats as well as to meter.

This definition is closely related to *Webster's Third New International
Dictionary's* definition regarding the rhythm of speech: "An ordered re-
current alternation of strong and weak elements in the flow of sound
and silence in speech, including the grouping of weaker elements
around stronger, the distribution and relative disposition of strong and
weak elements, and the general quantitative relations of these elements
and their combinations."[2]

Focusing on music, *Webster's* suggests that rhythm is "the temporal pattern produced by the grouping and balancing of varying stresses and the lengths in relation to an underlying steady and persisting succession of beats.''

In this sense, rhythm is very definitely related to pulse and meter, to the subdivision of beats, and to an organization of stresses and weaker sounds. Focusing on rhythmic patterns, the *New Harvard Dictionary of Music* says: ''Repetitive rhythms rooted in bodily movements, whether of work or of play, lie behind much of the world's instrumental music. . . . Repetitive need not mean monotonous, however. Repeating cyclic patterns may be very complex internally, for one thing; but in combination, even simple patterns may result in great complexity.'' Going on to examine west African procedures as a good example of this, the dictionary notes: ''Rhythms rooted in bodily movements are always fundamentally accentual; rhythms oriented toward speech have more varied orientations.''[3]

Graphing Rhythms

Rhythm has been defined here as the organization of sound and silences into recognizable patterns of proportional lengths in time.

Because the same rhythmic patterns can be notated several ways, it can be helpful to see the basic proportions in a graphically proportional way.

The following method is the one suggested by composer Lou Harrison in his *Music Primer.*[4] The possibilities for any given segment of time are

Sound ⬚X⬚

or

Silence. ⬚

Harrison's formula is: Rhythm $= 2^n$.

Graphing Meters

Here is a metric grouping of three beats:

Next an accent is added on every first of three in a series, and the meter is clarified by drawing vertical bar lines after every third beat:

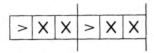

The graphing method emphasizes that the downbeat of every measure is simply a time slot. It can be silent as well as sounded, unaccented or accented.

Graphing Subdivisions

This should be done accurately. Use either large squares measured with a ruler, or graph paper.

Any beat can be divided into two equal halves, and each resulting time segment can be sounded or silent. For a measure in a metric grouping of two, these are the possibilities of sounds and silences if each beat is divided into four equal time segments:

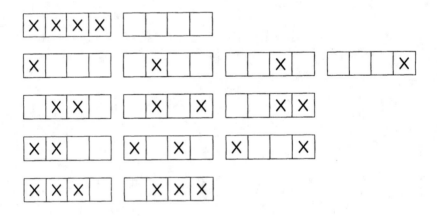

These are the possibilities of sounds and silences for subdivisions in triplets, for just one beat:

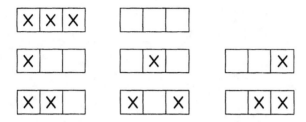

It should soon become clear that if the available combinations are joined, the possibilities for longer rhythmic groupings quickly multiply geometrically. Immediately, transfer these patterns to bodily movement.

Charts of Two Skips

Here is a graph of a skipping rhythm in which the hop provides a regularly recurring kind of feeling, based on a triplet subdivision with the second division being silent:

A sharper skip, with a briefer shuffle sound:

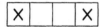

This last is the equivalent of a dotted note in traditional notation. It could be a dotted half, dotted quarter, dotted eighth, or dotted sixteenth; the proportions are the same, and each of these notations could in fact be played at varying tempos so that the resultant sound would be identical.

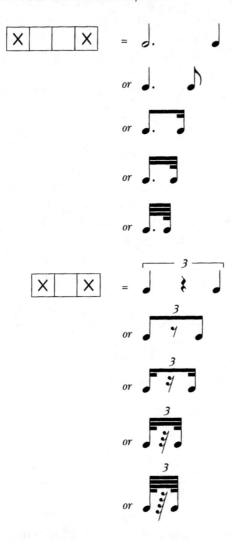

The same rhythm can be danced or sounded in music fast or slow or at any speed in between. The same rhythm can be played loud or soft. It can be played on one instrument or several together. It can be translated into musical sound using one pitch or several. Furthermore, the same graphed pattern of the first skip rhythm could be thought of as a grouping of three beats (with the first and third sounded and the second silent). Or it could be thought of as one beat subdivided into three equal segments (again, with the first and third sounded and the second time segment silent). The point is that no matter how it is analyzed and represented, the rhythmical pattern retains its proportions of sounds to silences whether played quickly or slowly, and regardless of how the sounds are divided among various instrumental timbres.

Effects of Timbre and Pitch

A listener's perception of rhythmic patterns in time can be greatly skewed by the addition of different pitches and tone colors. This was discussed in connection with drumming patterns, and is something for students to be aware of when trying to discern what the timing patterns are in music. Often this phenomenon can be explained in terms of resultant rhythmic patterns that the ear sorts out. We can distinguish a separate melody line if the same timbre recurs within a rhythmic overlapping of several different parts.

Polyrhythms and Cross Rhythms

Polyrhythm or *cross rhythm* indicates that there is more than one basic rhythmic pattern going on simultaneously in the music. It is also an important concept for dancers, for a choreographer may want one group of dancers to relate to a particular musical rhythm while a second group gears into another rhythmic aspect.

Often these interweaving patterns are the result of different subdivisions of the beat. For example, if in a piano work or in drumming the left hand is subdividing a beat into duplets while the right hand subdivides into triplets, they would relate as follows:

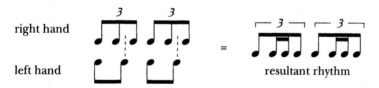

Notice the resultant, new pattern that emerges.

Another fascinating effect of timbre upon perception of rhythm can be experienced when a drummer's left and right hands play a paradiddle on two drums, or with two different tone qualities. Although the basic rhythm is steady eighth notes, the ear distinguishes the following two distinct rhythms, interesting because of the irregularity:

The polymetric organization of much sub-Saharan African music becomes quite intricate, for not only will different instruments be playing in different rhythms and meters, but the beginning of each pulse grouping may fall at a different moment in time so that the ear is constantly tantalized with shimmering resultant rhythms. This is one aspect of the additive techniques of African drumming that make it such a vibrant accompaniment for the dance. It must be emphasized that the procedures are quite different from European-based music. In the African traditions, fast beats are combined to make rhythms; in the European system, the basic beat is often slower and is not only combined with other beats to make patterns, but is also subdivided in many ways.

As discussed, the listener's impression of a rhythmic pattern can be greatly changed depending upon the instruments, or the tone color elicited from one instrument for the various sounds within a pattern. Additionally, each tone of a rhythmic pattern, or the entire pattern, can be played on any available pitches, which greatly increases the possibilities for creating interesting music from simple materials.

Some Four-Beat, Two-Foot Rock Feats

As an example of the effect of timbre, the graphing method can be expanded pictorially. Here are eight rock drumming patterns, using only two drum timbres plus a constant high-hat cymbal playing eight notes or duple subdivision of the basic pulse. The number of divisions will be limited to two per beat. It is recommended that each pattern be repeated a number of times.

Instead of the two drums, you could substitute any two objects, or use your hand tapping the tabletop contrasted with a flat stomp of your foot.

Some 4-beat, 2-foot rock feats!

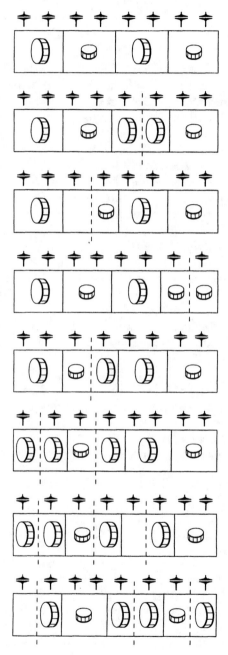

These modules can be repeated as many times as you want. They can also be mixed and matched in any order.

Listening for Rhythms

When dancers perform, they will probably not know how the sounds have been notated unless they have studied the score visually. The important thing for them to be aware of is the relationship of the relative lengths of sounds and silences within patterns. They want to be able to feel a beat, and to be aware of a regular meter if there is one. Next, dancers can listen for smaller subdivisions of beats, and then for distinctive rhythmic patterns of sounds and silences.

Once dancers can recognize the pulse, as well as the metric and rhythmic organization in a piece of music, they can deal with questions of how to move in relation to the basic pulse, the meter, or the rhythm, or some combination. If the movement is to acknowledge accents in the music, how will this be done? Or is the movement to contrast with distinctive musical accents? Furthermore, it is possible for the movement to have an entirely different metrical organization, and even to develop at an entirely different pulse rate or tempo than that of the music. Maybe the dancers are supposed to mimic the flow of the music, or maybe not. Maybe there is some direct relationship between a distinctive musical rhythmic pattern and choreographed movement, perhaps not. It is the choreographer's choice.

It may be helpful in grasping rhythmic patterns to represent them visually in a non-notational way upon first hearing. For example, one could use dashes in combination with vertical bar lines to indicate metrical structure. In the example below, read left to right. Small dashes on the bottom row indicate the regularly recurring beats within each measure. The varying dashes on the upper row indicate how long a tone is to be sustained. If there is a space, this indicates silence. For example, here is a phrase in a metric three:

in 3

Unlike graphing, this method cannot be accurate in regard to smaller subdivisions of a beat. But it can be quite useful in plotting out less intricate music, and in clarifying the general flow of music taken in by ear alone. Dancers can then immediately relate their physical movements to the relative durations, taking notice of the stresses and accents created by sustained sounds, and the surprises sometimes introduced by silences.

Poetic Meters

The poetic meters in written, verbal language would be termed rhythmic patterns by musicians. Many students have been familiarized with longs(——)and shorts (∪) and the following rhythmic modes or meters:

trochaic	— ∪
iambic	∪ —
dactylic	— ∪∪
anapest	∪∪ —
spondaic	— —
tribrachic	∪∪∪

Analogous patterns were a major ingredient in dance music of the Middle Ages, when melodies for currently popular group dances were cast in rhythmic modes to provide a structure for movement. Apparently the percussion accompaniment further underscored the metric structure, though of course we have no way of knowing precisely what the drumming was like.

Taking Dictation

Purely as a means of alerting dancers' ears to the details of rhythmic patterns, it can be helpful to take dictation and write down what is heard, in standard notation. The use of percussion instruments is particularly advised, and students can immediately use what they have written in music as a chart for movement patterns.

Students who wish to know more about the details of handwritten notation may want to consult the *Music Notation Primer* by Glen Rosencrans or Anthony Donato's book, *Preparing Music Manuscript.* Just as with verbal language, there is a distinct accepted grammar in notating rhythmic groupings, which is not always followed in fast printouts of today. However, the older practices were followed mainly as visual aids, so that performing instrumentalists could quickly identify familiar rhythmic patterns. This is akin to the chunking phenomenon that psychologists have recently explained. Basically, when taking rhythmic dictation, it is helpful if the underlying metric groupings and pulses are kept clear. To this end, musicians might tend to insert multiple rests that belong to different beats of a measure, to clarify where the pulses are. However, in many popular and jazz pieces of recent years, musicians are expected to be equally familiar with other methods of notating the same sounds.

Notation of Jazz Rhythms

Many of the rhythmic aspects of improvised jazz do not fit easily into standard notation. Often simplified approximations are written, and instrumentalists are expected to be familiar with aural performance practices.

There is only one basic fact that need concern dancers initially, namely that stemming from earlier swing styles, it became common convention to notate eighth notes as if they were equal in length, when the actual sounds are expected to be closer to uneven "dah-di" syllables—closer to a triplet figure consisting of a quarter note and eighth:

In certain Latin dances and in pop-rock music, however, the written

would be played straight, as even subdivisions.

Some Basic Rhythms for Dancers

For novices in taking dictation, it is perhaps best to begin with very basic, nonjazz rhythmic patterns such as the following. These can be played on any percussion instrument and repeated for verification. Advanced dictation would include tagging one pattern after another, with various repetitions. Students can reverse the procedure by composing original rhythmic patterns and playing them with body percussion. Here are some easy patterns to start with; more are suggested in the "Explorations and Assignments" section.

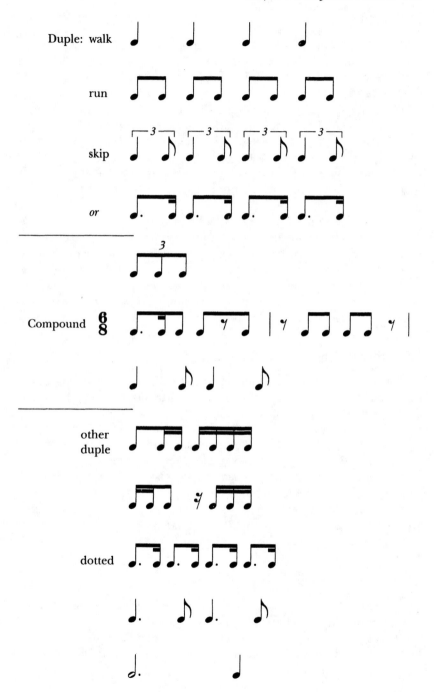

Ornamentation

It is important for dancers to distinguish basic structural patterns of timing as distinct from overlaid flourishes of ornamentation. These are devices used to draw attention to certain notes in a melody or accompaniment, or else simply to fill in gaps of a melodic contour.

Among the most common ornaments are the *trill* (a rapid alternation of two adjoining pitches), various *turns* (groupings of four or five notes adjacent to the main pitch), *glissando* (a fast sweep of intervening pitches between two non-adjacent pitches) and the grace note (single neighboring pitch played quickly so as to accent the main tone which follows). Ornamentation heard in electronic pieces is apt to be more complex.

For dictation purposes, it may be helpful simply to omit ornamental additions and concentrate on basic rhythms. However, sometimes musical ornamentation contributes a great deal to the character of a social or theatrical dance. One thinks of the central adagio pas de deux in *Giselle*, for example, where the extended ornamentation of the melody serves to maintain an intensity of flow at a slow tempo, as well as to create a sense of classic balance aesthetically.

Extracting Rhythms from Melodies

A good exercise in musical dictation consists precisely in taking down extracted melodies that are familiar from both classical and contemporary theatrical dance. Two books that may be useful for their extracts are Robert Lawrence's *The Victor Book of Ballets and Ballet Music* and Roger Fiske's *Ballet Music*, both listed in the bibliography. Students could also copy melodies themselves—for example from *Nutcracker*—and make up "name that rhythm" quizzes, presenting the class with only the rhythms extracted from their pitch relationships.

Equally if not more important for dancers to copy and understand are the rhythms found in accompaniment patterns. These often provide basic flow and support.

A Sampling of Social Dance Rhythms

Here are some rhythmic patterns that form the underpinnings of some preclassic, nineteenth-century, and contemporary social dances. These can be played on any instrument for written dictation, or transferred directly to bodily movement. Remember to set a basic beat first and keep the pulse steady in every case.

Typical rhythms in social and national character dances:

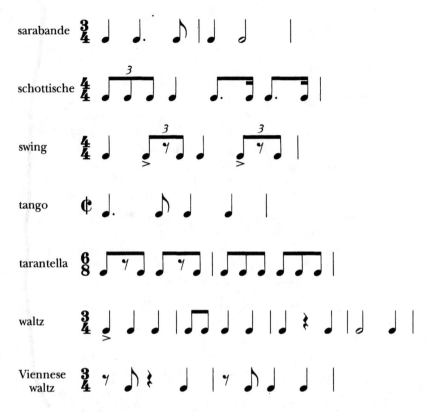

It should be mentioned that in music for many dance forms, listeners will not necessarily find particular rhythmic patterns; rather the distinctions often have to do with the choice of meter, tempo, and general flow of phrasing. For example, there is no single minuet rhythm.

Explorations and Assignments

1. Notate what you feel are mimicking rhythmic patterns for six locomotor patterns of movement. Discuss. What is the energy shape of each?

2. Devise six rhythmic patterns, variously making use of duplets, triplets, and quadruple subdivisions. Play them as body percussion, and extend them in dance movement.

3. Devise a rhythmic pattern using syncopation and rests. Play as body percussion and extend in movement.

4. In pairs or groups, practice listening to very brief rhythmic patterns, played percussively, and taking dictation. For nota-

tion, use dots and dashes, graphing, or standard musical notation. If the notated results are not an accurate representation, go back and listen to the patterns again. Concentrate on
distinguishing basic duplets, triplets, dotted notes, and various
combinations using sixteenth notes.

5. Demonstrate one social or traditional dance step, with its appropriate musical rhythm. Point out the important rhythmic
aspects of the dance movement in relation to the music heard.

6. Listen to selections indicated by the instructor, or the following suggestions, and compare the use of syncopation in each.
Clap the syncopations. Anton Dvorak: *Piano Quintet in A Major,*
last movement; Darius Milhaud: *Le boeuf sur le toit;* Scott Joplin:
The Strenuous Life; and available Renaissance dance music suggested by your instructor.

7. Watch a videotape of two waltzes and two mazurkas from the
classical ballet repertoire. What distinguishes them? Demonstrate the underlying rhythmic patterns in each.

8. View examples of a polonaise and a minuet. What distinguishes
them?

9. Choose several dances in **2/4** (can-can, coda, or gallop) and
compare the typical rhythmic patterns.

10. Compare two preclassic dance patterns in **4/4**.

11. Devise and play four different rock drumming patterns in
4/4, using only quarter notes, eighth notes, and rests.

12. Using a book of vocal music with familiar folksongs, tap out
just the rhythms of the melodies, noticing how they are notated.

13. With a group, devise a rhythmic pattern, and pass it around
the circle, keeping the pulsation and tempo constant. To
check for accuracy of reproduction, a tape recorder could be
used. What happens to the rhythm as it moves from person to
person?

14. Use the following rhythmic patterns for both drumming and
dance movement. In each case, repeat one pattern at least
eight times, keeping the tempo constant, with either a physical
or sounded accompanying pulsation to serve as markers in
time.

Try the patterns at different tempos. Transfer the rhythmic
patterns to your body, and create dance sequences that closely

mimic the timing of the musical rhythms. Movements need not be locomotor patterns; you could stand firmly and use your arms, shoulders, or your entire torso. Give particular attention to accurate beginnings of notes, to a continuing sense of underlying pulsation of beats, and to observing the full value of both notes and rests.

Copy several patterns on paper, this time adding markings for articulation, accents, dynamics, and tempo.

Choose three patterns and rewrite them using different note values but retaining the same rhythmic relationships. (For example, instead of a quarter note, use an eighth note, etc.)

Combine several rhythms to create a distinct motif, and improvise both music and dance movement based on the resulting pattern.

Create your own charts of rhythms by exploring further possibilities of subdividing beats, combining patterns, and substituting rests for some notes. Ties may also be added to notes to change the rhythm. Graph paper or a dash system may be helpful in working out the permutations, but they should also be notated in the standard musical system. Each measure can be considered as a module that could be combined with any other measure or measures to create a new motif.

Become familiar enough with these basic patterns so that you can write them down accurately upon hearing (by dictation). This is the continuing challenge for all dancers: what are the exact timings in the music that is heard while you dance?

For drumming, dictation, and movement improvisation:

Characteristic rhythmic components in duple meters:

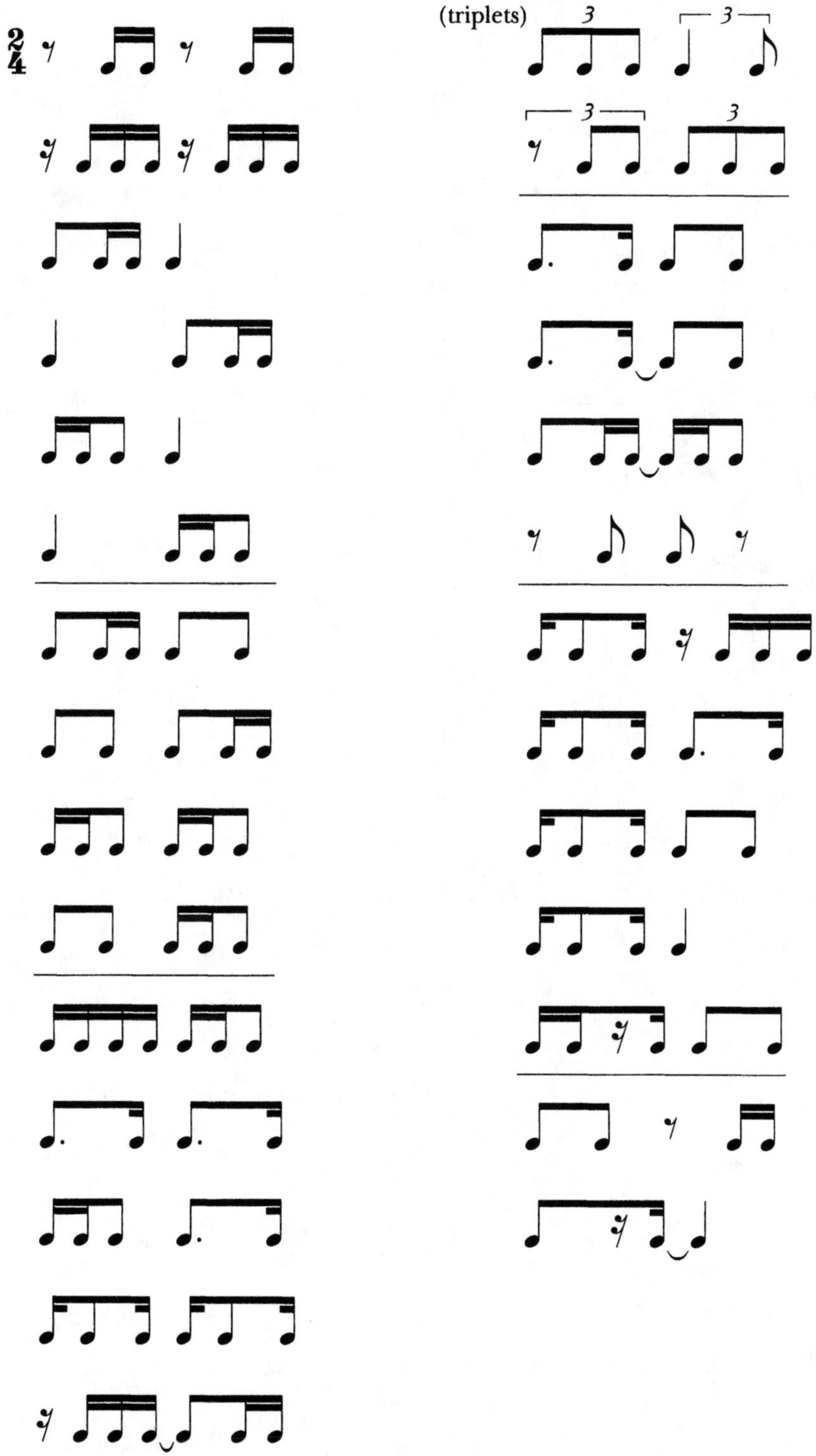
(triplets)

Typical patterns in common time.

etc.

Rests or ties can be added
on any beat or subdivision.

jazz
ride
style

Syncopated patterns

patterns with dotted notes

Triple meter patterns.

Asymetrical meters.

For variations, insert rests on any
beat or subdivision, or add ties.

Rhythms in compound meters.

In group percussion practice of all the preceding patterns, it is helpful if one person establishes a constant pulse, varied only with slight accents or timbre changes to mark downbeats. This provides an underlying metric framework for the specific rhythms. In solo drum practice, play the rhythmic patterns with your dominant hand, maintaining a regular pulse with the other to acknowledge the metric organization in some way. (One way is simply to play the downbeats of each measure nearer the center of the drumhead, the other beats nearer the rim.)

Advanced rhythmic training could involve combining two or more patterns for movement sequences. For example: keep one rhythm going in your feet, another simultaneously with your arms. Or isolate the timing of moving one shoulder, your head, the chest, the hips, and so forth. Dancers, like music, usually have more than one rhythm going on simultaneously.

The ways in which simultaneous rhythms combine with pitches result in the varying textures of music: the subject of Chapter 12.

chapter 10

PITCH, SCALES, AND MELODY

The dancer's body can be made an effective agent of musical discovery.

—Richard Kislan

This story is told by the cellist/improvising collaborator Gwendolyn Watson:

"Preparing for a workshop with a special guest choreographer, I eagerly set up my cello and various percussion pieces in addition to the piano, in order to be ready to gift her with some variety in music and sound for whatever movement situations she would present. Upon her arrival into the room, she looked over to my corner and the first words out of her mouth were 'No cello!' So I put the cello away. Next sentence to me was 'And no percussion!' " Watson proceeded to improvise on the piano: a single soft chord leading to a second chord. "Suddenly, the teacher's voice rang out from far across the dance floor 'And no melody!' Who was this person? Anna Sokolow."[1]

It is understandable what the choreographer/educator was after: she probably did not wish to have movement explorations be constrained in the studio by music that is too specific, too suggestive either emotionally or structurally. It has been proven time and again that unadorned human movement alone is sufficient for beautiful, expressive, powerful theatrical art. And if all one had to work with were rhythms, timbre, dynamics, and form, a great deal of interesting music could be made for dance use.

In the right theatrical context, however, a good melody can heighten the audience's awareness of what the dancers are doing onstage. Not that the movement mimics a melody; this rarely makes for

150

good choreography. But a melody can serve many dance purposes. Vaslav Nijinsky realized this when he chose Debussy's langorous flute solo that opens *L'Après-midi d'un faune.* Twyla Tharp realized this in a different way when she set her *Sinatra Songs.* And Alvin Ailey's signature work *Revelations* is framed indelibly by the vocal spirituals he selected. Undeniably one of the attractions of Martha Graham's *Appalachian Spring* is Aaron Copland's colorful instrumental setting of the Shaker tune "Simple Gifts."

Melody. One thinks of the threateningly foretelling theme of Tchaikovsky's *Swan Lake;* the unassuming yet effective and well-balanced melodies that Adolphe Adam composed for *Giselle;* the heroic dotted rhythm in the theme for *Apollo,* Stravinsky's score set by Balanchine; the trumpet solo that accompanies the ballerina doll in Stravinsky's *Petroushka;* Fred Astaire in his filmed performance of "Let's Face the Music and Dance"; or Paula Abdul's contemporary music videos.

In trying to grasp and remember melodies, it can be helpful to dancers to sing along when possible. While learning choreography, many dancers find it helpful to take tapes home to listen to and sing along with.

However, sometimes melodies seem to pass by too swiftly for singing along, or they have intricate rhythms that are difficult to replicate vocally. Sometimes dancers may not even be sure if there is a melody—or if there is, where it begins and ends. In such cases, the visual aid of scanning a score can provide a valuable shortcut for clarifying exactly what is happening in the music. It should also be observed that sometimes there is in fact no melody; the music may focus instead upon rhythmic play, or upon creating sound textures that might be analogous to changing cloud formations as a backdrop.

Pitch as Raw Material

The existence of all melodies—along with their accompanying harmonies, tone colors, and textures—depends upon the basic acoustical element of pitch. To back up a little, this must be examined simply as raw material for composers. As suggested in Chapter 9, any part of any rhythm can be assigned to any available pitch.

Harmonic Overtone Series

All pitches (the highs and lows in music) result from the varying frequencies in the cycles of sound waves.

In any particular tone, usually there is one predominant high or low sound, and we usually assign the pitch of the tone to this frequency. But objects can vibrate in many ways, producing not only the prominent pitch but also, simultaneously, higher frequencies that are called *over-tones* (or *harmonics* or *partials*). One may be aware of these with some instruments more than others, and their presence is in fact what accounts for the different tone colors of each instrument and each individual sound. Notation of pitch will be introduced shortly, but for future reference, here is an example of the lowest partials in the overtone series based on the fundamental of C below the bass clef. The series continues with upper partials coming at closer and closer intervals of pitch. It is hoped that a musician will demonstrate the sounds.

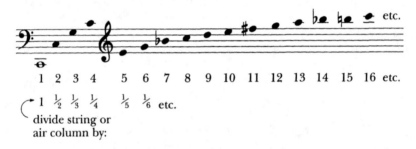

This is an unvarying series that can be produced, for example, on natural horns (alphorns, hunting horns, or French horns played without the valves). Many people experience the seventh and eleventh partials as being "out of tune," and in the sense that they have not been manipulated to fit our equal-tempered tuning system, this is true. A sample of harmonics can also be produced by lightly touching the string on a stringed instrument at certain mathematically precise points. The ratios are given in the chart.

The overtones seem to have a strong bearing on what people consider pleasing, as well as upon the way various tuning and harmonic systems evolved, and upon the way many familiar melodies are structured.

Intervals

The term *interval* refers to the difference in pitch between any two tones. In Western musical theory, intervals are measured by counting whole steps and half steps (or semitones, the equivalent distance between any two neighboring keys on the piano, regardless of whether they are white or black keys).

Octaves

The lowest-pitched tone in the overtone series is called the *fundamental.* The next tone is called the octave, because in our system of tuning, that is the eighth note of the diatonic scale systems. All this will be clarified a little later. What is important now is that the octave interval is the point at which human ears universally sense a special unity; we are aware that one note is higher than the other, but there is a particular congruence that allows us to perceive any replication of a melody at the octave, for example, as a true *doubling.* There is an acoustical basis for this phenomenon. The mathematical relation of a pitch one octave higher in tone to the fundamental is exactly double the frequency, and is produced by the sound source—with a string, for instance—vibrating precisely in half.

The chart indicates the precise mathematical points at which the string must vibrate to produce each succeeding overtone. These terms are not going to be explained in detail just now, but for future reference, the next overtone occurs at a perfect fifth, an interval very important in the tonal system that evolved in Europe. The next overtone is at an interval of a perfect fourth, also a strong relationship. Then come a major third, two minor thirds, and closer and closer tones at the interval of seconds. This information is emphasized only because the natural series of overtones does seem to have greatly influenced the development of both Eastern and Western systems of pitch heirarchy in regard to both melody and harmony.

More detailed definitions are to come, but for now, melody is considered the horizontal aspect of music, the single line of tones that progresses in time, indicated by left-to-right notation on paper. Harmony is considered to be the relationship of differently pitched tones heard simultaneously; hence the common reference to harmony as the vertical element in music, because that is how simultaneous pitches appear when notated in the Western system.

Consonance and Dissonance

These are terms with changing definitions, often depending upon shared cultural tastes and perceptions. But basically, consonance and dissonance refer to the impression that two or more simultaneously sounded different pitches make in regard to their impetus to move to other pitches. Consonant harmonies are perceived as stable, or complete in themselves. The ear accepts this quality particularly at definite resting places, either a pause within a musical section, or at the very end of a piece. Dissonant harmonies are perceived as more restless or unstable, with an impetus to resolve or progress to less dissonant combinations, and ultimately to consonance.

Perception of harmonic intervals depends upon the context in which they are used, in regard to consonance and dissonance. For instance, some centuries back, the *tritone* interval (equivalent on the piano B to F) would be avoided as a devil's sound; now it bears no curse. A hundred years ago, close intervals of a second were considered dissonant; now in some contexts, these are not heard as needing to resolve elsewhere.

Although consonance and dissonance refer basically to the vertical element in music, the construction of melodies in the tonal system is also tightly linked to underlying or implied harmonies, and to that sense of progression and resolution.

Dancers find analogies to consonance and dissonance in their kinesthetic sensations of tension and release. Balanchine, noted cook as well as choreographer, touched upon such contrasting sensations in his discussion of Stravinsky:

"They call his music dry or dissonant. What do they mean? After all, dissonance makes us aware of consonance; we cannot have the cool shadow without light. And we know that to find a wine too dry is merely to express a personal limitation."[2]

Pitch Can Be Selected

Concert A that orchestras tune to has a frequency of 440 cycles of vibration per second; the next higher A has 880; the A below the first one, 220, and so forth.

In between these recognizable points, where our ears identify higher or lower replications of similar patterns of tones, many pitches can be produced. Our voices easily slide, or glissando, from one recognizable pitch to its octave below or above, and so can stringed instruments.

Pitch, therefore, can be selected. Even the frequency of that tuning note, A has changed over time, though the letter name remains constant. In the eighteenth century apparently it was a bit lower than today, producing a mellower sounding ensemble than in·modern orchestras. This becomes a concern for dancers when they are presenting period reconstructions. For instance, in joint performances with Catherine Turocy's New York Baroque Dance Company, the Concert Royal Orchestra conducted by James Richman uses antique instruments or reproductions, and instrumentalists adjust their tuning to earlier practices. It does add a noticeable and charming flavor to the overall theatrical production.

Although dance students of today may be most familiar with a limited system of twelve pitches from octave to octave, other selections of available frequencies have been used around the world. If one listens to stringed or vocal music from the Middle East or India, for example, there will be pitches equivalent to between the cracks of our piano, or *microtonal* increments.

In the United States, one of the most dedicated explorers of microtonal pitch possibilities was the composer/instrument builder Harry Partch. Many of his discoveries about tuning and pitch were incorporated into his unique percussion and stringed instruments, as well as into his compositions for extended dance dramas. His work is carried on by the ensemble Newband, and their performances are recommended.

Just Intonation

When instruments are slightly out of tune, there is a lack of congruence in their sound waves, and this is experienced by the ear as *beats* or a wobble in the total sound (bearing no relation to rhythmic beats). In just intonation, instruments are tuned according to the harmonic overtone series, to eliminate the beats present in other systems. This makes the intervals of fifths and thirds particularly pure sounding. Among the composers well known in the dance field for use of just intonation is Lou Harrison, in his collaborations with Jean Erdman, Erick Hawkins, and others.

The disadvantage of this system of tuning, however, is that one cannot move around in pitch centers and retain the same relationships for the construction of melodies and harmonies. It is not possible to have all intervals pure in just intonation and still construct the kinds of melodies and harmonies that musicians have favored with other tuning. Consequently, the tuning system described next has been favored in European-based music for several centuries.

Equal Temperament

Most of the instruments commonly used in European-based musical styles make use of the equal temperament system of tuning, which includes small adjustments and accommodations to result in twelve pitches, each equally spaced a semitone or half step apart. The advantage of this is that the same identifiable melody can be *transposed* to start on any pitch chosen.

The available pitches on instruments such as pianos depend upon a good tuning. In order for dancers' ears to be properly trained, therefore, it can be a considerable help for studio instruments to be kept in good condition, and for the finest possible instruments to be provided in the first place.

With strings and winds (and of course, the voice), each note is constantly adjusted in performance, in consideration of how it sounds in the ensemble and depending upon the forward melodic function of particular tones in particular harmonic contexts.

A purposeful departure from equal tempered tuning is the effect of *bending* a note, or slightly raising or lowering the pitch of a note even while it is sustained. This is an important technique in jazz singing, as well as in playing wind and stringed instruments. Increasingly, nowadays, it is a possibility that is built into keyboard synthesizers, as well as an expressive option.

The Western System of Notating Pitch

The main reason dancers may want to learn the basics of pitch notation is to be able to scan a written score and visually follow along while focusing attention on melodies or accompaniment textures. Even some limited experience in reading scores may help students' dance activities later on. In some dance companies (such as Erick Hawkins's) the dancers regularly spread out the scores to study as an aid to learning the choreographic work.

The basics of pitch notation are fairly straightforward: a grid system is employed. Notes are read horizontally from left to right to account for the passage of time. The highs and lows of pitch are indicated vertically by placing note heads so they either fill spaces or are intersected by lines of a *staff*, which has five lines and four spaces, counted from the bottom up. Each line and each space represents the pitch equivalent of only the white notes on a keyboard, in order as shown on the chart, with alphabet letter names from A through G.

Accidentals

The pitches sounded by black notes on a keyboard can be indicated two ways, using symbols called *accidentals*. A *sharp* indicates that the pitch is the next semitone higher than the letter-note indicated; a *flat* indicates the next lower semitone pitch. A double sharp indicates that the pitch is to be a whole tone above the written note head; a double flat, a whole tone below. A *natural* sign serves the function of canceling out the sharp or flat. All accidentals appear to the left of the note affected, or else in a *key signature* at the beginning of a piece. If there are sharps or flats there, they indicate that those tones will be used for the entire section unless cancelled out by a natural sign before individual note heads.

staff:

clefs: C clefs:

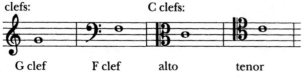

G clef   F clef   alto   tenor

accidentals: ♯   ♭   𝄪   ♭♭   ♮

sharp   flat   double   double   natural
                             sharp   flat

grand staff

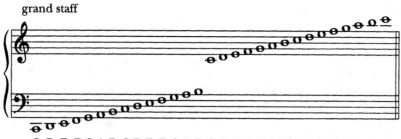

C D E F G A B C D E F G A B C D E F G A B C D E F G A B C

Clefs

The lines and spaces can represent different specific pitches, depending on which *clef* appears at the far left.

The G clef indicates that the second line from the bottom represents the G above middle C. This is the clef used for high-pitched instruments: flute, violin, clarinet, trumpet, horn, and so forth, plus, generally, the right hand for keyboards.

The F clef indicates that the fourth line from the bottom (between the two dots) is the F below middle C. This is used by lower-pitched instruments such as the bassoon, cello, tuba, plus, usually, the left hand for the piano.

When these two clefs are braced together, they form a continuous system used for keyboard instruments, called the grand staff.

The C clef is movable, and is most often nowadays used in the alto position for viola, with middle C on the middle line. When placed on the fourth line, the C clef is termed the tenor clef, used for higher notes of the cello, bassoon, and trombone.

For higher pitches above the staff, or for pitches below the staff, extra *leger lines* (or *ledger lines*) are added. For still higher pitches,

8ve — — — — — ⌐

indicates sounds an octave above notation. Similarly,

8ve — — — — — ⌐

indicates the actual pitch is to be an octave below that notated.

Playing Keyboard Instruments

Gregory Presley, a pianist formerly with the Martha Graham Company, tells his dance students at Florida State University: "Learning a musical instrument teaches more than a thousand years of theoretical information at the blackboard could."

Pianos are always a good choice for dance students to experiment with. Another excellent choice is an electronic synthesizer with many tone-color options, plus automatic rhythm and accompaniment selections. It is further recommended that students initially use the easy-read, big-note books with letter names printed on note heads. Also, you should get books of songs that are already familiar. Singing along while reading notation and playing a keyboard can help in developing a sense of interval relationships. For dancers it is such ear training that is most important, rather than virtuosity in playing instruments.

Relative vs. Absolute Pitch

As mentioned previously in regard to the tuning of instruments, specific pitches are of great importance to musicians. For people singing by themselves, however, or for dance students scanning written music visually, it is a *relative* sense of pitch that is helpful, and this is something that can be cultivated. Some dancers have found that the *solfège* system of singing is helpful. Borrowing tapes of the music to which you are rehearsing choreography and singing along with recognizable melodies may help in remembering both the music and the related choreography. Obviously this applies only to music that has discernible, singable melody; some music does not have this.

Scales: Chromatic and Otherwise

The word *scala* in Italian means ladder, and musical *scales* are ladderlike arrangements, from low to high, of all the pitches that are selected for use in a particular piece or section of a piece.[3]

Any available pitches can be selected for compositions and improvisations. If only the black notes of a piano are used, then those five pitches arranged low to high comprise the scale. This is among one of many such *pentatonic* scales that are very popular throughout the world.

If seven different pitches are chosen within one octave, then a *septatonic* scale is created, with the eighth note, the octave, being considered number one in replicating the same pattern at a higher pitch.

If all the notes within one octave on a piano are used in a piece, this produces the *chromatic* scale of twelve tones.

Pentatonic and Whole-Tone Scales

The choice of pitches, or scale, determines much about the flavor of a piece of music.

Pentatonic—or five-tone—scales are found in traditional music the world over, including music of native North and South America, the British Isles, Finland, Hungary, and Southeast Asia, as well as throughout China.

Among the most sophisticated uses of pentatonic scales are the ensemble pieces used for ritual dance dramas in Java and Bali. Because each village tunes its percussion orchestra differently, the scales therefore are not interchangeable, though they may be variations of related pentatonic forms. A second popular Indonesian scale form divides the octave into seven pitches. Some pentatonic scales have semitones; in others, the pitches are nearly equidistant. Typical examples of Balinese pentatonic and septatonic scales are included in the chart.

Whole-tone scales, as the name implies, have pitches equally distant: six different pitches to the octave. Combinations of whole-tone and pentatonic scale usage became attractive early in the twentieth century to certain French composers, including Debussy, Puccini, and Ravel. Because of the mellifluous sounds projected by these scales, they are also popular in the construction of modern day Orff barred-percussion instruments such as marimbas, xylophones, and metallophones. These are used extensively in music and dance education. Many of the multi-pitched instruments have removable bars so that one can construct varied scales simply by lifting the bars for pitches to be excluded.

Diatonic Scales

The *major* and *minor* scales most frequently encountered in European-based music of the last 300 years, as well as the *modes* of the Middle Ages and Renaissance, can be classified as *diatonic.* They all consist of various arrangements of whole steps and half steps within each form. For now, only a few common choices descended from European modes will be described.

Most familiar to our ears is the major scale, with half steps occurring between the third and fourth degrees of the scale and between the seventh and eighth (or octave). The pattern of whole and half steps produces two *tetrachords* (groups of four pitches), each comprised of these intervals, from low to high in pitch: "whole step, whole step, half step." The two tetrachords are separated by the interval of a whole step. The C major scale, which falls only on the white keys of a piano, is included in the chart.

There are several forms of minor scales, with the common denominator of having a half step fall between the second and third degrees, creating the minor third. The *natural* minor scale follows this pattern, with semitones between the second and third degrees, and between the fifth and sixth degrees. In the *melodic* minor, the semitones are from the second to the third degree and from the seventh to the eighth on the *ascending* pitches; but for *descending,* both the seventh and sixth degrees are lowered, resulting in semitones between the sixth and the fifth and third to the second. For the *harmonic* minor, semitones are between the second and third, fifth and sixth, and seventh to eighth, both ascending and descending.

The blues scale employs both major and minor third degrees as well as lowered fifth and seventh degrees, in addition to the pitches of the diatonic major scale. The added notes serve particularly expressive functions.

Contemporary Use of Modes

Jazz music makes considerable use of modes, dating to the Middle Ages in Europe, and in turn, related to still more ancient Greek forms. To figure these out, play only the white notes on the piano, starting on a different note for each mode. Notice that the whole and half steps fall on different degrees for each of the modes. It is these arrangements of whole steps and semitones that create the distinct flavors of various melodies based on the different modes.

Starting on white keys, the modes are: C, or Ionian (same as our major scale); D, or Dorian; E, or Phrygian; F, or Lydian; G, or Mixolydian; A, or Aeolian (same as natural minor scale); B, or Locrian (little used).

Scales:

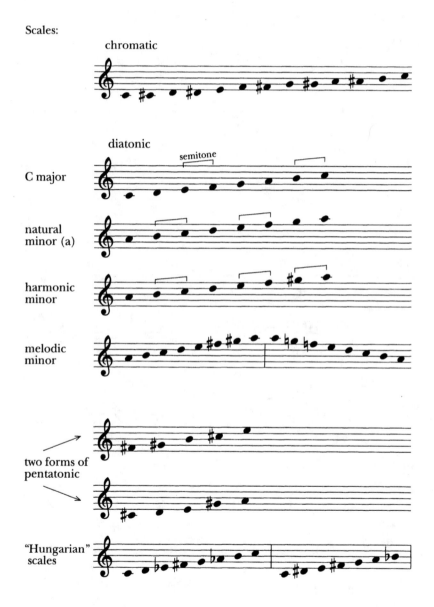

Scales, continued:

Hungarian and Synthetic Scales

Quite interesting flavors result from Hungarian scales. These can be heard in twentieth-century pieces by Béla Bartók and Zoltán Kodály, as well as in the *Hungarian Rhapsodies* of Franz Liszt.

   A choice of scale can lend an air of authenticity when a theatrical suggestion of a distinct place and culture is desired. For example, choreographer Sophie Maslow and her original collaborator for *The Village I Knew*, Samuel Malowsky, chose melodies based on middle-European scales to evoke earlier Jewish life. (The score was completed by composer Gregory Tucker.)

Synthetic scales can be made up by choosing any number of pitches as the basic material for composition or improvisation.

For an entire volume of scale forms, consult the *Encyclopedia of Scales* by Schafer and Colin (see bibliography).

Melody

Ragas

When students at the Martha Graham School begin their floor exercises, they are likely to hear pianist John Schlenck improvise music based on Indian *ragas*. These are more than simply pitch choices for scales; rather they are pitch seeds of melodic invention, to be intertwined with rhythmic patterns called *tala*. In connection with traditional rituals, ragas also had certain connotations of mood or ceremonies. The use of ragas is an ancient and intricate art, closely connected to dance in India. For an extensive introduction to the subject, see *The New Grove Dictionary of Music and Musicians.*

Melody Defined

Webster's first definition of melody is: "a sweet or agreeable succession or arrangement of sounds."[4] This doesn't tell the whole story, for there are ugly melodies that serve important emotional and dramatic purposes, including those for dance.

The dictionary's second definition is more general: "a rhythmically organized and meaningful succession of single musical notes or tones having a definite relationship one with the other and forming an esthetic whole."

In considering this definition, it is interesting to notice the derivation of the word melody: from the Greek word meaning "to sing," plus *melos,* meaning, among other things, limb or joint. The parts of the arm in fact suggest a good visual analogy to melody in music: there is an overall shape, but there are interior parts that can be angled or smoothed to present varying contours. Furthermore, the muscles can be tensed or relaxed and in so doing, can suggest or convey emotional states.

Similarly, melody in music (continuing the anatomical metaphor), is simply a succession of tones, with both pitch and rhythm, that form a recognizable shape and make a statement of some kind. It is the horizontal aspect of music. But as suggested already, the very choice of pitches in a melody often are related to an underlying sense of harmonic organization, to a sense of repose or a need for further motion, and to the aesthetic purpose of presenting a satisfying, proportioned, overall form. What we consider as melody, therefore, is not a random series of pitches and rhythms.

Melodic Contours

During performances, dancers onstage are usually most concerned with the tempo and the rhythmic aspects of the music. But the melodic contours can suggest a great deal in the way of expressivity. Something to notice and analyze in a melody is the general shape or overall contour. Is it smooth, progressing mostly by smaller (stepwise) pitch intervals? Or does it give a jagged impression, which may result from the use of wide leaps and large intervals in the pitches plus the interjection of many rests or silences varying in duration? In regard to duration in real time, is the melody brief? Or does it go on at some length without pause?

It is both instructive and enjoyable to listen to recordings of music from the dance repertoire and draw doodles suggestive of the overall melodic lines. In doing this, do not try to represent every note or each change in pitch, but rather the generalized outline of the beginning, middle, and end. Notice: do the pitches stay in a limited range of high and low or encompass a relatively extensive range?

Doodling shapes, splattering dots on a paper, creating swerving lines, engraving zigzag angles, inserting sudden spaces: all these are visual suggestions that composers sometimes use to get started in creating melodies. Upon occasion, such graphic directions for melodies have served as scores for collaborating musicians in dance works.

Speaking very generally, in most music of the world, melodies consisting only of large leaps in pitch are uncommon. More favored are melodies in which there is a grouping of pitches in a certain range. There will be skips, but these are balanced by stepwise motion closer by. And in extended composed music of the West, melodies tend to have a direction; they are going somewhere; there is a point they are trying to reach; there is a sense of tension and release.

Effects of Register

The quality of any melody can be vastly affected by changing the pitch *register* in which it is played. Register refers to the general high or low range in pitch. A good example of this is the famous pas de deux from

Swan Lake. In the first hearing of the grand adagio, the melody appears in the violin, quite high and vibrant. As the dance progresses, the same melody is placed in a lower register and given to the cello, with the violin now taking an obbligato countermelody. What happens musically does not mimic the dance movement, but parallels the idea of a love duet.

Hints for Improvising Vocal Melodies

Most people like to sing familiar songs but would feel at a loss if asked to make up a tune of their own. How are melodies composed? Sing any pitch, preferably not in your extreme high or low registers: the melody has begun.

From there, the choices are to go either up or down in pitch. The next pitch can be very close to the first one, or the singer can skip the nearby possibilities and leap to a more distant pitch. For the next note, the singer can continue in the same direction (up or down), progressing either in close stepwise fashion, or again by a leap. Alternatively, a melody could turn and go in the reverse direction. And of course, at any point any pitch could be repeated, using any rhythms you choose.

Spinning out of a melody could continue in this fashion, note by note. Or one could speed up the process, and sing according to a drawn, linear melodic curve. Such an overall arc or form injects a forward thrust and energy; making up a melody becomes less of a note-by-note affair and more of an expressive vehicle.

Add dynamics. For example, a useful model is to start at a moderate level, then crescendo until a peak is reached in the melodic contour, and finally retreat gradually to a conclusion.

Another method of forming a melody is to mimic the accents and nuances in any spoken sentence of any language. This automatically adds rhythm to a melody.

Yet another way is to use the rhythm of poetry, as a basis, but to leave the choices of pitch wide open. An interesting project might be to take the lyrics of a favorite popular song and improvise original melodies for the same words—and then add contrasting or supportive dance movement.

In regard to counts, a melody could be created that would directly complement dancers' counts for any phrase length. This is a very good way to get started in composing tunes: there are only eight beats, and within that, there is a beginning tone, a rhythmic idea, some sort of goal, and either a gradual end or an abrupt stop. Generally speaking, the most effective melodies limit the palette in regard to both pitch patterns and rhythmic patterns. The listener can absorb just so much new material.

Consequently, the ear and the mind perceive a cohesive form better if there is an initial idea (or ideas) that are expanded in various related ways.

All these techniques of improvising melodies provide a handle for understanding the process of musical composition. Dancers may not want to embark on large-scale composition projects, but just as one cooks to learn culinary arts, similarly, dancers can profit by spending even a half hour experimenting with inventing melodies of their own. A good inspiration is an electronic synthesizer hooked to a tape deck, plus computer equipment that will instantly notate and even print out whatever you are improvising on the keyboard. You may not immediately hit upon something suitable for use in a dance piece, but in any case, such explorations may help when it comes to grasping and understanding not only the melodies that are heard in other music, but also a little something about the compositional process.

In addition to hands-on or voices-on experience in making up melodies, you might explore the musical literature for theatrical dance, focusing solely on melodic content. As you watch videos or live performances, ask yourself: What effect does the presence or absence of a recognizable melody have upon the choreography or the performance of individual dancers? How does the style of the melody seem to relate to the overall flavor of the dance work? And is there any way of telling which came first, melody or dance?

Explorations and Assignments

1. Using drinking glasses or soda bottles with varying amounts of water (possibly colored with food dye for further recognition), devise a pentatonic (five-tone) scale that pleases you. Improvise an eight-beat pattern using only several rhythms. Improvise a twelve-beat pattern; a nine-beat pattern.

2. For group experimentation: in a circle, "pass a pitch" around, matching it with any method of vocalization. Octave doublings are allowed for the comfort of male and female voices, but otherwise, the pitch should not change. How accurately was it passed? Check with a tuned instrument.

3. Also with group vocalization: establish one pitch that is in a comfortable range for all singers. Everyone first sustains the same tone in unison. Then singers may enter and exit, using any articulations and dynamics.

The experiment may be repeated, adding various pitches that are comfortable for men's and women's voices. Each group, however, sticks with its particular pitch. This time, in addition to varying the articulations and dynamics, singers may add any rhythmic patterns on the repeated pitch.

4. Spend some time at a piano or electronic keyboard. Notice the arrangement of black and white keys, and the repetition of the same arrangement with each octave. Learn the names of all the notes, and relate these to written notation. Experiment with various intervals, singing along to learn the pitch differences between any two notes within one octave.

5. Pick out one tune by ear on a keyboard instrument.

6. Learn to play two folk songs from notation, using a big-note keyboard book that has the letter names written on the note heads.

7. At a keyboard, play a major scale. Play a pentatonic scale (all on black notes). Play a whole-tone scale. Play the chromatic scale. Have a musician show you how to construct the three kinds of minor scales, and a blues scale. Make up your own scale and write it in pitched notation.

8. Doodle a line contour on paper and use it as a general guide for an improvised vocal melody, using nonsense syllables.

9. Using available scores from theatrical dance works, draw lines on paper to represent the general contour of three melodies. What is the general effect created by the shapes? Do they relate in any way to a sense of climax, or tension and repose? If possible, view a videotaped performance danced to one of these melodies. Does the choreography relate in any way to the melodic lines? In your opinion, should it, given the context of a particular style?

chapter 11

HARMONY

Abstract dancing is analogous to abstract music. The same elements are there—the tone, rhythm, melody and harmony, with the addition of the kinesthetic appeal only possible in dance.

—Doris Humphrey

If melody involves the use of various pitches consecutively in time (which can be represented horizontally), then harmony can be defined as the use of the same basic scale pitches, but simultaneously.[1] This is usually represented visually as the vertical dimension of music. Sometimes a functional harmonic underpinning can be implied in various ways even without being completely present at any particular moment in the music.

Intervals

As discussed in connection with melody, an interval is the distance between any two pitches, and the same interval term would be applied whether one is considering horizontal melodic motion or vertical harmony.

In the Western system of tonality, intervals in the diatonic scales are measured by counting half steps and whole steps (semitones or whole tones). The distance is measured from the lower-pitched note to the higher one. The accompanying chart shows intervals available in the diatonic system, with the inverted intervals that result if the higher pitch is positioned lower. (If inverted, seconds become sevenths; thirds become sixths; fourths become fifths; fifths become fourths; sixths become thirds; and sevenths become seconds.)

Intervals:
interval

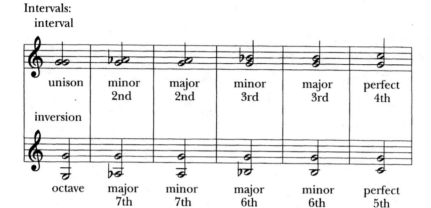

inversion

interval

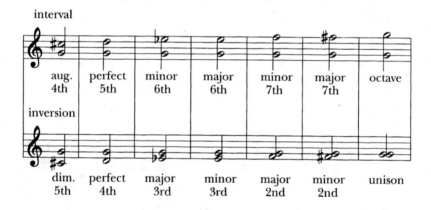

inversion

enharmonic equivalents

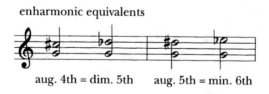

aug. 4th = dim. 5th   aug. 5th = min. 6th

Chords in diatonic harmony

C major – Tonic triad

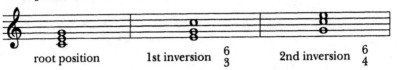

root position   1st inversion $\begin{smallmatrix}6\\3\end{smallmatrix}$ 2nd inversion $\begin{smallmatrix}6\\4\end{smallmatrix}$

Triads

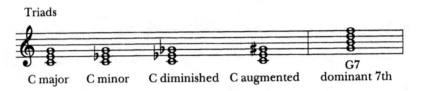

C major   C minor   C diminished   C augmented   G7 dominant 7th

Triads in C major

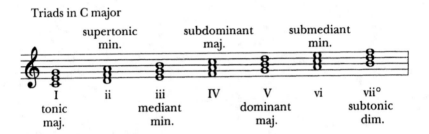

supertonic min.   subdominant maj.   submediant min.

I   ii   iii   IV   V   vi   vii°
tonic maj.   mediant min.   dominant maj.   subtonic dim.

Triads in C minor

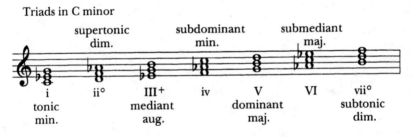

supertonic dim.   subdominant min.   submediant maj.

i   ii°   III⁺   iv   V   VI   vii°
tonic min.   mediant aug.   dominant maj.   subtonic dim.

Fourths, fifths, unisons, and octaves are considered *perfect* intervals. Seconds, thirds, sixths, and sevenths are major if they coincide with tones found in the major scale of the lower note. An interval a semitone smaller than a major interval is called minor; if it is yet another semitone smaller, it is *diminished.* If it is a semitone larger than the major interval, it is *augmented.* Because of enharmonic possibilities using accidentals, it can be seen that identical-sounding intervals can be notated in several ways, and the choice usually depends upon a tone's function in relation to the harmonic or melodic progression.

In the common-practice era of Western tonality (roughly from the late seventeenth century through the early twentieth century in Europe and the New World), perfect intervals, thirds, and sixths were considered consonant. Dissonant intervals—those deemed restless and in need of some resolution to a consonant interval—were seconds, sevenths, ninths, plus all augmented and diminished intervals.

A practical use of the measurement of intervals can be seen in the keyboard parts to Baroque instrumental pieces, in which a single bassline (the *basso continuo*) is provided, with numerals used as a shorthand indication of harmonic intervals upon which the musician was supposed to improvise and embroider.

Chords

A *chord* is a structural harmonic device, consisting of three or more simultaneous pitches with different names. (Octave duplications are not relevant in this case.) Chords can have just three tones, or more, with multiple doublings of component pitches in different registers, or on different instruments.

Formation and Analysis of Triads

Basic chords in the Western tonal system are built on *triads,* or chords comprised of three pitches, with both the lower two and the upper two forming intervals of thirds. The varying uses of major thirds (C to E, for example, an interval of four semitones) and minor thirds (C to E flat, an interval of three semitones) give distinct flavors to different chords.

Major triads are comprised of a lower major third, plus an upper minor third. *Minor triads* are comprised of a lower minor third and an upper major third.

Diminished triads consist of two minor thirds. *Augmented triads* consist of two major thirds.

These are the basic harmonic structures found throughout the 300-year common-practice period of Western music. However, much of our popular and art music continues to adhere to these basic harmonic customs.

A triad in *root position* has the main note in the lowest placement; the other intervals measure a third and a fifth above the root. If the lowest pitch name is moved to the highest placement in register, the triad is in *first inversion position*. The intervals, measuring from the new lowest note, are a sixth and a third; hence the figured bass indication of six-three. For the *second inversion* of a triad, the intervals measured from the lowest note become six-four. If any of these tones are altered from the usual pitches found in the diatonic scale, this is indicated by the use of accidentals.

Triadic Progressions

As a shorthand indication for both analytical and performance purposes, Roman numerals are assigned to each degree of the scale (formerly, using upper and lower case to distinguish between major and minor triads). This system of analysis allows any piece to be transposed to any other key, simply by substituting the appropriate alphabet letter names for the new key.

Alternatively, for performance purposes, alphabet names are used for exact pitches, using *maj.* to indicate major, *min.* for minor chords. Diminished chords are indicated by *dim.*, and augmented chords by *aug.* Alternatively, a superscript circle ° indicates diminished; a + indicates augmented.

In major keys, the major chords are I, IV, V; minor chords are ii, iii, vi. The diminished chord is vii°.

In minor keys, i and iv are both minor chords; V is always a major chord; ii°, iv°, and vii° are diminished; and III+ is augmented.

Examples of the usefulness of abbreviations for harmony are the many fake books that fully notate only the melodies of popular songs, indicating chords that can be filled out on keyboard or guitar.

All this can probably be understood a little better if a musician demonstrates at the keyboard and dance students construct their own intervals and chords. Most important is simply to listen to the differing qualities of major, minor, augmented, and diminished chords.

Quartal Harmony

In the twentieth century, composers such as Paul Hindemith have constructed their music using quartal harmony: that is, chords built on intervals of a fourth instead of a third. And a very beautiful vocal tradition from the southern states is heard in Sacred Harp singing, which often combines quartal and tertial harmonies with hymn melodies in the tenor voice.

Extended Chords

Triadic formations can be extended simply by adding further intervals of thirds: sevenths, ninths, elevenths, and thirteenths. The flavor of each can be varied according to the choice of major or minor third. (These are indicated in analysis by the use of accidentals for the altered pitch intervals.)

Most prominent of the seventh chords is the dominant seventh— the equivalent of G-B-D-F if the tonic or home-base key is C. In common practice, it is felt to contain an impetus to *resolve* or progress to the tonic, or home key center.

Extended harmonies were explored by composers such as Wagner, Richard Strauss, Debussy, and Ravel. Extended chords are essential to creating the rich flavors of contemporary jazz. For a thorough compendium of chord possibilities transposed to all keys, see some of the popular piano publications listed in the bibliography; they provide both notation and pictorial representations of chords played on keyboards.

Tonality

Composers generally are not concerned with rules at the moment of conceiving new works. Yet in analysis after the fact, one may discover certain preferences in harmonic progressions that lend distinctive flavor. For instance, the harmony of Brahms becomes quite recognizable over repeated hearings. The harmony in Arnold Schoenberg's serial music gives a different impression, because it is not based on triadic formations or traditional concepts of tonal pitch relationships.

In the very broadest sense, tonality can imply a feeling of pitch center, or home base in any system of organizing harmony. What developed in Europe as common practice has come to be labeled the tonal system. It is based on the idea of a *tonic* home base and a strong *dominant* (the perfect fifth seven semitones above the main tone) that pulls towards the tonic. In the key of C, the dominant is G.

Next in the heirachy is the *subdominant* (the pitch a perfect fifth or seven semitones below the tonic). In the key of C, this is F. Next in strength and importance are the chords on the second (*supertonic*) degree of the scale and the sixth. The chord with its root on the third (*mediant*) degree of the scale is even weaker. And finally, there is the chord built on the seventh (*leading tone*) degree of the scale. This is a diminished chord with a distinctive flavor, particularly because its root is that seventh, or leading tone that also helps lead back to the tonic. So although this isn't used as much as the tonic or subdominant, it is also a strong chord, and one that is very useful in establishing a key center.

Throughout this discussion, one could refer to the chart of natural harmonic overtones. There seems to be a definite relationship, and also with the intervals considered consonant or dissonant.

In connection with the discussion of equal tempered tuning in Chapter 10, it was explained that pitch can be regarded as a relative aspect of music, and that the same melodic patterns or harmonic progressions can be transposed with any other pitch as a tonal center. The twelve possible *keys* each have their own key signature, and are related in a *circle of fifths*, as shown on the chart. To figure out the key in a key signature with sharps, take the last sharp to the right, and count up one semitone. The piece may be in that key if the scale is major—or it may be in the *relative minor* key, which begins on the sixth degree of the major scale. To find the home key in a flat signature, count back one flat from the last flat: that will be the pitch of the major key. The relative minor key begins on the sixth degree of the major scale.

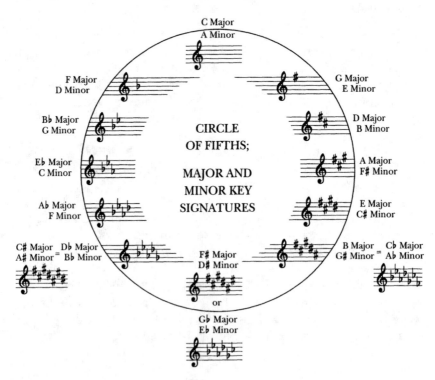

Frequently, pieces in classical concert music have no poetic title, but instead are identified by the key (Sonata in A Major; Symphony in D Minor). Therefore, the ability to recognize the signatures may be handy on occasion, particularly for choreographers.

Cadences

Moments of harmonic resolution or repose are called *cadences*. These are used prominently to delineate phrases or other sections in a piece of music, and they may also function as important structural marking points for choreographers and dancers. Harmonically speaking, these resolutions may be either partial pauses (*semicadences*) or very conclusive resting places (*full cadences*), and they can be clothed in many rhythmic garments.

The two-chord "A-men" at the end of church hymns is an example of a simple *plagel* cadence, from the subdominant to the tonic. At the conclusion of classical symphonies, the dominant-tonic was often emphasized to such an extent that exaggerated caricatures have become a staple of comedians.

For all cadences, the important aspect is that the chord or chords directly preceding the final chord provide a real feeling of impetus towards that goal of a resting place. Cadences often act as an analogy to punctuation in language. They serve to divide both brief and longer sections within an extended piece of music. They may verify for the listener the intended key center of the section just concluded, and they frequently emphasize progression from dissonant to consonant intervals.

However, music need not end in a restful manner, nor even upon a tonic note. One very effective way to end a piece is by resting on the dominant, leaving the audience in a state of suspension. More usually, a cadence on the dominant functions as a *half-cadence*, followed by another phrase, which may progress to a final tonic. A cadence that does not progress as expected but to some other chord instead is termed a *deceptive cadence*. Among other things, this can prove useful in changing keys (modulating).

For the purposes of most dancers, individual chord changes in harmony have modest effect. The harmonic rhythm is often more pertinent than the specific pitches of the chords themselves. Also important to notice are the cadences. Many choreographers in the past have related the structure of dances to these points of pause and repose.

Modulation

Music remains centered in the same pitch for the duration of a piece in some traditions around the world. Often this is a result of instruments used (for instance, with a pentatonic xylophone, there is little choice).

With increased availability of pitches, one of the endless avenues of creation in terms of harmony is to change keys, or *modulate.* This can be done in two ways: either as a total surprise (just start playing in another key) or by finding a *common chord* that can fill simultaneously different functions in two key systems.

Modulation provides a freshness for the listener, so that even if a melody and accompaniment are played in exactly the same way, they will seem transformed by the difference in pitch. Pianists in dance studios often make use of this technique for lengthy combinations across the floor. Sometimes modulating even a semitone higher will increase the energy felt by the dancers.

Modulation also serves an important structural function. In sectional dance music, contrasting material may be cast in different key centers, often with the final section returning to the original key. In extended concert forms, particularly the *sonata allegro* of symphonies and chamber music, modulation is an expected device that serves to delineate both the development and the return of original themes.

Polytonality

At the keyboard, if a pianist plays in one key with the left hand and another with the right hand, a *bitonal* mix results. Or this could be attempted with two people at one keyboard.

Bitonality is only one kind of *polytonality,* the presence of multiple keys simultaneously. This has become a source of exploration for many contemporary composers who seek to expand the harmonic palette of their music. Our ears are used to the phenomenon now and often find the contrast refreshing. But earlier in the century, the composer Camille Saint-Saëns wrote the following in a letter to Darius Milhaud (composer of scores for *Le boeuf sur le toit, La crétion du monde,* and many other ballets): "I am grieved to see that you are opening the doors to all sorts of bedlam aberrations and trying to force them down the public's throat when it protests. Several instruments playing in different keys have never produced music, only a babel!"[2]

Today, concert audiences accept polytonality, as well as an absence of any tonal center.

Atonality

The twelve-tone system (found in the early twentieth-century music of
Arnold Schoenberg, Anton Webern, and Alban Berg and in the works
of many contemporary composers) is a compositional procedure that
departs from the tonal system that predominated in Western music for
three centuries or so. The composer Judith Lang Zaimont goes a step
further and states that "in truth, atonality is not in any sense a compositional method but rather a philosophic guide to the act of composing.
Because new principles of organizing materials had to be developed for
virtually every piece, each composer's atonal works are apt to be quite
individualized."[3]

Analyzing particularly the short works of Webern, one finds that
there is no heirarchy of *tonic-dominant,* no expected progressions according to common-practice tonality. Instead, all available twelve pitches
from equal tempered tuning are involved. Once the order of any particular *tone row* is established, it becomes the basis for the whole composition, both melodically and harmonically. In strictly serial twelve-tone
works, the pitch sequence does not repeat until every tone in the row
has been used up.

Atonal music has been successfully used for theatrical dance, and
its style can vary greatly depending upon the rhythmic content delivered
by the composer. For example, Stravinsky's first atonal ballet score, *Agon,*
still manages to sound like Stravinsky. It is possible to use twelve-tone
procedures and sound like jazz—or even like centuries-old common-
practice tonality.

A Provocative Viewpoint
on Tonality and Atonality

In using the tonal system as an analogy for political and other aspects of
life, Czech author Milan Kundera in *The Book of Laughter and Forgetting*
included a thought-provoking contemplation. Relating what his father
had taught him, he compared the tonic note to a king; dominant and
subdominant tones were right-hand men. Other scale tones were similar
to dignitaries that had special relationships further down the line, and
chromatic notes were analogous to guests from other courts. Kundera
suggested:

> *Since each of the twelve notes has its own job, title, and function, any
> piece we hear is more than mere sound: it unfolds a certain action before
> us. Sometimes the events are terribly involved . . . princes from other*

courts intervene, and before long there is no telling which court a tone belongs to and no assurance it isn't working undercover as a double or triple agent. But even then the most naive of listeners can figure out more or less what is going on. The most complex music is still a language.[4]

When Schoenberg began composing in a way that produced a sense of atonality, Kundera went on to observe, the former feudal system of privileges was completely abolished. Each tone was subjected to the strict discipline of being equal with all others. It was as if a single empire had appeared by decree. Kundera wrote:

Perhaps the sonorities were more interesting than they had been, but audiences accustomed to following the courtly intrigues of the keys for a millennium failed to make anything of them. In any case, the empire of the twelve-tone system soon disappeared. After Schoenberg came Varèse, and he abolished notes . . . along with keys, replacing them with an extremely subtle play of sounds which, though fascinating, marks the beginning of the history of something other than music, something based on other principles and another language.[5]

Students may want to listen to various atonal pieces to decide for themselves whether they agree or disagree with Kundera's viewpoint. Furthermore, does the compositional invention of Varèse constitute another language, or just another style of music? And if there are no longer any expected relationships between tones, then does the listener have to examine each atonal piece on its own terms to ascertain what the music is all about?

The present exploration continues with an aspect of harmony particularly imbedded in the tonal system, and of relevance to choreographers as well as to performing dancers.

Harmonic Rhythm

The *harmonic rhythm* in a piece of music has to do with the way a progression unfolds over time. This can be analyzed and charted in terms of timing notation. The harmonic rhythm will usually not coincide beat-for-beat with the rhythmic patterns of a melody or accompaniment parts, except in the case of hymn tunes, when there is often a change of chord for every syllable sung.

In contrast to such frequency of harmonic change, for example, are the expansive harmonic rhythms in the works of J. S. Bach. In the first movement of his *Brandenburg Concerto No. 3 in G,* for example, there are lengthy sections where the underlying harmony is constant. This serves to build tension, particularly when the harmony sits on the dominant chord. When the tonic is finally reached, the release from tension is all the more effective.

Particularly when choreographing, dancers may want to focus some attention on the harmonic rhythm in music. It is not necessary to be able to analyze the specific chords in harmonies, but it is relevant to be able to recognize the pace of harmonic change as well as moments of cadence in harmony, for these become structural elements in building an edifice of sound.

Most often, the harmonic rhythm will support the flow of a main melody or melodies, and the structure of a melody is therefore closely linked to the harmonic framework. In common practice styles, the more predominant pitches of melodies often outline basic harmonic chords of the underlying accompaniment.

Clusters and Other Dissonances

In an extension of the idea of a chord being simultaneously sounded pitches, *clusters* consist of multiple adjoining pitches. Henry Cowell is usually credited with introducing these into concert music, with his piano pieces such as *The Tides of Manaunaun* and *Tiger*. These are notated with indications of the outer limits, and are to be executed with the forearm, fist, or flat of the hand, depending on the size of the cluster. The technique of clusters has been transferred to other instrumental writing as well. With the introduction of electronic sound sources, microtonal clusters are possible. Often, with such a broad conglomeration of sound, the effect comes to be more rhythmic or percussive rather than focused on pitch. In any case, the listener's impression is certainly altered from the kind of pitch awareness one has with purely triadic harmony. In the first place, the sense of consonance and dissonance has changed. It used to be felt that seconds were dissonant, needing resolution to thirds or unisons, for example. But if the total harmonic texture of a piece consists entirely of clusters (in an extreme case), then perhaps some seconds would be heard as less dissonant than others, and consonance would be determined by the context.

Another keyboard example of a different kind of increased dissonance in harmony is Hindemith's *Suite 1922*, based on popular dance forms of the time. Hindemith's approach was to make use of traditional concept of tonality, but to extend it. This can be heard in a Hindemith work that continues to be popular with ballet audiences, *The Four Temperaments*, composed for George Balanchine and the New York City Ballet.

New Pitches, New Harmonies

Certainly one of the major thrusts of twentieth-century composition has been to enlarge composers' palettes of available pitches and the way these are used both melodically and harmonically. Among the pioneers in this respect was Edgard Varèse, whose music was used with great theatrical effect by Hanya Holm and other choreographers.

As Robert P. Morgan observed in his study of *Twentieth-Century Music,* in the later music of Varèse:

> *Pitch is no longer necessarily the musical element of primary significance. The focus of compositional activity has shifted to nonpitch elements—not only timbre but also rhythm, registration, dynamics, and texture—and the music's character and logic are determined at least as much by the structuring of these elements as by that of the pitches.*[6]

Commenting further on the music of Varèse, Morgan offered a summary that could be applied to the later works of other composers as well:

> *The principal focus is on the general textural and timbral effect rather than on specific motivic or harmonic details. There is no clear distinction between melody and accompaniment. The individual notes are often not conceived as parts of "lines" or "harmonies," but as constituents of what the composer called "sound masses," whole configurations of notes that work together to produce a generalized sonic character. . . .*
>
> *Starting with the most basic features of his materials—instrumentation, registration, contour, rhythmic shape, etc.—he attempted to devise formal contexts in which they could function as "sound objects"—as plastic events to be shaped, combined, and fused by the composer, much as a sculptor works with physical materials.*[7]

In light of such an approach, dancers may be faced with several listening challenges: to follow the main harmonic rhythms and cadences in music that is tonally organized, or, with some contemporary music, to ascertain if the specific pitches are intended to be a prime consideration in the first place. Alternatively, attention could be focused instead upon other musical elements such as rhythmic patterns, timbre, or texture.

Explorations and Assignments

1. At an electronic synthesizer that has chord patterns, experiment with various progressions. Start with the familiar: C major—F major—G major. If the equipment will expand these into various patterns of accompaniment, push the buttons and listen to the different effects of rhythm in spreading out the same chords.

2. Have a pianist demonstrate the basic accompaniment patterns of bass-and-offbeat; arpeggios; various melodic ornamentations such as trills, mordents, grace notes, and so forth. How many ways can the person play a C major chord? Play some variations of your own, using only the pitches of one chord.

3. At a keyboard, play any triad and keep repeating it as a pulsation. When you feel a need for some harmonic diversity, change only one note, by stepwise motion, and continue pulsing the resulting new chord. Change another note to a neighboring tone. Repeat the process, this time plotting the harmonic rhythm of what you do.

4. Listen to a choral hymn, one movement of a Bach Brandenburg Concerto, and an excerpt from an opera by Wagner. Discuss your impressions of the underlying harmonic rhythm. What effect could these various approaches have upon choreography?

5. Analyze the points of cadence in two piano ländler by Schubert or other brief dance form. Why are the cadences and phrasing regular and clear in many forms of music based on social dances? How would you as a choreographer today tend to relate to such points of cadence? Demonstrate in movement.

chapter 12

TEXTURE

The ballet with the best chance of immortality is the one with the best music.

—Roger Fiske

Eliot Feld has choreographed an intriguing ballet for his company titled *The Relative Disposition of the Parts.* This work explores the seemingly endless patterns that can be made with just two arms, two legs, a torso, and a head—plus ways in which these possibilities can be multiplied by altering the placement of other dancers in space and in connection with delayed timing of variations.

The title could serve equally well as a definition of texture in music. One thinks of analogies in regard to fabric: is it bumpy, is it smooth? Monochromatic in color, or variegated? Consistent or intricately woven in contrasting raw materials? Is the eye drawn to one particular spot, or more likely to form an impression of the total repetitive pattern in weaving?

Similarly, with music, texture has to do with the overall consistency and relationship of the various ingredients—rhythm, melody, harmony, and tone color. It has to do with what gets highlighted, what functions as a supportive accompaniment, and the relative weight of simultaneous melodic lines at any particular moment. For dancers, musical texture can determine the overall impression of flow, and it may well gain more attention than the specific pitches of a melody. Texture can be present even if melody is not. At the most simplistic level, texture could answer questions such as: How thick or densely packed is the music at any particular moment? Or, how sparse is it?

Often the texture of music reflects idiomatic techniques of specific instruments, and such tone colors may become a means of distinguishing various compositional ideas. Tone color will be discussed in the next chapter. For now, the focus is on general relationships that emerge as a result of how harmony is filled out rhythmically. Another focus of attention is the degree of emphasis given to various melodic lines or accompaniment patterning and choice of register.

In musicological studies, the basic choices in layout have been grouped generally into four kinds of textures: *monophonic,* or single melodic line with no other moving harmonic parts; *homophonic,* in which there is one predominant melody and a supportive harmonic accompaniment; *heterophonic,* in which several variations of the main melody occur simultaneously, thus providing accompaniment for the main theme; and *polyphonic,* in which several strands of individual melodic lines occur simultaneously. Additionally, a separate category is included here for music that has harmonic and/or rhythmic texture, but no melody. This seems to epitomize certain kinds of sound scores that have been used for contemporary theatrical dances as well as for episodes that act as dramatic transitions between set dances, or as sound effects for staging. *Sound collages* come under this heading.

Unaccompanied Melody: Monophony

Music that is monophonic consists of a single melodic line, which may or may not be doubled at the octave or in another register. Particularly with traditional vocal music in India and the Middle East, an instrument may shadow the singing either exactly or with some added ornamentation. In such cases, the very choice of ornamentation will serve to define and flavor the overall texture. Additionally there may be some purely percussive accompaniment. Harmony may be implied in the melody by the choice of scale or mode, and by phrasing and cadences, but there is no vertical accompaniment that offers progression to varying harmonies.

This distinction about the harmony is introduced because there is a considerable heritage of traditional melodic music from around the world that makes use of some kind of *drone* effect. A drone consists of a pitch or several pitches (usually in the lower register, but possibly occuring higher as well) sustained as a nonvarying presence throughout an entire section or piece (although the tones may be renewed by articulations at various points). Perhaps most familiar are the bagpipe drones that accompany Irish and Scottish melodies used for traditional dancing. A particularly common drone consists of a perfect fifth.

Monophony has proven a splendid tradition for dance. Some of the few written European pieces surviving from the thirteenth century are the single-line examples of the *estampie.* These have been recorded in our own time by a number of early-music ensembles who add their own percussion accompaniment.

Contemporary composers have drawn from monophonic traditions, employing them in their scores for modern dance. For example, Peggy Glanville-Hicks drew from monophonic styles of Greece and India and collaborated a number of times with John Butler. Alan Hovhaness drew from studies of Indian music, but also from Armenian traditions, and these influences can be heard in his music for Erick Hawkins, Jean Erdman, and other choreographers. One particularly beautiful section of monophonic writing is the violin solo (with accompanying drones) in the section of wrestling with the angel, from *God the Reveler,* commissioned from Hovhaness by Erick Hawkins.

Consistent with his view of embracing music from the whole world, the late Henry Cowell composed dozens of scores for choreographers earlier in the century, and some of these include monophonic sections. Of this composer's score for *Trickster Coyote,* the choreographer Erick Hawkins mentioned: "Melody has charm, and it relates very much to being at one with the world."[1]

Another recent piece of choreography that includes monophonic music is Eliot Feld's ballet *Frets and Women,* to compositions by Lou Harrison, including a number of guitar pieces (hence the "frets," the bars marking off sections on the neck of the instrument).

Of Violins and Dancing Masters

For students who wish to explore European styles of melody used for traditional dancing, there exist many published regional collections, such as the harp and fiddle tunes of Ireland.

The solo violin has long been regarded a sufficient provider of music for centuries of dancers. In colonial times in America, for example, a much sought-after itinerant dance master/composer/violinist was Pierre Landrin Duport. Today, the Library of Congress houses his manuscript notebooks of tunes played for Martha Washington as well as for social balls up and down the eastern seaboard.

For something like twenty-one editions and generations of dancers on both sides of the Atlantic, the tunes collected by John Playford were the source to turn to. For dancers of today, these older monophonic dance tunes provide a rich store of material for reconstructing historic styles.

Vocal Monophony

In addition to all the instruments of the world that can play unaccompanied melodies for dancers, one source of monophonic music that can have powerful theatrical effect is the sound onstage of a live human voice, whether the dancer's or someone else's.

Recorded unadorned vocal solos are also heard during dance concerts nowadays. For example, Wendy Perron included tapes of Sonya Cohen singing *a capella* (unaccompanied) in a concert dance titled *Will I Rise*. Perhaps even more effective would have been the presence of a live singer—an option open to student choreographers and performers.

Among the visiting companies to make expressive use of the solo voice is the Inbal Dance Company from Israel, for instance in their portrayals of the lives of traditional Yemenite women. Delight in new love, the rhythm of daily work, jealousy when a husband takes a new wife, grief upon losing a loved one—for all these evocations, one could wish for no other accompaniment to the dancers' movement than the expressive quality of a solo voice singing. "The dancer is our contemporary," says director Sara Levi-Tanai. "But her feet remember days gone by."[2] So does her singing voice.

Such performances, of course, have to be choreographed so that dancers can breathe. However, in conjunction with improvisations in movement, it could prove fruitful for dance students to also improvise by vocalizing with wordless syllables. With such experiments, it may help to be reminded of some of the variables discussed so far: pulsed or unpulsed flow, spiky punctuated articulation or smoothly connected melodies. In pitch choices: stepwise to close intervals, or a melodic line that jumps around. In dynamics: stay at one level or change gradually, adding accents at any point. In regard to tone color: use different syllables, or control the size of the mouth–sound box by changing the shape of the lips. The tongue can be used in clucking or "tsking." As to rhythm: lock into repeating patterns, or have constantly changing or unrelated durations.

For such an improvisation to grow into something that could be called art, dancers can call upon their personal intuitive sense of whether the sounds are expressing something or adding in some other way to the total effect of dance movement. If there is no real melody and the voice is used more as provider of rhythm or isolated sustained tone quality, then such vocalization would not come under the heading of monophony, but would fall into some categories of pure texture that will be discussed subsequently.

Melody Plus Accompaniment: Homophony

In styles that are strictly homophonic, there is only one melody, along with harmonic parts that move along more or less in rhythmic lockstep with the melody. Most hymns fall into this category, as well as some arrangements for barbershop quartets. It should be noted that the melody does not always have to be in the soprano or highest-pitched part or voice; it could be in the bass, the tenor, or the alto. In any case, it is always given dynamic prominence.

In the literature of Western concert music, as well as in scores for ballet and modern dance, the texture of a single melody plus supportive harmonic accompaniment is very familiar. Distinctive textures depend upon the character and flow of the highlighted melody and upon the disposition of harmonizing pitches among various instruments, registers, and rhythmic patterns. The same melody can be harmonized in different ways, and the accompaniment arranged to present the melody in an entirely different emotional light.

For countless examples of music used in theatrical dance, the specific rhythmic patterning of the accompanying harmony provides energy and flow in kaleidoscopic stylistic possibilities. The literature of music for classical ballet offers excellent examples of how subdivisions in the musical beat can be arranged to form ongoing patterns that function as the floor for both the melody and the dancers.

For students who wish to see what such patterns look like in notation, it may be helpful to have a musician point out pertinent accompaniment textures while following a full score or piano reduction and listening to a recording or the sound track of a video. Even without much practice in score reading, a novice can learn to spot ongoing patterns of groups of notes, and these can be related to the sounds heard. The whole point of such an exercise would be to consider the effect that different textural patternings can have upon choreography and dancers' performances.

Among the accessible works that provide many examples of accompanied melody are Mozart, *Divertimento No. 15* (as choreographed by Balanchine); Minkus, *La Bayadère* and *Don Quixote;* Delibes, *Coppélia* and *Sylvia;* Tchaikovsky, *Sleeping Beauty, Nutcracker,* and *Swan Lake;* Offenbach, *Gaité Parisienne;* Stravinsky, *Petroushka;* Copland, *Rodeo;* Joplin, *Maple Leaf Rag* (and other piano pieces, as choreographed by Martha Graham).

In all these scores, the context of the dance must be considered. If the section is essentially one of dramatic events (such as the appearance of the bad fairy and her rats in *Sleeping Beauty* or the entire section of the fight with the mouse king in *Nutcracker*), the purpose of the music may be akin to sound effects. In such cases, the musical portion can be considered as pure texture without melody. The melody-and-accompaniment patterns will occur in set sections of formal dances.

In each case, things to look and listen for include: the melody, the bass line, the rhythmic relationship between bass and inner voices, grouping of subdivisions in relation to both the meter and each individual beat, and distinctive rhythmic patterns that continue over a considerable period of time.

Accompaniment Patterns

The following frequently used patterns are best demonstrated directly by a musician, but the listing can serve to focus attention upon textures that dancers may become aware of in many styles of music used for choreographed theatrical performances.

BLOCKED CHORDS

Here the same chords are repeated in exact arrangement, often for percussive effect. A familiar use of this type of accompaniment in popular rock music of today is for slow ballads.

SINGLE-NOTE BASS LINES

Just as a blocked chord can be used rhythmically as well as in harmonic terms, so too a single pitch can function both as a rhythmic force and as a suggestion of harmonic movement.

In Baroque ensemble music, a written basso continuo, or figured bass, was provided, usually played by both cello and harpsichord. In addition, the keyboardist was to use that single line plus the shorthand numerals underneath (representing the intervals of the desired harmony), and fill out the harmony by improvising.

In jazz combos of this century, the plucked walking bass has become an important ingredient of ensemble playing, one that lends both rhythmic and melodic interest even while it too suggests harmonic progressions.

BASS AND OFFBEATS

This procedure consists of using single bass notes on strong beats of the music, followed by *offbeat chords*. These are regular subdivisions of the beat, or weaker beats of the measure, which fill in the other tones of the harmonic chord introduced by the bass note. Good examples are waltzes in "oom-pah-pah" fashion or marches, codas, galops, and cancans in duple "oom-pah" alternations. Thousands of show tunes use this texture, plus all of early ragtime piano pieces.

ARPEGGIOS, OR BROKEN CHORD FIGURATIONS

An arpeggio is simply a harplike, consecutive succession of the pitches of a chord, in contrast to a simultaneous sounding.

Broken chords do not have to appear in the order of their pitch, low to high. Composers can make any arrangement they please. One common one is the Diabelli bass, particularly popular in the Classical era. The pattern is basically, in terms of pitch, a rhythmically even grouping of four: low-high-middle-high. A more spread-out pattern of low-medium-high-medium is the distinctive dotted-rhythm bass that accompanies tangos. Another common pattern is broken chords in triplets: low-medium-high.

Rhythmically, any basic chord can be divided into duplets, triplets, groups of fours, sixes, eights—or combinations of these, with syncopation or ties or rests within any particular beat. Typical sections in which to hear and see this procedure include the grand adagios of the ballets. Something for dance students to consider is the flow of the accompaniment in relation to the release of energy in the melody. This should be related, in turn, to the visual effect of the choreographed movements. In every case, the question may be asked: How does the particular accompaniment pattern serve to support the overall flow and impression of the dance itself?

Spacing and Register

The spacing of pitches, in relation to their octave position, is also important in determining the overall texture of a piece of music. For example, one strong characteristic of Beethoven's symphonies is the way in which he distributed pitches to various instruments in different registers. In our own century, both Copland and Stravinsky used spacing and register in ways that give their compositions distinctive flavor.

Antiphonal Procedures

Call and Response; Solo and Tutti

Although statement and reply patterns can be considered important aspects of overall form, they are being treated here as textural qualities.

Vocal call and response forms very likely stem from ancient rituals in many parts of the world. A leader intones a vocal statement or chant, and the group responds in unison. The practice of alternating solo voice and group voices continues today, most notably in gospel singing.

In instrumental music, the practice of changing from solo to ensemble texture (within one piece) has led to the orchestral *concerto*. Additionally, in the jazz practice of allowing each member of an ensemble to take a turn as soloist (although often the rest of the ensemble will continue playing), a single instrument often commands the full floor during breaks between choruses.

The early Baroque *concerto grosso* emphasized the difference in texture between a small group of soloistic performers (the *concertino* section) and the *tutti*, or *ripieno* sections when the full orchestra played. Corelli wrote many such works, as did Vivaldi. Among the most familiar concerti grossi are the six *Brandenburg Concertos* by Bach, used by choreographers such as Murray Louis for modern dance works. A contemporary concerto grosso composed by Ralph Vaughan-Williams was choreographed by Sallie Wilson. Her beautiful double pas de deux resulted: *The Double Wedding*.

The word "concerto" implies a single virtuosic soloist highlighted in an orchestral setting. When the soloist is in the foreground, the orchestra will function as accompaniment. There are also typically sections where only the soloist plays, in unaccompanied *cadenzas*.

Although some theatergoers wonder whether there is a danger in a virtuoso instrumentalist upstaging dancers if a concerto is used for collaborative purposes, there are many successful examples. Pennsylvania Ballet has in its repertoire a Khachaturian piano concerto choreographed as *Underlight* by Dane LaFontsee; Balanchine set a Tchaikovsky piano concerto; recently, Peter Martins set Charles Wuorinen's score with a virtuosic solo by cellist Fred Sherry; Paul Taylor used the double concerto of Bach for his *Esplanade;* Eliot Feld's first ballet, *Harbinger,* was set to a Prokofiev piano concerto.

Vivaldi wrote 425 concertos. Mozart wrote 23 concertos for piano alone. By and large, the instruments favored for concerto soloists have been piano, violin, and cello. Yet there also exists a less extensive but still beautiful literature for winds. Mozart wrote a flute and harp concerto as well as four famous concertos for horn; the concerto repertoire for bassoon, oboe, clarinet, flute, trumpet, and saxophone is quite extensive. Student choreographers searching for less familiar yet interesting music might do well to investigate the concerto literature for some of their favorite instruments, and consider collaborating with students from the music department.

Related to vocal call and response is a liturgical alternation of massed choirs. The acoustical effects of doing this with groups of instruments placed in varying locations of a cathedral were exploited by Giovanni Gabrielli in his Renaissance works for brass choirs.

In the twentieth century, Alberto Ginastera placed twenty-two horns around the balconies of the Metropolitan Opera House, for his opera *Bomarzo.*

Probably the contemporary composer who has most exploited the possibilities of antiphonal textures is Henry Brant. In fact, one of his orchestral pieces is titled *Antiphony.* Other compositions that use these techniques are Brant's *Atlantis, Ceremony, The Children's Hour, Dialogue in the Jungle, Words Over Fireworks, The Grand Universal Circus, Hieroglyphics,* and his *Violin Concerto with Lights* (which included lighting in the antiphonal designing).

For their staged works, choreographers might want to consider using either commissioned or extant music that is strongly antiphonal. The placing of instrumental groupings around a performance space would seem to offer attractive opportunities for interactions with dancers, particularly if a sense of total theater is desired and if the performing venue is interesting architecturally or acoustically.

Such multimedia events need not be confined to works of great activity or bombast, or experimental aesthetics. All the other aspects of music continue to interact with dance, of course. For example, there is nothing so beautiful as the sound of many human voices all singing pianissimo, coming from different parts of a performing space, and one could envision the use of antiphonal vocal choirs to create moments of great peace or heightened emotion in the dance. Or the peaceful music could be used to offset a contrasting or even tragic drama or atmosphere onstage. Or the onstage action could be peaceful while the music is dissonant and restless, in an antiphonal texture.

Additive Percussion Textures

Among the most compelling musical companions for traditional and social dancers are the additive percussion textures created by drummers in West Africa, Brazil, and the Caribbean islands.

As touched upon briefly in the discussion on polyrhythm, the key to producing these textures seems to lie in the procedure of adding many different instruments, each with individual patterns. If each player contributes an essential rhythm but starts the pattern upon a different beat, a multilayered impression results because the individual metrical patterns do not coincide at exactly the same point. Consequently, the listener hears *resultant* rhythms and tone colors that are not present if each drum pattern is isolated and listened to alone.

Excellent samples of additive percussion styles can be heard during concerts of the Chuck Davis Dance Company (which tours out of Durham) and during the annual three-day festival of *Dance Africa!* at the Brooklyn Academy of Music. Concert dancers as well as those who are studying traditional regional styles might also consider the effects of additive procedures in other styles of percussion playing.

The foundation of these textures is a very fast basic beat and a process of building with individual cyclical patterns that combine to produce variegated and vibrant textures of rhythm and timbre. The American drummer Mickey Hart offers a succinct explanation of how this is achieved:

> *The idea here as elsewhere in African culture, is to fit one's own personal rhythms seamlessly into the flow of the whole. You might call this rhythm sharing. Musically the rhythm of each drum in an ensemble is comparatively simple, consisting of endless variations on duple and triple time. It's only when these rhythms are combined that the complexity becomes impressive, threes beating against fours, throbbing and pulsing, creating a kind of bodily tension in listeners that is best released by dancing.*
>
> *Most of the drums in an ensemble will be engaged in purely rhythmic cycles, laying down the beat for the dancers. But there is usually one drummer, the master drummer, who will be drumming coded signals that tell the musicians and dancers when to start and stop various patterns, and woven throughout will be the commentary of the master drummer.[3]*

Contemporary Western composers have become intrigued to explore these procedures and resultant textures, and to incorporate them into their tools for composing concert music.

Additive procedures can be employed with instrumental textures other than percussion, of course, and the process is also found outside of Africa. Commenting on such traditions in the Indian subcontinent, for example, composer Philip Glass told *Ballet News:*

> *In Western music we take time and divide it, whole notes into half notes into quarter notes, but in Eastern music they take small units and add them together. We divide, they add. They also form large structures out of an additive process. Then there's a cyclical process, where you have something that lasts maybe thirty-five beats and then begins again. So you join cycles of different beats, like wheels inside wheels, everything going at the same time and always changing.[4]*

Minimalist Procedures

In recent years, procedures that have come to be labeled *minimalism* have proven fruitful for composers and choreographers alike. The analogies are that the parameters of materials are quite tightly limited, and that the creators work out various permutations and possibilities.

In music, minimalistic procedures involve the combination of limited rhythmic patterns and limited harmonic means, with multiple repetitions going on while gradual changes are introduced. Yet the results can be quite complex-sounding textures that have proved quite suitable for theatrical dance purposes. The artist who comes to mind most in this style is Laura Dean, and all her dances are recommended, both those for which she composed the musical scores herself, and those for which she drew upon the compositions and percussion performances of Steve Reich.

In a similar approach to texture, Eliot Feld's *Aureole* and *Aureole II* offer fascinating kinesthetic companionship to Reich's music. Lar Lubovitch's *Tabernacle* is another effective minimalist dance, to Reich's *Tellhim*. And at New York City Ballet, Jerome Robbins', choreography for *Glass Pieces* (to a score by Philip Glass) offers the additional visual suggestiveness of a gridlike backdrop.

While the word "minimalist" does not do justice to some of the thought that goes into composing many of the pieces so labeled, nevertheless, the term seems to convey the idea of certain kinds of musical procedures that greatly interested choreographers in the 1980s. The reactions of audiences have varied, as suggested by the following excerpts.

Here is David Koblitz writing in *Dance Magazine*, in an article called "Minimalist Music for Maximum Choreography":

> *Why has minimalism become the musical* lingua franca *of a whole generation of choreographers? That this music provides a steady, insistent pulse is no doubt an important factor, since even in experimental circles, it is no longer unfashionable to set dances "to" music. And because that pulse is continuous and undifferentiated, the music doesn't act as a rhythmic straitjacket to the choreographer—virtually anything is possible. The answer may also have to do with the fact that the style is generally rooted in traditional scales and harmony and therefore can maintain a level of abstraction without sacrificing comprehensibility. The music doesn't impose itself on the dance. A choreographer can use its repetitive strands as a formal device or can choose to ignore its structure entirely, using instead the music's streamlined, open textures and sensual surfaces as a kind of high-tech sonic wallpaper.*[5]

Dance critic Anna Kisselgoff, of the *New York Times*, offered another opinion on minimalism in concert dance works:

> *Everyone knows that repetition—in patterns, steps, rhythms—has accompanied the rise of so-called minimalist music; that in fact, it is the chore-*

ographers who have helped make composers such as Steve Reich and Philip Glass more visible than they might have been initially.

. . . [But] today, repetition . . . has become invasive, if not pervasive, in dance. The first question is whether repetition is leading choreographers to reduce their vocabulary. The second is whether a paucity in the movement invention is responsible for the recurring use of text and speech—as compensation—in dance.

. . . The hypnotic effect of such pieces creates tensions in the audience that a public cannot withstand permanently. Repetitive dance pieces cannot, paradoxically, be seen over and over again. In the end, the eyes need a rest.[6]

Heterophony

Minimalism is closely related to the kind of heterophony successfully practiced for centuries in other cultures, notably in the gamelan music of Indonesia. Particularly on the West Coast, but also on Eastern campuses like Cornell and Wesleyan, students are enthusiastically playing in gamelans, the kind of musical ensembles that are used for dance dramas in Indonesia. The textures heard in both the Javanese and Balinese styles are essentially heterophonic—that is, consisting of a brief main melody that is simultaneously varied and played in many parts, creating a vibrant and shimmering backdrop for the dancers in their traditional ritual-dramas.

These sounds have greatly influenced a number of American composers in the dance world, notably Lou Harrison, who composed the score that the late choreographer Robert Joffrey used for his dance titled *Gamelan,* but using Western instruments. Harrison also composed the music used for Jean Erdman's *Solstice,* and has drawn on gamelan techniques in other scores used by Erick Hawkins and Mark Morris.[7]

Polyphony

In polyphony, performers are rather equal. There is not the division between soloist and accompaniment that exists in homophonic music. In polyphony, although a vertical sense of harmony may be present in varying degrees, one is always aware of individual melodic lines that could be separated and sung or played alone.

A basic distinction can be made between polyphonic music in which each voice really is independent harmonically from the others (as in a considerable portion of the Renaissance vocal literature as well as the music of twentieth-century composer Charles Ives), and music in which there is an underlying and interrelated harmonic organization (as with music of Bach and other Baroque composers). The latter kind of texture is usually referred to as *contrapuntal.* Either approach can offer interesting musical companionship for theatrical dance.

Various contrapuntal procedures will be discussed further in Chapter 14, on form. For now, it is sufficient to note that as far as textures go, there could be a simple duet: two lines of counterpoint, either sung or played on instruments, but each recognized as a melodic line. Other voices can be added for textures of three-part, four-part, and five-part counterpoint. Or the texture could be thicker.

When listening to contrapuntal music, it can be both instructive and enjoyable to focus attention on a single line. Then play the music again and follow a different melodic line. Dancers can then mimic what they hear, or create yet another contrasting melody, this time in movement.

Choreographers, including George Balanchine and Mark Morris, have created many beautiful dances using contrapuntal music. In watching some of this repertoire, one might notice the rate of rhythmic flow in various parts of the music and in the dance as well. And in regard to the texture of the dances onstage, one might notice if there is any attempt to mirror the stylistic flow of separate yet related melodies.

Sound as Collage and Effects

Some sections of classical ballet scores as well as some entire twentieth-century compositions can be considered as pure texture. This can offer a splendid aural backdrop for dramatic pantomime, or for abstract dance.

Much of the effect of choreography by Alwin Nikolais stems from his use of sound as collage. Instead of analyzing his composing in traditional terms of phrases, melodies, and so forth, one tends to use descriptive or almost poetic words about the sounds he created. Audiences have an awareness of sprinkles of tone color, or huge blobs, or a dense block, or wisps. In regard to textures, analogies with clouds come to mind rather than musical terms from other centuries: cumulus clouds, storm clouds, mare's tails, fast blowing or in a band, or a tiny one isolated in a sky of blue.

With certain contemporary styles of composition, theatergoers aptly seek analogies in painting. The musical *Sunday in the Park with George* by Stephen Sondheim certainly comes to mind. The show deals with the Impressionist painting of Georges Seurat, and the visual images are effectively mirrored in a kind of musical pointillism, as well as in many of the staged movements of the actors.

Lucia Dlugoszewski's scores for Erick Hawkins also provide a special kind of energy plus textures that cannot readily be analyzed in traditional terms. Among the Hawkins dances with scores by Dlugoszewski are: *Cantilever II, Here and Now with Watchers, 8 Clear Places, Early Floating, Geography of Noon, Lords of Persia, Black Lake,* and *Angels of the Inmost Heaven.* In addition, as this book goes to press, Dlugoszewski is still working on her score for a new Hawkins piece, *Many Thanks.*

Another leading contemporary composer known for his imaginative use of instrumental timbre and texture is George Crumb. His *Black Angels* was used for choreography by Constantin Patsalas for the National Ballet of Canada.

A major textural work that comes to mind is John Cage's music used for Merce Cunningham's *Beach Birds.* In this, the listener does not expect melodies and harmonies. The visual dance onstage transports the audience to the realm of experiencing what it must be like to be birds together by the ocean. So the varying aural textures—again, wisps or blobs of sound—are quite effective, and it would be entirely beside the point to talk of form, melody, or harmonies in the traditional sense. Reviewing the premiere, Anna Kisselgoff of the *New York Times* wrote:

> *Mr. Cunningham's works are sometimes perceived as hermetic, removed from reality. The paradox is that he and John Cage, his musical adviser, have long insisted that art can incorporate the sights, sounds and processes found in the real world. Thus, "4³," the Cage score that prompted the creation of "Beach Birds," is full of silence, and Mr. Cunningham's choreography is full of stillness.*
>
> *A work like "Beach Birds" pierces the riddle. Its beauty lies in the poetic value of the images, which offer a vision of heightened reality. Any shore scavenger will recognize the dancers as birdlike, fishlike and shell-like. "Beach Birds" is a so-called accessible piece, but its creatures onstage are super real. . . .*
>
> *"4³" was commissioned . . . for the James Joyce/John Cage Festival and its occasional watery sounds have to do with the idea that Joyce was going to write a novel called "Ocean."*
>
> *The musicians—David Tudor, John D. S. Adams, Takehisa Kosugi, Michael Pugliese—add more sound via rattles and an amplified violin. The group occasionally freezes; movement, like pebbles thrown into water, is dropped into the stillness.*[8]

In closing this overview of texture in music for dance, it seems appropriate to include an observation made by Malcolm Goldstein in the *Dictionary of Contemporary Music:*

There is today a new awareness of sound as a physical phenomenon. Anyone who has heard a very low-cycle sine wave or a highly amplified group of instruments has experienced the tangible feeling of sound against the body, of sound as an atmospheric disturbance heard with the ears but also received with the whole body. Texture in this context can be thought of as energy structures.[9]

Explorations and Assignments

1. The group is divided into sections, spaced far apart in the studio. Jointly, devise a brief chant melody that will be used as a response. Taking turns, a solo leader can improvise a melody on any thoughts of the day. Expand the experiment to include movement, making use of the concepts of antiphonal music and widely spaced groupings of dancers.

2. As a group project, and drawing upon individual listening, assemble brief musical passages that exemplify the following textures: unaccompanied vocal melody, melody with ornamented shadowing, unaccompanied violin (or fiddle) piece, an Indonesian gamelan piece, a contrapuntal piece for multiple instruments, a contrapuntal keyboard piece, a choral work, a contemporary sound collage. Demonstrate or discuss briefly the ways you might want to choreograph using each piece, focusing on numbers of dancers and their spacing on the stage. Are you inclined to find any relationship between the relative density of the musical texture and your desire for a certain amount of space around each dancer? Why or why not?

3. Either while viewing videotapes or in your attendance at live dance performances, notice the musical textures and how they relate to the choreography. Describe one instance that you found particularly effective in regard to the relationship between musical texture and the dance onstage.

chapter 13

TIMBRE, INSTRUMENTS, AND SCORE READING

Modern dance means new movements, and new movements require new sounds. Just as the whole world of movement is material for dance, so are all sounds material for music.

—Barbara Mettler

So significant is timbre (or tone color) as an element of music that it can be regarded as both a tremendous asset to the work of the dancer, or upon occasion, as a problem.

Professionals and students alike remark on their surprise when a rehearsal piano is replaced by other instruments in a chamber ensemble or full orchestra for performances. Textures that sound monochromatic or consistent on the keyboard can seem totally different when distributed among many instruments. Variety in timbre that could be only hinted at by dynamics and accent on the piano may suddenly present a totally different soundscape and a new energy for the dancers.

Among the differences are that the piano cannot sustain a tone for very long when articulated softly, and in any case, there is a diminution. By way of contrast, with winds and bowed strings, there can be considerable changes of nuance within a single tone. Furthermore, a pianist has only two hands, necessitating choices when it comes to reducing large-scale orchestral textures.

Many choreographers prefer to rehearse with tapes precisely so that dancers will became accustomed to the specific timbres that will be heard in performance. Particularly with new music that is highly layered in texture, tapes can assist dancers in recognizing changes of instrumentation that serve as cues for choreographed dance movement.

Yet a rehearsal pianist provides the advantage of being able to stop and start repeatedly, and some choreographers prefer to hear the music reduced to its structural form, stripped of instrumental nuances and timbres. Martha Graham, for one, stated in her memoirs:

> *I like to work from a piano score of the composer's music. He conceives it for an orchestra of however many instruments there are in his vision, then reduces it to a piano score from which I feel most comfortable working. At other times I will work in silence, blocking out movement before I find a piece of music, and then sometimes it works and other times it does not, and I have to discard things. For example, with* The Rite of Spring *I had known the music very deeply for years, but in preparation for my 1984 version I listened to the recorded music over and over again, so that by the time my first rehearsal came, I worked in silence to the music I now felt in my body as well as heard in my mind. I worked closely then with the pianist, asking him to guide me through the first reading of the music and subsequent readings, to notate the change of instruments for me.*[1]

The effects of instrumental coloration can be fully appreciated, for example, by looking at a piano reduction of the Minkus scores for the ballets *La Bayadère* and *Don Quixote,* with their straightforward, recognizable, and often predictable patterns of melody and accompaniment. Yet when heard performed in orchestrations by conductor John Lanchbery, the same wallpaper patterns of musical materials take on vibrant new life.

In the concert chamber music repertoire, an interesting study of timbre effects occurs in Elliott Carter's *Eight Etudes and Fantasy* for woodwind quartet. The same pitch is played as the flute, oboe, clarinet, and bassoon enter and exit, creating different dynamics and rhythms even though the pitch remains constant.

Overtones at Work

The acoustical explanation for varying tone colors has already been discussed in connection with pitch and dynamics. The distinctive qualities of each instrument, each player, and any particular note sounded all depend upon the relative distribution of the spectrum of harmonic overtones as a tone progresses in time, plus the amplitude, which accounts for dynamic changes.

Sounds can now be analyzed electronically, and many have been electronically synthesized. In fact, with the latest sampling equipment, one could take a single note sung by a singer, and use that tone quality as the timbre while changing the pitch up and down a keyboard. Such techniques are raising interesting questions of ownership and copyright: if one records the recognizable quality of a single tone from a famous singer, for example, does one have a legal right to use this as the basis for a composition? Until such questions are settled in court, dancers who wish to sample timbres for their choreographic collaboration might wish to limit themselves to the sounds of singers and instrumentalists who give explicit permission.

Vocalization

Although singing while moving obviously presents breathing considerations for dancers, vocalization in various styles has long been a staple of the theatrical dancer. The history of the Broadway musical would have been different without dancers who could also sing! The same can be said of Hollywood musicals: who would want Fred Astaire lip-syncing to someone else's voice?

In the world of opera, singers may have some movement required of them, but the real dancing is more often relinquished to specialist performers. Among contemporary multimedia performance artists, however, proficiency in both singing and dancing is welcome. The art of Meredith Monk is perhaps the most demanding example of this. Students who wish to prepare for such possibilities might cultivate their own voices, not only with singing in traditional ways, but also by experimenting with jazz scat singing, as well as using all conceivable vocal techniques as means to achieve various timbres.

Some of the techniques often overlooked are flutter tonguing (making an engine like sound by rolling the tongue) falsetto registers (pitches about an octave above the usual male range), and rhythmic panting. *Sprechstimme* is a technique of singing-speaking sometimes called for by avant-garde composers. *Melisma* is extended vocalizing that distributes one syllable over many notes. Whistling is often effective; whispers can be made very theatrical as well.

Among the more traditional and formal uses of several voices in contemporary dance styles, Annabelle Gamson chose the vocal quartets of Brahms for her lovely work for women dancers, *Tanzlieder.* Extended choral works as well as opera excerpts can also offer beautiful companionship for modern dance. For example, Lar Lubovitch achieved a sympathetic setting of Bach's cantata "Jesu, der du meine Siele," transformed into the dance *Of My Soul.* Choreographer Danny Grossman's *Ecce Homo* (inspired by the art of Michelangelo), uses Bach's Cantata No. 78. The same choreographer's *Bella* (set for two poignant dancers and a motionless wooden horse inspired by Chagall) is heightened by an effective use of arias and choral ensembles from Puccini's *La Bohème* and *Madame Butterfly.*

Then there is the solo voice with myriad possibilities of accompaniment: Eliot Feld choreographed his stirring *Adieu* to songs of the nineteenth-century composer Hugo Wolf, accompanied by piano. Songs of the chanteuse Edith Piaf were arranged by Paul Chihara for the San Francisco Ballet production of Michael Smuin's *Hearts;* Peter Martins choreographed *Songs of the Auvergne,* with the singer onstage with New York City Ballet, to perform Cantaloube's beautiful settings of French songs. Another dramatic inclusion of the singer occurs in Antony Tudor's *Dark Elegies,* to Mahler's Kindertotenlieder. More recently, Dan Wagoner created a modern dance solo with a uniquely intimate feeling in his *Songs to Dance,* with composer/pianist William Bolcom onstage to perform his own commissioned music with Joan Morris singing his setting of poems by George Montgomery.

Chants also offer fresh material for choreographic purposes. The street songs and chants of urban childhood were a main ingredient of Donald McKayle's powerful modern dance *Games.* Jawole Willa Zollar also makes effective use of chants in choreography for the Urban Bush Women.

When songs with words are used, a literary and specific expressivity is imposed on the dance itself. The meanings of words should not be ignored. Even if the songs are in a language unfamiliar to the dancers, the explicit meanings should be explored in translation.

Consider, for example, flamenco guitarist/composer Paco Peña's *Missa flamenco,* a stunning work that includes guitar, solo voice, chorus, and the sound of clapping hands, all drawn from the flamenco style of music and dance. If you wanted to choreograph this work, what considerations do the cultural connotations of style raise, along with the specific religious meaning of the words?

Main Types of Instruments

A brief survey of instruments in relation to their dance uses is included next. For extensive details concerning the techniques and literature for various instruments, consult *The New Grove Dictionary of Musical Instruments.* It is suggested that students listen extensively to solo instrumental literature if they wish to become acquainted with the idiomatic characteristics of each instrument in turn. Also important for dance students is to notice the effect of instrumentation upon choreographic works seen both in theatrical performances and on film.

In addition to the human voice and percussion instruments already explored, the main groupings of musical instruments include the following: keyboards, flutes, reed woodwinds, brass, harps and other plucked strings, and bowed strings. Other music makers are tape recordings of natural sounds and electronic synthesizers.

Pianos and Harpsichords

For most dance purposes, the acoustic keyboards of practical interest are piano (with its hammer action) and the harpsichord (with pluckers). Pipe organs are acoustically related to flutes.

Because of its versatility in providing a variety of textures plus a percussive element for dance classes, the piano is probably the instrument most familiar to dance students. The solo literature for this instrument is extensive, and its repertoire is a resource that continually attracts and serves dance artists.

A solo piano onstage has been masterfully incorporated by Jerome Robbins for New York City Ballet, in his *Dances at a Gathering, Other Dances,* and *The Concert,* as well as for his setting of Bach's monumental *Goldberg Variations.* Eliot Feld set his very first ballet, *Harbinger,* to Prokofiev's G Major piano concerto; his later *Intermezzo* uses the Brahms opus 117 and 118 piano pieces with the same title, plus the opus 39 waltzes.

In the earlier modern dance repertoire, Valerie Bettis's *The Desperate Heart* has the solo dancer circling in passionate frenzy around the piano, which is center stage. The music, by Bernard Segall, is alternated with a spoken poem. A modern dance classic that continues to be in the repertoire of the Limón company is Doris Humphrey's *Day on Earth,* set to Aaron Copland's Piano Sonata. More recently, the jazz stylings of pianist Don Pullen provided a deeply emotional setting for a masterpiece of our own time, Garth Fagan's *Until, By, and If. . . .*

Piano four hands was a favorite combination of the modern dance pioneers. Musicians Ruth and Norman Lloyd began their collaborations with Doris Humphrey and Charles Weidman by touring and playing performances. Two pianos set the musical stage for Kurt Jooss's powerful ballet *The Green Table,* and the effect of the antiwar portrayal owes much to the starkness and doubling of the piano sounds, in the powerful score composed by Frederic A. Cohen. Stravinsky multiplied such effects even more by using four pianos plus percussion and chorus for *Les Noces,* choreographed by Bronislava Nijinska.

Harpsichords most often figure in performances of Baroque music, but contemporary composers such as Lou Harrison have also made use of them for dance scores. When used for live performance, care must be taken to amplify the sound adequately so it can be heard in the back of the theater. Recently, the choreographer/dancer Danny Grossman used harpsichord suites by François Couperin for his solo work, *Curious Schools of Theatrical Dancing,* with a recorded performance amplified electronically.

PREPARED PIANO

One of the original contributions made by the late John Cage was his youthful invention of the tack piano and the prepared piano. The former transforms a regular piano into something reminiscent of a harpsichord, by placing thumb tacks in the hammers. For the prepared piano more elaborate means are employed, including placing of various objects either on or between the strings. Both the pitches and tone qualities are thereby changed.

John Cage's cameo *Sonatas and Interludes for Prepared Piano* date to 1946, but they still sound fresh today and are recommended listening. The composer explained that the inspiration for his experimentation was the need for coming up with a score for a student's dance. Today, Cage's prepared piano music can be experienced as a score for Jean Erdman's videotaped dance *Daughters of the Lonesome Isle.*

Other uses of prepared pianos can be found in the compositions of George Crumb. And two other composer/collaborators for dance have achieved particularly noteworthy results from prepared pianos: Lou Harrison, in his scores for Erick Hawkins and Jean Erdman; and Lucia Dlugoszewski, in her extensive work with Erick Hawkins. Dlugoszewski called her particular invention the timbre piano, and it differs from Cage's invention in a number of respects, notably in using bowing on the strings.

Other experimental techniques do not require changing the piano itself, but rather manipulating it in new ways. For example, in his *Aeolian Harp,* composer Henry Cowell directed the performer to hold keys down silently while variously plucking, hitting, or strumming the piano strings with the hands and fingers. In the repertoire of modern dance, Cowell's *Banshee,* choreographed by Jean Erdman, was a unique concert use of the piano at the time of its composition.

Dance Uses of Flutes

One has only to look at Greek vases with their depictions of dancing figures and pipers to realize that the link between dancers and flutists is an ancient one. This connection was reawakened in modern ballet by Vaslav Nijinsky's use of archaic poses in his choreographic setting of

Debussy's *L'Après-midi d'un faune,* which opens with a long, langorous flute solo.

Among the flutes, there are three sizes used in the orchestra: the piccolo, the usual full-sized flute, and the longer alto flute. Familiar to theatrical audiences around the world, the flute solo marks the beginning of "Tea," the Chinese dance in *Nutcracker.*

Among contemporary American composers who have used the flute more experimentally are Otto Luening (including his *Sonority Canon for Two to Thirty-Seven Flutes*) and Henry Brant (whose *Angels and Devils for Flute and Flute Orchestra* might inspire choreographers).

Equally stunning is the use of a solo wooden flute, which adds such a beautiful element of melody to the dances of native North Americans. This instrument is included in the programs of the American Indian Dance Theatre. In South America, vertical flutes are an integral part of every Peruvian band, for example.

In the Middle Ages and Renaissance in Europe, recorders came in many sizes and often accompanied social dancing. The recorder was used for concert music through the early Baroque repertoire as well, and was often a part of the ensemble accompanying colonial dances in America.

The horizontal, side-blown wooden flute can draw on a wide solo literature. In the very popular performances and competitions for Provençal dancing in France (the style that predated ballet), the simple accompaniment of tabour (drum) and flute is all the music that is needed.

Panpipes are among the other members of the flute family. Consisting of end-blown reeds or hollow wood such as bamboo, they were named after the god Pan. Such pipes existed not only in Europe for thousands of years, but also among the ancient peoples of South America. The use of panpipes in Peruvian bands is particularly haunting. One ensemble that specializes in keeping up traditional styles of music used for dance in Peru is Inkhay, which employs both multiple sets of panpipes and vertical flutes. Panpipes can also be heard in many traditional Greek and Irish musical bands.

Another instrument long associated with dance are the bagpipes. The air from the mouth is blown directly into the wind bag for storage, and in turn is pumped by pressure from the arm into several pipes—one or two providing a harmonic drone automatically, and one with more airholes for fingering melodies. These can be heard to best advantage at festivals of Irish and Scottish dancing.

Metal whistles have become a standard addition to studio dance musicians' collections. More interesting whistles are the pottery types from Latin America, developed in pre-Columbian days and formed into artistic shapes, with several holes for production of multiple pitches. Then there is the ancient whistle instrument still practiced by some musicians in dance: cupped hands.

Reed Instruments

The slow saxophone solo in Jerome Robbins's setting of *Glass Pieces* is a stunning concert use of this instrument, without vibrato. Another striking theatrical appearance of the saxophone is in Prokofiev's *Lieutenant Kijé*. Among recent collaborations involving saxophones have been the joint works of choreographer David Dorfman and composer/saxophonist Dan Froot. Another source of collaboration that dancers may want to investigate are saxophone quartets. This combination dates from the turn of the twentieth century, and by now there is a considerable literature plus a number of virtuoso ensembles.

The oboe has a wide and beautiful literature dating from Baroque chamber and orchestral works (as in Bach's Brandenburg Concerto No. 1) and including such late Romantic compositions as the Saint-Saëns Sonata for Oboe and Piano. In the modern dance repertoire, Jean Erdman's *Transformations of Medusa* has a score for oboe and piano, originally by Louis Horst and arranged for recent revivals by Eliot Sokolor. The second movement of Bizet's Symphony in C (choreographed in its entirety by Balanchine) features an extended oboe solo.

The English horn is a relative of the oboe, with similar qualities but in a lower range. A familiar example of its tone is the solo in the slow movement from Dvorak's *New World* Symphony.

The still deeper-pitched bassoon may be less noticeable as a soloist in orchestral texture, but it is invaluable as a member of the common grouping for woodwind quintets. Its sound, for concert audiences of all ages, has become linked with the grandfather part in Prokofiev's *Peter and the Wolf.* Stravinsky's *The Rite of Spring* includes an unusual eerie sound of the bassoon in the high range. Bassoon and oboe are notably paired in the scene from *Swan Lake* where the prince is alone, contemplating. The musical conversation between the two instruments seems to suggest an inner questioning on the part of the prince.

The clarinet was recently featured in Lar Lubovitch's quite beautiful choreography for *Concerto Six-Twenty-Two,* drawing its title from the posthumous Koechel catalogue listing of Mozart's Concerto For Clarinet and Orchestra, K. 622. The bass clarinet is featured in the Moor's scene in Stravinsky's *Petroushka.*

WOODWIND QUINTETS

The woodwind quintet usually includes the horn along with flute, clarinet, oboe, and bassoon. The contemporary literature for this combination is extensive, and since the grouping is popular among classical musicians, it would seem to offer attractive opportunities for collaboration with dancers. For much less money than the price of a full orchestra, choreographers could offer their audiences live music with a warm and wide variety of timbres, at least for one piece on an evening's program. Generally speaking, chamber players (because they perform without conductors) become habituated to paying attention to details of ensemble, and this kind of alertness could be applied to collaboration with dancers as well. One attractive example is *La Cheminée du roi René* by Darius Milhaud, in the style of older French dances.

Brasses

This family of instruments has encompassed many inventions over the centuries. The most common in use nowadays are the trumpet, cornet, horn, trombone, and various kinds of tubas. Most brass players can play more than one instrument. Trumpeters also commonly play cornets—and some of them will also master the higher ranges in pitch with tiny clarino trumpets, which are especially useful for playing Baroque concertos. The lower-pitched flugelhorn is popular with jazz players, and there is now an in-between instrument called the frumpet.

Among the works from the Baroque trumpet literature, the *Brandenburg Concerto No. 2* was used by choreographer Murray Louis for his *Bach Suite*. More recently, choreographer Garth Fagan collaborated with the versatile trumpeter/composer Wynton Marsalis for *Griot New York*, a full-evening work.

Among the beautiful horn solos heard in the ballet repertoire are the melodies in *Sylvia*, by Delibes. In this ballet, the horn calls serve to establish a dramatic forest setting. Also a favorite is Mendelssohn's lovely nocturne from *A Midsummer Night's Dream*—for instance, in Sir Frederick Ashton's setting for the Royal Ballet of London.

Trombones generally come in two sizes: tenor and bass. A favorite of jazz artists, the trombone works well in the dance theater for Alvin Ailey's *Pas de Duke* and George Faison's *Suite Otis*. Jawole Willa Jo Zollar collaborated with trombonist/composer Craig Harris for a number of brief works, and added other instruments for *Heat*.

Tubas are perhaps the most misunderstood instrument among the brasses. Because some—like the sousaphone—are so large, there exists almost a stereotypically bombastic characterization of the sound. Heard in solo contexts, tubas are actually not loud instruments. One sousaphone silently took visual center stage recently in Eliot Feld's choreography to *The Unanswered Question,* to music by Charles Ives. As an antidote to the stereotypes of tubas, students might enjoy the jazz stylings of tubist Howard Johnson.

With all the brasses, the various effects possible with mutes are extensive. There are many ensemble groupings that can be effective for dance purposes. One classic is José Limón's use of Gunther Schuller's Symphony for Brasses and Percussion, for the choreographed work *The Traitor.*

The Big Band Sound

At the height of the big-band era, every city had numerous dance halls, each with live music for social dancing. The best of these developed a style that was easily transferred to professional stage presentations. A sampling of what these were like was offered by the Broadway production *Black and Blue,* in which a fast-paced glittery succession of ensemble jazz and tap dance, vocal solos, and big-band sounds provided a polished revue of the type that won wide audiences earlier in the century.

Jazz Combos for Dances of Today

Jazz combos often consist of piano, bass, drums, trumpet, with someone doubling on saxophone and clarinet. The instrumentalists must know how to improvise on charts of basic harmonies or tunes, and possibly to give vocal renditions as well. Because they know how to fashion their music instantly, such musicians can often learn to work very well with dancers.

Tap dancers and jazz combos go together almost automatically. For a recent season at the Joyce Theater in New York, Brenda Bufalino and her Tap Dance Orchestra had a jazz trio onstage and thoroughly meshed with the sounds of the dancers' footsteps.

Strings

Instruments of the string family can be divided generally into two groups: those that are usually bowed in performance, and those that are only plucked. In the first category are the Western orchestral strings (though plucking or pizzicato technique is used quite often to good effect). And when double basses are used in jazz combos, they are apt to be exclusively plucked.

BOWED STRINGS

In Western orchestras, string sections are comprised of violins, violas, violoncellos (cellos), and double basses.

As Romantic ballet developed, violins and cellos were selected for many beautiful adagio solos. One thinks of the long violin solo accompanying the big pas de deux in *Swan Lake;* for the musical repeat, the melody is given to the cello, and the violin continues in a beautiful obligato—an effect that makes for splendid aural intertwinings with the partnering onstage. Another instance of a cello solo featured within the orchestra is the slow opening from Weber's *Invitation to the Dance,* as transformed by Fokine into the classic ballet *Le Spectre de la rose.* Unaccompanied cello was used by composer Ezra Laderman for his score for Jean Erdman's *Fearful Symmetry.*

Though it was composed as a concert work, *The Lark Ascending* by Ralph Vaughan Williams has a stunning violin solo to which Alvin Ailey choreographed one of the most beautiful dances in the modern repertoire. One of the favorites in the Balanchine repertoire continues to be *Concerto Barocco,* set to Bach's Concerto in D Minor for Two Violins.

Violas and basses are more apt to bolster the general string tone in an orchestral context. Yet there is an interesting passage in Stravinsky's *The Rite of Spring* that uses six solo violas to achieve a unique tone color.

The double bass is not usually thought of as a solo instrument, yet it has been used by concert dancers as the sole accompaniment for their choreography, and with good effect. For example, New York choreographer Catherine Mapp set her solo *You'll Never Know Dear* to an increasingly emotional double bass line played by composer Harvie Swartz, dedicated to coal miners and their families. In country-and-western and jazz combos, the bass is a familiar sound, almost always electronically amplified for balance, and almost always played pizzicato.

CHAMBER MUSIC FOR STRINGS

There is a large body of literature for string trio, which consists of violin, cello, and viola. There are also many piano trios, with violin and cello. It would seem that both these combinations would lend themselves well to choreographic collaboration, offering a variety in tone colors with few players. Dance students who are embarking on choreographic projects are urged to inquire about both student trio ensembles and local professional groups. Either may offer attractive collaborative possibilities, and as far as forming an impression of the qualities of the sounds, not even the best CD recordings can match a live performance.

The same advice applies to string quartets, consisting of two violins, viola, and cello. The concert literature for this grouping is enormous, and spans several centuries of styles. Among the modern ballets set to string quartets is the masterpiece by Todd Bolender, now director of the Missouri Ballet, called *The Still Point*, set to the only quartet by Debussy.

STRING ORCHESTRA

This strong combination has proved attractive to choreographers. For example, Balanchine's first ballet created in America was *Serenade*, to the music of that title by Tchaikovsky. An exquisite modern example is Samuel Barber's Adagio for Strings, which actually is an enlargement of a movement for string quartet. This has been set by a number of choreographers, including recently by Daniel Job for *Above*, an unusual work performed jointly by the Tom Evert Dance Company and Cleveland Ballet Dancing Wheels (which includes handicapped performers).

There is a large body of Baroque music written for string orchestra.

Finally, it should be emphasized that bowed strings make up the backbone of the modern orchestra, with extensive timbre additions of winds and percussion. Among the best theatrical use of massed strings are in the three ballet scores by Tchaikovsky: *Swan Lake, Sleeping Beauty,* and *Nutcracker*. Also masterful is the full orchestral use in the ballet scores by Stravinsky (including *Petroushka, The Rite of Spring,* and *Firebird*).

PLUCKED AND STRUMMED STRINGS

Harps, lutes, and traditional guitars are all plucked or strummed with the fingers. Steel-stringed guitars and mandolins are usually played with picks.

Because of its ubiquity in popular music of today, the guitar is easily available to student choreographers. The live presence of even one guitarist can add considerably to dance performances.

The guitar found a lasting partnership with Spanish dances, particularly flamenco styles, continuing today in the mariachi bands of Mexico. Guitar ensembles can be seen in performance with dancers of the Ballet Folklorico de Mexico.

As with the lute, the guitar also has a long history of association with preclassic and classical dance forms of the British Isles as well as of Italy. Many of the written Italian and English keyboard works of the Renaissance show the influence of strumming and variation practices of both guitarists and lutenists. These practices were carried to the New World, where the guitar was used even in formal colonial dance balls.

Another instrument that has been a favorite since the Renaissance is the mandolin. Now associated with old-timey bands in this country, it was formerly much used for concert music. Murray Louis made a stunning choreographic solo for himself to Vivaldi's Concerto for Two Mandolins.

A less virtuosic strummed instrument is the Appalachian dulcimer, which is held in the lap and played with a pick (often to accompany folk singing).

Venturing abroad, one might meet relatives of the guitar and dulcimer: for example, the sitar from India, which has a very long tradition of playing for dances. Certainly among the foremost performers on this has been Ravi Shankar, who has popularized the sitar in the West as well. Also esteemed is sitarist Ustad Vilayat Khan.

In Japan, a very beautiful plucked instrument (larger than the dulcimer) is the koto, heard in virtuosic concerts across the United States played by Shinichi Yuizi, for example. In the Russian tradition, the balalaika, usually a triangular-shaped instrument, is common. It comes in different sizes and can be combined to form a whole orchestra: an unusual sound.

As an orchestral instrument, the harp is often used effectively for dramatic ballet: for instance, in the introduction of Tchaikovsky's *Waltz of the Flowers* from *Nutcracker*. Choreographers might also consider the combination of harp with various wind instruments. For example, a particularly beautiful combination was that of cello, harp, flute, and drums used by composer Lou Harrison in his score for Jean Erdman's dance work *Perilous Chapel*.

HAMMERED DULCIMER

Linking the technology of plucked dulcimers and harps with the later mechanisms of harpsichords and pianos is the hammered dulcimer. This instrument is descended from types known in ancient Persia. There are a number of modern relatives, including the Hungarian *cembalon*, played with mallets. This was used to virtuosic effect in the Hungarian State Dance Ensemble's U.S. tours recently. Two cembalon players seemed especially to enjoy goading the dancers onstage to ever increasing speeds, in a virtuosic arrangement of Liszt's Hungarian Rhapsodies.

In the British and North American folk traditions, the hammered dulcimer has remained popular. Played with light wooden mallets sometimes covered with felt or leather, the instrument lends itself to a variety of styles, from accompanying historical reconstructions of the dances of John Playford, to mountain clogging contests where contemporary tunes are played. Among the virtuoso players of today is Walt Michael, who composed and performed the music for *Molly's Not Dead,* choreographed by the Pilobolus Dance Theater.

Full Orchestra

Instrumentation for full orchestra may vary depending upon the piece. However, the standard literature calls for pairs of flutes, clarinets, oboes, and bassoons; three trumpets, four horns, three trombones, and a tuba; string sections of first and second violins, violas, cellos, and basses; a timpani player, and other percussion. A harp or piano is a common addition to the general texture. And there are expected secondary instruments: piccolo, bass clarinet, English horn, contrabassoon, cornet, Wagner tuba, and saxophone.

The great Romantic ballets of the nineteenth century took advantage of the enormous variety in tone color available from a full orchestra. Consequently, some of the classic scores for ballet require some forty to sixty musicians for performances. This is a major concern nowadays in a society where ballet companies are not subsidized by a czar, and when the fees set by the musicians' union can add up to an enormous expense whenever a full orchestra is involved. The finances become such an overriding concern that usually programming and rehearsal schedules are partly dictated by how many musical personnel must be on hand. Finances also dictate how much rehearsal time is available, and often this may mean that the first time the dancers hear live orchestral sounds will be in the actual performance.

In the ballet repertoire, the works of Delibes, Tchaikovsky, and Strainsky offer notable orchestration. Outstanding among the repertoire of modern dance are the orchestral scores either commissioned or used for choreography by Martha Graham, including *Errand into the Maze,* by Gian Carlo Menotti; *Cave of the Heart,* by Samuel Barber; *Herodiade,* by Paul Hindemith; *Diversion of Angels* and *Seraphic Dialogue,* by Norman Dello-Joio; *Judith, Night Journey,* and *Voyage,* by William Schuman; *Acrobats of God, The Owl and the Pussy Cat,* and *Embattled Garden,* by Carlos Surinach—and the list could go on.

This treatment of instrumental groupings for theatrical dance purposes is necessarily cursory. The main point is that there is a vast repertoire of musical literature available to student choreographers, plus many unusual instruments and combinations that have yet to be widely used for collaborative works. And for dancers performing onstage, the ability to recognize the various instrumental timbres and entrances is always an asset in both rehearsals and theatrical performances.

Scanning Instrumental Scores

Visually scanning a notated musical score in an analytical way may help to increase dancers' awareness and understanding of what it is they are hearing. Even without being able to play an instrument, students can learn to follow the main aspects as well as discover interesting details.

If an analytical focus on the basic form and musical materials is desired, then piano reductions may be easiest to deal with initially. Vocal scores are particularly recommended because of the added ease of locating one's place by noticing the words. Works for string orchestra or a small chamber group such as a woodwind quintet, with its distinctive instrumental timbres, might be good choices for a second experience in following scores. Subsequently the specific idiomatic instrumental timbres heard in orchestral performances can be studied in full score.

It must be mentioned that particularly with commissioned scores or arrangements made for particular dance companies, full scores are not usually published or available to the public. And even for so long-lived a classic as *Giselle,* there is still no published orchestral full score (only a piano version). Therefore, when material is selected for study purposes, it is best for dancers to investigate what materials their libraries can match up in the way of available videos, sound recordings, and published scores.

General Layout of Scores

Musical scores are read horizontally for the passage of time. Everything that occurs vertically in the same measure is heard simultaneously.

The layout on the page attempts to suggest relative pitch registers by locating higher parts first as one goes from top to bottom of a page. Vocal scores are generally "SATB"—that is, soprano, alto, tenor, and bass, reading from the top of the page. In small ensemble pieces, parts for higher pitched instruments are placed nearest the top of the page. In works for string orchestra, parts for first and second violins occur at the top of the page, and reading down one finds violas, cellos, and double bass parts.

Similarly, the placement on the page in full orchestral scores is high- to low-pitched within each family of instruments, reading vertically. Traditional scoring places woodwind parts on the topmost staves of a page: piccolo, flute, oboe, English horn, clarinet, bass clarinet, saxophones, and bassoons. Next come brasses, with horns being first, even though they are not the highest in pitch. Then come cornets and trumpets, trombones, and tuba. Percussion parts are indicated next, including timpani. Then comes harp, and finally the bowed strings: first and second violins, violas, violoncellos, and double bass.

The staves of the various sections of the orchestra will generally be connected with bar lines drawn through, as a visual aid to locate these family groupings of instruments. The initial braces at the left of every page provide an additional guide for the eyes in grouping related instruments.

Initial Markings to Spot

Before beginning to listen to a recording, flip through a score intended for dance use and notice a number of general things. How many movements are there? Are they long or short? (Look for double bar lines, titles, or numbers of movements.) Within movements, you may see boxed numbers now and then at the top of the page. These are usually measure numbers, which are useful for rehearsal purposes as well as for analytical study. Alternatively, boxed numerals or alphabet letters are indications for rehearsal purposes and may not coincide with measure numbers.

Look for important directions at the beginning of a score. The titles of subsections often suggest important information abut mood and dramatic or choreographic purpose.

To the left of the first page, and at the beginnings of various sections, are tempo markings, which could be in Italian, English, German, French, Russian, or another language. It is helpful to look these up in a music dictionary.

The abbreviation "*M.M.*" stands for Maelzel metronome, with a clocked tempo reference. For example, Stravinsky marks the beginning of *Petroushka* as follows: "Vivace. M.M. ♩ = 138." This prepares you for something extremely fast, with quarter note beats (in **3/4**) going by at a rate of 138 per minute.

A time signature may indicate a consistent meter (but look ahead to spot multiple changes in meter). A key signature will be present if the work is tonal; if there is none, perhaps the work is atonal, or it could be in C major or A minor.

Dynamic markings are easy to spot. These have been discussed in Chapter 7. Flip through a score and notice: is this piece essentially a quiet one (*p*) or loud (*f*) or are there changes in dynamics? The relative dynamic levels of various instruments may also alert students to which instrumental lines should stand out more. Notice where the melody is, what the balance of the accompaniment should be. Also notice any distinctive-looking rhythmic groupings.

Pitch Indications

As explained previously, in Western notation all instruments use a five-line staff to indicate pitch. Lower pitches appear vertically lower on the staff. The clefs indicated at the beginning of each line will determine the precise pitches. For tonally centered works, a key signature will appear on each staff before the first measure in each page. Various instruments may have different key signatures because they are transposing instruments (including clarinets, saxophones, various trumpets, cornet, horns, and English horn).

It is not expected that newcomers to scores will follow each pitch exactly moment to moment. However, when initially scanning scores, a generalized sense of pitch can be both adequate and helpful. First, dancers might simply notice the general range: high, low, or changing? One might also notice if changes in pitch occur in predominately stepwise progressions (for example, a line to the neighboring space) or by larger leaps.

Following Melodies and Bass Lines

Singing along with slower familiar melodies is a good way to work on one's skills of score reading. If dancers have already performed in *Nutcracker* or a musical show with an available score, these are good materials for listening and simultaneous visual study of the printed music. An experienced musician pointing out prominent melodies as they are heard also helps the eyes to focus on the page and to keep moving as events in the musical sounds progress.

Also helpful in developing this skill are available excerpts from scores (such as a series published by Norton) with coordinated recordings, and with prominent material highlighted in yellow. Unfortunately, to date, there is no published compendium geared specifically to the musical literature of theatrical dance.

Identifying Various Instrumental Parts

Normally pages of published music include only those instruments that are playing for the particular section—with the exception of the very first page, which usually lists the entire instrumentation called for during the course of the complete work. This listing can serve as an important reference for dancers, and is a good thing to observe when beginning study of any score or recorded work.

Once a solo melody is heard, students might try to follow the corresponding line in the score, hopefully with the help of an experienced musician who provides a moving pointer. It is enough if you can follow the general contour of a melody. Get a sense of the tempo and pace at which it progresses, and the visual outline in terms of highs and lows of pitch. Notice whether it has a fairly steady rhythm, or whether there are many ornamental notes or a variety of rhythmic patterns.

Then go back and listen again, this time focusing on the other instrumental parts. The bass line, usually appearing in both the cello and double bass parts, is often a good second choice, since it often provides a continuity plus implications for supporting harmony.

Accompaniment Textures

For striking visual representation of accompaniment textures, the ballets by Stravinsky and Tchaikovsky are excellent examples. Often the repetition of figurative rhythmic patterns have a distinctive look on the page.

Other Coloristic Aspects

For special instrumental coloration, look for specific directions such as *muted* in the brasses, or *col legno* (with the wood of the bow) in the strings.

Look for *cresc.* and *dim.,* which indicate changes in dynamic levels. Look for accents and sudden *sfz* marks. In regard to articulation, look for staccato dots that indicate a crisp style, or else long curved lines that indicate legato, or smoothly connected playing. (But remember that in string parts, slur marks indicate bowing.)

It is recommended that several styles of music be followed in score form, including something for strings alone, such as the brief William Boyce Symphonies (used choreographically by Paul Taylor for his *Arden Court*); the *Ancient Airs and Dances* arranged by Ottorino Respighi (used by Agnes de Mille for *Three Virgins and a Devil*); or Stravinsky's *Danses Concertantes, Petroushka,* and *Firebird.* Finally, the three scores by Tchaikovsky should be examined: *Swan Lake, Nutcracker,* and *Sleeping Beauty.* The Stravinsky and Tchaikovsky are excellent examples of how the tone colors of the full orchestra can be used to support the dramatic dancing onstage. Notice where the various techniques of the instruments are used as suggestive sound effects, as distinguished from the more abstract forms of set dance sections. Aaron Copland's *Appalachian Spring* is another good choice, in the full orchestral version.

New Technology, New Sounds

Musique Concrète

In earlier times, composers who wished to introduce interesting new timbres into their performances practically had to go into the furniture-moving business. In 1923, for example, George Antheil broke with what was considered polite concert traditions, with his *Ballet mécanique*. It made use of eight pianos, a pianola, eight xylophones, two doorbells, and airplane propellers. His 1927 version required sixteen pianos and added car horns and anvils.

With the invention of tape recording at mid-century, musicians explored the compositional possibilities of taping natural sounds and manipulating them to create new timbres and new pieces, called musique concrète. One enjoyable example is *Dripsody*, by the Canadian composer Hugh LeCaine. The entire piece is based on the sound of water falling into a sink.

With even more accessible tape equipment available to students today, sound collages have become an important source of inspiration for composers and collaborating choreographers. For example, one particularly stunning dance presented at a festival of the American College Dance Association in Washington, D.C., was *Scrimshaw II (The Lighthouse)*, choreographed by Tryntje Shaph and danced by Karen Johnson. The taped score by Lisbeth Woodie included the sounds of waves, roar of wind, squeaking of pilings, and cries of gulls. Imagine a lonely setting with a singular dancer, and the prop of one lantern as she waits for someone who does not appear on the horizon: a most effective evocation in movement and sound.

Electronic Synthesizers

The timbres that become available with electronic marimbas, drum pads, and hookups for electric guitars, winds, and keyboards are being used for both dance performances and studio class work. The drawbacks of using some technological equipment in the dance studio have to do with the time it takes for adjustments, and with what some musicians perceive as a lack of nuance. Still others question the imposition of "now" sounds upon such dance traditions as Graham or Limón techniques, which evolved in direct relation to distinct viewpoints and stylistic tastes in music.

So when new technology, new sounds, or new musical styles are considered, their appropriateness for a particular choreographic aesthetic should also be of concern. An interesting question to ponder: does such music energize dancers in the style intended—or should dance techniques be allowed to evolve and change according to the musical impulses suggested by whatever is heard in class? Timbre alone can introduce aesthetic questions when specifically historical dance styles are concerned.

Live or Taped Performance?

For choreographic purposes, the contemporary technology of various electronic synthesizers, computers, and multitrack recording offers affordable and exciting compositional and timbral possibilities for theatrical dance collaboration. The danger, in fact, seems to be rather that with so much attention given to the electronic timbres, dancers may be overlooking equally effective collaborative opportunities that are available with modest forces of older acoustical instruments, or with singers.

Dancer/choreographer Tandy Beal's musical partner, Jon Scoville, delights in taping sounds for electronic collages and works compositionally with many kinds of synthesizers. Yet he is also known for his percussion playing, and for his inventions of new instruments. Commenting on the choices available, he observes:

> *I feel electronic music is so powerful and seductive and so artificial—all at the same time—that if I am working exclusively in my studio and am wrapped up in that kind of sound and energy, it behooves me to get out and just take simple hand drums and things like that into the dance classroom and reestablish my connection with older traditions. It revitalizes what I am doing musically. Moreover, there is a tendency with electronic music to get pretty gauzy. You can get such nice string washes and big, reverberant sounds that you can disguise ideas that are limited, by making an envelope of profound dress. But if I am in a class with just one or two conga drums, trying to get different qualities out of them, I realize that it's a tradition that goes back thousands and thousands of years.[2]*

Another musician who has wide experience with dance students is the composer/educator Pia Gilbert, formerly professor at UCLA, recently at The Juilliard School. Voicing her concern about the pervasive use of taped music for dance performances, she suggested that just as we have Muzak surrounding us in daily life, the effect of using nothing but taped music for performance raises the question of whether theatrical dancers would consider presenting Danzak to their audiences.

And yet, there are many good reasons why dancers continue to make use of tape recordings. First and most often cited is cost. Especially for small modern dance touring companies with tight budgets, the added cost of hiring a chamber ensemble, let alone a full orchestra, is prohibitive or at least daunting. Major ballet companies are more apt to feel that full orchestral presence is demanded by aesthetic traditions, funding patrons, and paying audiences alike. Yet regional ballet companies may perform to tapes because they cannot meet the costs of live music or because the logistics of rehearsal with new musicians cannot be adequately arranged.

Yet there are admirable exceptions. In Miami, the civic ballet under Thomas Armour always managed to have live orchestra for its recitals. And in modern dance, Erick Hawkins could be an example to all in the way he has insisted upon always having live music for all his performances. The company proudly includes this information in all its publicity.

For students and other emerging choreographers with little time and little money, the prospect of dealing with a collaborating composer and collaborating conductors, instrumentalists, and so forth may seem too daunting when scheduling is added to the ingredients. And so it often seems convenient to use tapes.

One positive aspect is that by using recordings, students open whole realms of music as possible ingredients for theatrical dance works. Favorite music that is known very well by the choreographer can be used. Dancers can rehearse to the exact tempos and instrumental timbres that will be heard when they are onstage. All these may be positive points, from the dancers' view.

A cautionary note that should be sounded in connection with the use of recorded music, however, is that dancers check out the performing-rights situation for whatever music is selected as part of a theatrical dance work. If it is a nonprofessional student work in question, university and college administration can best answer questions about what is legally permissible in each venue.

Affordable Alternatives

Despite all the ready arguments given by dancers who use taped music to the exclusion of anything else, it should be noted that even the best CD recordings can never match the quality and timbre of live musical performances, to say nothing of the immediacy of interacting with performers onstage. Dancers feel an increased energy with live music, and audiences often sense that performances with live music are more unique; there is less of a museum quality to the total experience.

Consequently, when planning performances, dancers might give some thought to cultivating collaborative relationships with music students as well as with professional musicians and consider the inclusion of even one dance with live music on each program.

Some affordable alternatives to tape might include small instrumental combinations: a single percussionist, a local rock band, a solo flute or violin, a two-piano duo, a string trio, a flute quartet, a woodwind quintet, a string quartet or sextet, a jazz combo, a singer with piano or double bass and percussion, a group of student dancer-musicians playing found instruments of a percussion nature, a guitarist amplified with a mike, or the sound of the dancers' own voices.

Other possibilities that students may want to explore are joint performances with student or community musical groups: bands, orchestras, chamber ensembles, choirs, or solo recitalists on various instruments. Often local departments of recreation, arts councils, libraries, chapters of the musicians' union, and museums will assist in funding joint performances. And increasingly, through funding from such sources as Meet The Composer, professional dance artists have opportunities not only to perform with live musicians, but also to collaborate with outstanding composers, for new choreography.

Another potential source of collaboration that dancers have not taken advantage of are the societies within the music world. The annual *Musical America* lists organizations that focus on individual instruments: societies for horn players, violists, barbershop quartet singers, amateur chamber players, guitarists, harpists, jazz improvisers, and so forth. As noted previously, the International Guild for Musicians in Dance may prove to be especially helpful to students in the dance world.

Many of these groups regularly sponsor workshops and if dancers have a predelection for certain instruments, these gatherings offer unusual opportunities to hear new music and meet musicians. Some of the players are still students, and if they were approached by dance students, the result could very well be some affordable, collaborative performance possibilities.

Without leaving many campuses, it does seem that college music departments are producing a surfeit of able instrumentalists and composers, and that part of *their* training should be precisely the experience of collaborating with dancers. It is in the interest of the music students to do so at least once in their four years of training. Many musicians who have gone on to specialize in work with dancers feel that such experiences should be required of music majors as part of their academic coursework.

What is the opposite of live music? Is that something dancers really want for their performances?

Explorations and Assignments

1. Using a portable tape recorder, collect sounds with which to make a taped collage for a brief dance. Explain your reasons for choosing certain types of sounds in relation to the particular dance.

2. Select one melodic (nonkeyboard) instrument and explore the solo literature via recordings. Make a list of at least five pieces highlighting the instrument as soloist. Next, explore the literature for mixed ensembles that feature your chosen instrument. For example, if you have chosen the flute, find out about unaccompanied pieces, flute concertos, works for flute and electronic tape, flute and harp pieces, flute quartets, and finally, choirs of flutes.

    In class, present one recorded excerpt about a minute long that you consider typical of the tone quality of the instrument. Demonstrate a movement that reflects that quality of the tone.

3. Discuss: What are some affordable sources of live musical performance for dance in your area? What are some existing groupings that might be effective? (Consider solos, duets, trios, quartets, chamber and jazz ensembles.)

4. Select a brief musical score (one to five minutes) for a dance you have seen and follow the score while listening to a recording. Repeat the process, and with each hearing, focus on a different aspect of the music: instruments, special effects, bass line, melody, metric and rhythmic organization, dynamics.

5. Attend a live performance of a Tchaikovsky ballet, or view a videotape. Afterwards, listen to a musical recording and follow the published orchestral score. As you recall the staging, were there particular moments when the choice of instrumentation was important to the dramatic or emotional unfolding of the dance itself? Notice any particular patterning that seems idiomatic to specific instruments.

6. Listen to three short contemporary works created entirely with electronic sounds. Discuss: If you were working with a composer who had a synthesizer, what qualities of sounds would you be interested in making use of for a staged dance?

chapter 14

FORM AND COMPOSITIONAL PROCEDURES

In general, we should attempt to develop . . . a natural sensitivity to the structure of music so that [dance students] will take [their] cue for starting, stopping, or changing movement from the music and not from the teacher.

—Martha Hill

To put it bluntly . . . form is one of the composer's chief means of averting the boredom of his audience.

—Percy A. Scholes

Thus far, this survey of musical ingredients has included pitch, duration, loudness, and tone color, with considerations of how these materials can be expanded into rhythmic patterns, melodies, harmonies, and varied textures.

How are these ingredients fasioned into lengthier works of music? What are some successful procedures for composing? What are some of the general formal structures that can be recognized by ear? And how do choreographers make use of musical structure, as a collaborative support or as a contrast to the formal structure of their dances? These are among the questions explored in this chapter.

Listening for Structure

The art of composing music could be called a process of organizing sounds: of limiting and selecting sounds to be heard in the first place, and then manipulating them in various ways. If the main structural aspects of compositional procedures and form are defined broadly enough, they apply to many styles of music and may give dancers one approach to understanding what they hear.

Generally speaking, the most common active procedures for creating lengthy music are *development, repetition, contrast, variation,* and *imitation.* These are aspects that dancers can listen for, using scores upon occasion to help clarify how the music is organized.

It should be mentioned that one may not be able to discern the overall form of a musical piece upon just one hearing. It may be helpful for dancers, upon each repeated hearing, to be listening *for* something. For example: What motifs seem important? Are there important tempo changes or other demarcations of contrast?

It may be helpful to tap out rhythms as original material is introduced. Singing along is also a good aid when possible, and this in itself may alert students to shifts in general register or key centers. The more specific descriptions of the music that dancers can provide for themselves, the more aware they may become of both the unique details and the overall structure of a work. For example, it is helpful to count the exact number of main beats in a brief section, as well as the number of repetitions of larger sections, and to chart these in some way on paper. When learning music for choreographic purposes, it is particularly important to become aware of the planned points of coincidence between music and movement.

Notice, too, the exact instrumentation or character of electronic timbre, for this may provide a clue to the structure of the music. Does one instrument have a complete melody? Or does a melodic line seem to jump around from instrument to instrument? If the same melody is repeated, is it played by the same or a different instrument? Does it have a different type of accompaniment texture with each repetition or transformation?

Form as Result of Process; Form as Mold

Musical form can be regarded as the result of certain working procedures, with the structure flowing directly from the unfolding choices made by the composer as a work progresses. With such music, the word form is perhaps best thought of as a verb. Examples of this category would be some freely contrapuntal fantasies of the Baroque era, character pieces of the Romantic era, contemporary minimalist pieces, and many collaborative scores written for specific theatrical dances.

But form is also a noun, and a generalized structural outline (much like a preliminary architectural sketch) can exist even before specific combinations of sounds are composed. Particularly with traditional dance forms, a preexisting plan can serve as a mold into which composers can pour their own new material. Such forms in dance music can imply strict counts, specific choices of meter, a definite pattern of phrases and longer sections, and even the general texture and characteristic rhythmic motifs. Examples of this kind of music include the extensive collections of traditional European social dances. Instrumental concert suites based on dance forms (such as the suites by Bach and Handel or many movements in the serenades and divertimentos of Mozart) tend to be much freer; nevertheless, the basic inspiration of the earlier dance forms are evident.

In turn, the beginnings of instrumental dance music in Europe have been traced by musicologists to some of the existing poetic forms and vocal music of the Renaissance. Joseph Machlis, for example, in considering a 1551 publication of pavans, galliards, allemandes, branles, and other types collected by Tielman Susato, comments: "It was through dance pieces such as these that Renaissance composers explored the possibilities of purely instrumental forms. From these humble beginnings sprang the imposing structures of Western instrumental music."[1]

A familiar contemporary example of using counts and phrase structure of dance movement as a mold are the musical improvisations that studio pianists improvise to fit the dance instructor's directions during daily technique classes for ballet and modern dance. In addition, popular songs and musical show tunes are often cast in regularly phrased sections of identical counts, as are songs that follow certain strophic structures of poetry. Hymn tunes also exhibit an expected format of phrasing, cadences, and texture, all related to the poetic format of the words.

An extension of this procedure of structuring composition was the collaborative method favored by Petipa and Tchaikovsky. The choreographer provided detailed scenarios for the composer, and in that broad sense, the general form and length of the music (as well as the meters and emotional spirit) were cast before it was composed.[2]

Nowadays, composers for theatrical dance are just as likely to map out their plans in terms of real time, using a stopwatch to clock choreographic movements that have already been devised (though usually not totally set in a final version). In such cases, the musical form may be closely linked to the sections of the dance itself, and may be unique to a particular work.

Undetermined Aspects

When the structure and planned content of sounds of a piece are left to chance, this has come to be labeled *indeterminant music*. The term implies two possible procedures: first, that the composer has used chance methods such as dice to determine various aspects of a work; or second, that some important variables are left to the choice of performers. For instance, the rhythms might be specified but the choice of pitch left open; or the pitches might be notated but not the rhythms.

It should be mentioned that many styles of music have incorporated undetermined elements in performance. Certainly in traditional west African drumming for dances, the exact combination of sounds will vary from occasion to occasion, though consistent drum patterns will accompany specific dances. In European Baroque ensembles, there was the figured bass framework for keyboardists to use in filling out the harmony however they could. Later on, in classical concertos, the cadenzas provided opportunities for creativity on the part of the soloists. Subsequently, composers from Beethoven's time on preferred to write out cadenzas exactly.

But improvisation has persisted. Dancers who are fortunate to have live musicians in their technique classes are probably familiar with sounds that have been tailor-made to fit their movement needs or impel them to greater effort.

Improvisation is also at the heart of jazz. Frameworks of melodies, harmonies, phrase lengths, or counts will be charted or communicated verbally before performance. But how these are elaborated upon is a matter for individual creation on the part of the performing instrumentalists and vocalists. It should be mentioned that improvisation does not necessarily imply total on-the-spot inspiration or creativity. On the contrary, many improvising musicians practice their improvisations a great deal before public renditions.

Turning to concert music in European styles, in the last several hundred years it became common practice for separate instrumental parts to be written out, closely specifying pitches, rhythms, dynamic nuances, articulations, phrasings, tempo, and nuances of tone color. The performer still had a job to do in working up a good rendition in terms of both style and technique.

In the twentieth century, however, instrumental performers may be presented with a kit of some sort provided by the composer: perhaps some guidelines that provide choices of pitch but leave the rhythmic patterns up to the performers. Or perhaps the parameters and the order of pitches will be provided, with the tempo and the dynamics to be determined by the instrumentalists. This approach can be particularly fruitful if a close collaboration of dancers with improvising musicians is desired. It also opens the possibility of having slightly different or considerably different music for each live performance.

Contemporary Western composers who have explored the possibilities of indeterminant music have often seemed fascinated with games and numerology. Those in the dance world think immediately of John Cage's experimental collaborations with Merce Cunningham. Another example: one of composer/conductor Leonard Bernstein's last works was an ambitious foray into indeterminate procedures for an orchestral concert work that readily suggested dance movement. *Jubilee Games* was premiered at Lincoln Center with the composer conducting the Israel Philharmonic Orchestra.[3] Focusing on that orchestra's fiftieth anniversary, Bernstein made use of the Biblical reference to seven sabbaths of years (in Leviticus 25:8–17) and structured the entire first movement, "Free-Style Events," on the number seven. The composer provided many parameters, but left many choices to the orchestral players. For example, a selection of vocal notes for several seven-note scales or mode groupings could be made by the instrumentalists, but the registers were specified, as was the 7/8 meter, phrase structure, and both direction and duration of pitches and dynamics. One section had no written notation at all (hence the "free-style" of the title). Yet even the improvisations were framed and dictated somewhat by the inclusion of several prerecorded taped reprises that were immersed in the texture of the live playing. The second movement, titled "Diaspora Dances," was set in a meter of 18/8, and the sounds did suggest that real dancing might very well enlarge the experience of an audience on some other occasion.

In regard to this discussion of form, it is pertinent to observe that if a tape were used for such a piece, then the work immediately would have a distinct set combination of sounds and silences, in effect a set form, while it was the composer's intention that details of every performance be different within the general structure he provided. The same can be said of using taped performances of jazz improvisations: the music acquires a fixity that was not intended by the musicians. In both situations, the immediacy of a unique performance for a specific audience is lost. Something for dancers to think about too.

Classical Indian
Procedures of Raga and Tala

The classical traditions of Indian music include compositional procedures that have attracted a number of Western composers who collaborate with contemporary choreographers. Moreover, perhaps harking back to the precedent of Ruth St. Denis, the inclusion of Indian-based styles has not seemed inconsistent to contemporary Western dance artists. Consequently, if one visits the Martha Graham School, for example, one is quite likely to hear pianist John Schlenck spinning out lengthy and elaborate improvisations that combine aspects of both European and Indian procedures.

The scope of this book precludes any detailed presentation of Indian composition. But in very broad outline, the traditions can be said to rest upon two components: *ragas* (the pitch basis), and *talas* (rhythmic cycles). Unlike the Western concert aesthetic in which the functions of composer and performer have become separated, in the Indian practice, the instrumentalist in effect becomes his or her own composer, within some parameters. As such, the performance experience might be more akin to the jazz improvisations of our own culture rather than to the experience of concert artists who memorize existing repertoire and then present their interpretations.

For instrumentalists, the choice of basic raga is crucial, determining not only the pitched melodic material for a performance, but also a general emotional expression as well. What ensues is determined by only a general framework. One example was explained to Western audiences by sitarist Ustad Vilayat Khan and tabla player Ustad Zamir Ahmad Khan as follows:

> *The basic form for the interpretation of a* raga *is made up of four parts:* Alap, Jor, Jhala, *and* Gat.
>
> Alap *is a slow introduction in which the performer contemplates the* raga *note by note composing phrases, at first quite simply, . . . but gradually becoming more and more complex as he extends . . . over the whole range of the instrument.*
>
> *In the* Jor *section the artist introduces a rhythmic pulse. The improvisations become more and more extended—eventually with very fast staccato passages called* Tans, *full of rhythmic subtlety and requiring considerable technical virtuosity.*
>
> *In* Jhala *the artist starts playing triplets and quadruplets on the drone strings at high speed, against which he plays phrases on the melodic strings, mostly in syncopation.*
>
> *The* Gat *section is really in rondo form with the main subject being a previously composed motif (usually traditional), which is set to a recurring rhythmic cycle called* Tal. *The* tabla *player enters now and accompanies the melody instrument to the end of the performance. . . .*
>
> *It is usual for this whole movement to be comprised of two* gats, *one slow and one fast. Near the end of the performance the melody instrument goes into* Jhala *again to bring the performance to a climax.*[4]

Total Control and Serialism

In contrast to such compositional and performance procedures, electronic equipment allows a composer to determine everything that is heard by audiences. There is total control of all aspects and all ingredients of the music. In such cases, the play of creativity takes place privately; dancers and audiences hear only the final result, and (depending on the skill of theatrical sound crews), the music will be exactly the same for every performance.

Many dancers choose this kind of musical partnering for purely economic reasons. Others prefer to work with tapes that can be depended on for precisely the tempo in which the choreography was developed. And in the case of electronic composition, if a composer wants to select exact sounds and mix them in multitrack taping format, then of course there is no longer any such thing as a live performance; the taped version is the one and only form.

In various styles, composers may use numerical charts not for chance, but as an aid in structuring their works. In strict serialist music of this century, for example, a composer will create an order for the twelve available notes of the chromatic scale. This tone row will then serve as the basis for both melody and harmony. According to this process of composing, the pitches recur in the same order (but they can be used either in the vertical harmony or in the horizontal melodic lines). Composers sometimes block out a serial control of other aspects as well, such as dynamics and rhythmic permutations, by means of charts.

Composers are constantly coming up not only with new musical ideas, but also with new procedures for eliciting or working with musical materials. Space here does not permit detailed descriptions of all the methods currently practiced. It is a good groundwork, however, for concert dancers to understand the traditions of form in European-based music. Attention will now be turned to some procedures that have been commonly used by many composers in building musical structures that may last anywhere from a few minutes to several hours.

Building Blocks

Motifs

The germinal seed or motif of a musical work is a brief, limited idea: it could be a rhythmic pattern, or a set of pitch relationships, or a short pattern combining both rhythm and pitches along with a suggestion of texture.

For examples of motivic material in the literature of music for theatrical dance, it is instructive to listen in rapid succession to just the beginnings (perhaps the first two or four seconds) of many pieces. Notice what makes each motif distinctive: the pitches, the rhythm, the general flow?

As far as analogies with dance movement are concerned, students could find no better examples in the use of motif in choreography than the entire repertoires of the Feld Ballets or the New York City Ballet, or in contemporary styles, the works of Paul Taylor, Laura Dean, and Mark Morris.

To continue with the next building block in much concert and popular music, the focus will be initially upon music that has a texture of a definite melodic foreground and an accompanying background.

Phrases

After motifs, the next-sized building section in the structure of much Western music is the *phrase*. Generally speaking, phrases are to music what sentences are to prose. They present an idea. They have shape and fluctuation in emphasis, and they have a definite end with some kind of punctuation.

To build a phrase, a composer can repeat the opening motif in some way (for example, rhythmically the same but with different pitches). Alternatively, a distinctive motif in the initiation of a phrase may be balanced by less interesting material in the latter part of a phrase.

Although here a phrase is being considered as a single melodic line, the underlying harmonic rhythm contributes an important impetus. Often the harmony of a phrase will be static or change only occasionally in the initial moments of a phrase. As the musical line continues, the pace of the harmonic changes will often increase as a melody nears a climax or a pause. If the pause is a momentary one analogous to a semicolon, it may be accompanied by related functional harmony that creates the impression of a half-cadence. Such a phrase is labeled an *antecedent* phrase. It would be balanced by a subsequent phrase that comes to a complete halt the equivalent of a period in speech. This is called a *consequent* phrase, and it is concluded with a full cadence. Two phrases paired as antecedent and consequent make up a *period* in musical form.

The sense of harmonic rhythm (the pace at which the chords change) is extremely important to the sense of melodic phrasing and overall form. A static harmony as well as progressions with perceived dissonances can both build up tension and prepare the listener for some kind of harmonic resolution. Good examples of this effect can be found in many of the concerto grosso forms of the Baroque era—for instance, in the first movement of Bach's *Brandenburg* Concerto No. 3.

For stunning examples of how the phrasing in music can be acknowledged with positive effects upon choreography, students are urged to see performances of dance works by George Balanchine and by Paul Taylor. Notice when the choreographic patterns coincide with the musical phrases, and other moments when the dancers will continue over the musical phrase, or as intentional contrast to the musical structure.

Sectional Forms

Among the most attractive musical forms for social dance purposes are pieces with definite sections, which are often repeated, either immediately and exactly, or else with interspersed new material and a few changes.

For purposes of analysis, musicians have found it convenient to use capital letters to indicate overall sections of pieces. A form that is AABB, therefore, has an initial section that is repeated, followed by a second section based on new material and probably with a different key center, which is also repeated. Some analysts might simply indicate AB as the overall structure.

Binary Dance Forms

One need go no further than AABB in order to discover a common structure for traditional European dance music. Take, for example, the piano ländler of Franz Schubert. These are often used in ballet classes because of their clear phrasing. Here is a general outline of structure Schubert used as a mold for hundreds of charming and individual pieces in 3/4 meter, dances that were the forerunner of the later waltz. The same structure is found in his écossaises, which were dances in duple (2/4) meter.

The overall form is *binary*, or two-part. Each piece consists of two sections, each eight measures in length. The first section is played, then repeated. The second section is played, then it too is immediately repeated exactly. The distinct motif is found in the first two measures, and the initial brief phrase is precisely four measures long, with a half-cadence feeling. The next four measures come to a firm cadence in the home (tonic) key. Then the entire first section of eight measures is repeated. In analyzing the form, musicians generally represent this whole section by the alphabet letter *A*.

The second section, *B* in such an analysis, departs from the home key center for four measures, and the last four-measure phrase in each piece wends its way back harmonically for a satisfying conclusion and a final cadence in the home key. The overall structure of these Schubert pieces, therefore, can be analyzed as AB or AABB if you wish to indicate the repeats.

In such brief pieces, listen for the motif ideas, the sense of regular phrasing accompanied by harmonic cadences, the repeats of the sections, and highly metric rhythmic organization. These features can be heard in thousands of dance forms, though the length of the phrases will vary. Eight, however, seems to be a very attractive number among European dances.

Other dances were not always symmetrical in regard to the repeats. For example, in the extensive *Playford Dances* printed in many editions over the course of a hundred years or so, many of the tunes will open with a phrase of eight counts, and then this same material is repeated. A second contrasting section with a new motif lasts eight counts, and the first four beats are repeated exactly, but the last four beats are a return to the rhythmic idea of the first section. Then, the second section (eight measures or sixteen beats) is repeated totally, apparently to accommodate the steps of the longways dances. Such a format could be considered *asymmetrical* binary form.

In many binary dance forms, an important feature is a harmonic modulation to a different key at the end of the first section; the second section then wends its way home for the final cadence. In regard to thematic material, in binary forms, the motivic choices are usually complementary, and are related for the two sections, rather than being starkly contrasting.

Many of the preclassic court dances were cast in binary forms. Readers are referred to Louis Horst's study, which offers not only a survey of the main types from previous centuries, but also comments about choreographic forms of the modern dancers earlier in the twentieth century. The dances covered in his *Pre-Classic Dance Forms* include the pavane, galliard, allemande, courante, sarabande, gigue, minuet, gavotte, bourree, rigaudon, and passepied.

Ternary Forms

These are also dubbed song forms, because the structure exists in vocal music so often. Continuing with the alphabetic manner of analysis, ternary forms have three sections, with the first and third closely related: ABA. Or there may be variants, depending on the repetitions: AABA, for example.

In all these small sectional forms, the harmonic organization is usually quite predominant, with clear modulations to the dominant or other closely related key, and a complementary return to the tonic at the end.

Ternary form can be heard today simply by listening to country and western songs and Broadway show tunes on the radio.

Preclassic Dance Forms

Traditional and European court dances inspired extensive composition of suites of instrumental dances. The individual dances were distinguished by meter and tempo as well as by general character of rhythmic patterns. But many shared the same sectional format of either binary or ternary layout. In addition, a third contrasting *trio* section came to be added to certain dances such as the minuet, resulting in this related form: AABBCCAB.

Such sectional dance pieces offer excellent examples for the study of set forms, because the phrasing is usually relatively clear. They are also excellent examples of the developmental procedures that serve as composers' tools: how to make the most of a brief motif. Good examples exist in the Elizabethan keyboard works included in the seventeenth century collection called the *Fitzwilliam Virginal Book,* as well as the later suites of Bach and Handel.

A second principle of composition is contrast, and in early seventeenth-century suites, this was provided mainly by pairing or grouping dances that had different meters, tempos, textures, and general flow. The dozens of suites written by Bach in the eighteenth century generally began with a freely contrapuntal prelude, followed by a flowing allemande, a faster courante, a slow sarabande in triple meter, perhaps a minuet and trio, and a final fast gigue in **6/8**. Some of the suites also contained bourreés and gavottes, both stately dances in **4/4**. It should be observed that the tempo of the instrumental minuets was apparently quicker than that taken by French court dancers previously, and that considerable liberty came to be taken with the phrase structure of other dance-based forms.

The lovely orchestrations that Ottorini Respighi did of Renaissance dances (*Ancient Airs and Dances*) have been used by several choreographers, including Agnes de Mille for her *Three Saints and a Devil.* A modern homage to the older dance suite forms is Ravel's *Le Tombeau de Couperin,* which was choreographed by Balanchine. The movements include the preclassic forms of forlane, rigaudon, and menuet.

In the repertoire of the Classical era, Mozart's serenades and divertimenti are attractive precisely because the individual sections are short and each one has a distinctive character. A continuing favorite in the repertoire of New York City Ballet, for example, is Balanchine's setting of the entire Divertimento No. 15. These compositions were intended as light works for various court occasions, but they include many dancelike sections.

Modern Dance Use of Set Forms

Choreographer Jean Erdman describes the approach of her mentor Louis Horst in using preclassic dance forms for modern dance purposes.[5]

> *We had to learn the exact preclassic dances, from the books. And we did them in dance. Then we had to take the same piece of music and do a contemporary dance to the structure of the music. We had to find a theme that was contemporary, not in the style of ancient dance, but a contemporary movement theme that was harmonious with the musical theme. The dance had to be harmonious not only in the way it was structured—the rhythmic patterns and everything—but it was also to be harmonious with the spirit of the old dances. For instance, the pavanne had a very slow and very strong and straightforward kind of quality. So when the contemporary movement came in, you'd keep that quality, but you'd do entirely different movement with it.*
>
> *Next in the training, we had to do archaic, taking off from the ancient Greek vase paintings. Louis Horst utilized the idea of the stylization of the paintings to help the dancers learn what style was—because when you're in ballet, you have a style given. You're in Spanish dancing; you have a style. You don't even think about it; you learn the style. But in contemporary dance, you have to create a style.*
>
> *So putting new movement to old music was the first part. Then when we got into the archaic, Horst used Satie and various composers, and then when we got into Impressionism, Expressionism, he used Debussy and Mompou and other contemporary composers of that time.*

In each style, Erdman points out, the students were taught how to relate to the structure of the music, so that they would be able to structure choreography similarly. This allowed for a wide range in the choice of the musical flavors employed for dance.

In describing Horst's method of teaching, Erdman observes:

> *He wouldn't let us just Mickey Mouse the music. He'd play the music maybe once or twice, and we had to take down the counts, the measures, and the phrases, and go home and do a dance, without any music. Then it was possible for the dancer to work entirely without music: to have an idea, in silence. A dancer could, if she had an idea, bring it into choreographic form, then have the composer come, see the form, and write the music for the dance—just as it had been the other way round.*

Classical Rondos

The concept of developing melodic material from brief motifs, and of structuring sectional pieces by means of distinctive harmonic cadences and phrase lengths, was extended in the late eighteenth century to include the *rondo* form. These are good pieces for testing a listener's mental recall, for the original thematic material keeps returning (usually in the same key), interspersed with contrasting themes. A typical format might be: ABACBA, or an extended ABACADA.

One contemporary dance use of a classical rondo is Lar Lubovitch's choreographic *Concerto Six Twenty-Two,* a setting of Mozart's concerto for clarinet and orchestra. A recent dance choreographed by Peter Sparling for the Ann Arbor Dance Works uses the title *Rondo,* and the movement patterns themselves acknowledge recurring aspects of David Gregory's sound score.

Ragtime Forms

Classic American piano rags came to have an expected general sectional form. For instance, Scott Joplin's famous *Maple Leaf Rag* follows this plan: AABBACCDD. Each section contains sixteen measures of 2/4, with first and second endings. Section C is labeled Trio and lies in a related (subdominant) key. The last section makes its way back to the original key, providing the spice of a little harmonic ambiguity along the way.

Often rags would have a four-bar introduction, for instance in *Solace,* Joplin's Mexican serenade. In later rags, four measure breaks were sometimes introduced after the B sections. But with slight variations, the general format of piano rags lent itself to thousands of individual creations, many of which are enjoying tremendous revival in recent years. Other popular forms can usually be analyzed in this sectional way.

Sonata Form

The Renaissance use of the term *sonata* served merely to distinguish instrumental music from vocal works. But by the Classical era, the term sonata was reserved for instrumental pieces that followed a definite sectional form, with general expectations about the harmonic relationships. Sonata form was used for musical movements within larger works for solo instruments, chamber ensembles, and orchestras. The format continues to serve composers of the twentieth century.

The overall form of a classical sonata is introduction, exposition, development, recapitulation, and coda.

The exposition always begins with a theme in the main key, followed by a second theme in a related key, plus some transitional material and a brief closing theme. The exposition is then repeated, exactly. The development section, as the name implies, works with the main thematic material to stretch it and recast it in various ways, especially by modulating to many different keys in often dramatic ways. The recapitulation brings back the original order and group of themes, this time all in the main tonic key. The final section, or coda, ends conclusively in the original key.

Symphonies

The sonata form became the favored general plan for opening allegro movements of classical and Romantic symphonies, which to this day form the backbone of repertoire for orchestras in concert halls. The allegro was often preceded by a slow introduction.

Following the fast first movement in sonata form, a slow movement usually is more free in structure, with an emphasis on arialike melody. This is usually followed by a minuet or the faster **3/4** *scherzo*. Final movements of symphonies are usually the fastest in tempo, and if cast in **6/8** meter, they may be reminiscent of the final gigues of dance suites. Not infrequently, the final movements of symphonies are in either rondo or sonata form.

Isadora Duncan is usually credited as the first modern dancer to make use of symphonies for theatrical dance, drawing upon orchestral works by Beethoven, Tchaikovsky, Schubert, Gluck, and others. At the time, her choice of concert music was quite controversial. Perhaps her taste has been somewhat vindicated by all the audiences who continue to applaud the use of classical pieces in the choreography of George Balanchine, Paul Taylor, Mark Morris, and others. Some prime examples are Taylor's *Mercuric Tidings* and Balanchine's *Scotch Symphony*, works set respectively to symphonies of Schubert and Mendelssohn. Other examples are settings of Prokofiev's *Classical* Symphony as a ballet with the same name, by Todd Bolender; and as a modern dance titled *Plod*, by Dan Wagoner. The use of this piece is of particular pertinence in this discussion of classicism, for it is an early work of Prokofiev, one he wrote to be more academically correct than many earlier classical symphonies were.

Variation Forms

Variation forms depend on the process of repetition: either exact repetition of the counts, or the repetition of a bass line melody, or the repetition of a melody itself, or at times just the harmony.

Most simple is the structural device of *ostinato,* a brief pattern in the bass line that recurs. Good examples are the various bass patterns in the familiar *boogie-woogie* piano pieces of earlier jazz. The entire third movement of Lou Harrison's *Symphonie No. 3* is in fact titled "Large ostinato."

Extending the principle is the *ground bass,* in which an entire bass melody will be repeated over and over to form the structural basis for an entire work. Perhaps the most famous example is still Henry Purcell's aria for Dido's lament, "When I am laid in earth," from the opera *Dido and Aeneas.* This was used for a beautiful contemporary pas de deux choreographed by Dan Wagoner.

There are many types of variation forms, but the common denominator is that something is repeated over and over as a framework. That something may be the bass line; it may be the outlines of a melody; it may be the harmonic progression; or it may be the rhythmic organization. Choreographers using such music may choose to mirror the structure in some way, or to offer movement sections that contrast to the variations—or ignore them entirely.

Among the preclassic forms of continuous or nonstop variation, the chaconne was based on a harmonic progression (often tonic-dominant-subdominant-dominant). A supreme example of this is the chaconne from Bach's D Minor Sonata for unaccompanied violin.

Closely related was the passacaglia, in which the bass line melody might occur in upper voices during repetitions, and be changed substantially in other ways as well. A choreographic setting that made modern dance history was Doris Humphrey's dance to Bach's Passacaglia in C Minor. This can still be seen on film. A totally different passacaglia is Anton Webern's opus 1, which was used by Dan Wagoner for his dance work *Dolly Sods: After the Flood.*

Variation was an important procedure in the Elizabethan keyboard compositions collected in the *Fitzwilliam Virginal Book.* Among them is John Bull's set based on The Spanish Paven, with typical metrical changes as well as in the rhythmic flow. In the Classical repertoire, variations came to be more sectionalized, with brief pauses between the variations. The separate sections often took on distinctly different characters, with different meters, tempos, modes, and textures. Each variation of an entire tune could very well stand alone as a short piece. Mozart excelled at this form, and his works offer many examples. In the Romantic literature, variations were often a vehicle for virtuoso extemporization and composition alike. Franz Liszt wrote many many variations on opera arias, for example.

To go back to an earlier example of the estampie from the thirteenth century: only a handful of written examples survive. The melodies are quite interesting, and occur in regular, metric *puncta,* or phrases, that are immediately repeated. These have been recorded by several early music groups, with elaborations in instrumentation and rhythmic percussion. But of the actual variations that were played, and of the actual percussion added, we can never be sure. Harking back to that tradition, the contemporary composer Lou Harrison has written *An Estampie for Susan Summerfeld* as the second movement of his *Symphonie No. 3.*

Jazz sets that go on for twenty minutes or so are basically a series of variations on the main tune. Sometimes this tune may seem to be lost in the general texture, and sometimes it is in fact the harmonic structure rather than a melody that provides the form around which instrumentalists improvise.

Methods of Variation and Development

To vary a given musical idea, composers can make changes in the melody itself, in the accompaniment patterns, in the rhythmic organization, or in the instrumentation. Similar procedures can be used to extend thematic material in a developmental or imitative form (as distinguished from sectional variations that retain the original counts).

These techniques include the following possibilities:

- Transpose motif to a different key.
- Change the register of the pitches.
- Put the melody in the bass line.
- Put the bass line in a higher instrumental part.
- Double the melody at various intervals of pitch.
- Keep the melody but change the harmonic progression that supports it.
- Change the texture (for example, from homophonic to monophonic).
- Decorate the melody with ornamentation (trills, grace notes, turns, etc.).
- Change mode: major to minor.
- Substitute rests for some of the tones.
- Alter the tone color by changing instrumentation, or the manner in which the same instruments are played.
- Change the articulations.

- Change the dynamics.
- Rhythmically, use a different meter.
- Introduce a new tempo.
- Apply the same pitches to a different rhythmic pattern.
- Retain the same rhythm, but use different pitch patterns.
- Add accents in new places.

These are all specific things to listen for in musical variations composed in many styles.

Also in terms of timing, *augmentation* and *diminution* are useful techniques. In the former, the same theme is elongated in timing. For instance, one could double the time values so that an original quarter note would become a half note, and so forth. In diminution, the reverse procedure takes place.

Structurally, various themes can be reintroduced in any order the composer chooses (except in theme and variations forms). This flexibility, in conjunction with choreographic movement, presents challenge and considerable possibilities in collaborative work. Choreographers need to consider the total effect of having musical material reintroduced in various ways. If the listener recalls certain musical themes, will they necessarily be associated with specific movement themes as well?

Contrapuntal Music for Theatrical Dance

Among the most interesting musical works choreographed for dance are those created in conjunction with contrapuntal music. This kind of music has simultaneous melodic lines that retain an individual continuity even when played alone. The style is a great contrast to homophonic writing, where one melody is in the foreground while an accompaniment has a varying, sometimes intermittent quality.

The presence of several simultaneous melodic parts often seems to inspire choreographers to employ complementary procedures in movement. The results can be rich intertwinings of many dancers and designs in space. Good examples are Jerome Robbins' ballets *The Musical Offering* and the *Goldberg Variations*, both set to music by J. S. Bach. Among the early modern dancers, Doris Humphrey was particularly noted for her sense of form in using contrapuntal music, for instance in her settings of Bach's Fantasy and Fugue in C Major and the Fugue in C Minor. Drawing attention to analogies in music and choreography, she even titled one dance *The Pleasures of Counterpoint*, with two subsequent sequels.

Contrapuntal Procedures

As in music with melody in the foreground and a distinctly different accompaniment in the background, among the basic materials for contrapuntal composition are motifs. These are developed by techniques of adding pitches, repeating the rhythmic motif using different pitches (sometimes in *sequences,*) modulating to different key centers, and so forth.

Of particular interest in contrapuntal music is the relationship between the flow of the independent voices. This may be *parallel,* if instrumental parts or individual voices progress in more or less continuous relationship separated by a constant size of pitch interval; or *contrary,* if one goes up while the other has a general downward direction; or the patterns may be *oblique* if one part remains fairly stationary while the other has a definite direction one way or the other. *Similar* motion implies the same general flow of direction, but with specific intervallic pitches varying.

Imitation: Free and Canonic

A technique that is apt to come into play frequently for contrapuntal music is *imitation.* Basically, this practice can be grouped into *free imitation, canon,* and *fugue.*

In the first category, as the term suggests, imitation of one voice by another may happen only briefly, switch back and forth between parts, or occur simultaneously.

With *strict* canon, one part exactly repeats the opening line (or *dux,* leader), in the manner of the children's game "follow the leader." However, the imitative entrance can occur at varying intervals of both time and pitch.

Canons can be exact, or free. Interesting variants are *mirror* or *inversion* canons, in which a melody line that goes up a major third in the original dux goes down a major third in a subsequent voice, for example. *Retrograde* or *crab* canons copy the original, note for note, but going backward. Combining the two procedures, one gets retrograde inversion: upside down and backward. The ratios of timing may be kept intact, but either augmented or diminished in note value. (As already explained in connection with variations, a quarter note becomes a half note for augmentation; the reverse procedure applies for diminution.) In *mensuration* canons, the same melody appears simultaneously in several voices, with different rhythmic pacing in regard to time values.

In movement, canon has proven a valuable choreographic tool as well. Among contemporary choreographers, Mark Morris and Eliot Feld are particularly skilled in devising canons in movement. Morris has one work called *Canons in 3/4*, actually set to waltzes played by the pianist Harriet Cavalli; Feld has a work called *Canon* set to music by Steve Reich.

Fugue

The imitation in fugue is more closely structured in regard to pitch and key relationships. But this is still a developmental form in that the exact phrase lengths may be varied, and the total structure grows directly out of the specific thematic material, which may be quite lengthy in its initial statement. (This is in contrast to sectional forms of set phrase lengths and interior cadential pauses. Fugues are more apt to go straight through with little or no pause.)

The general procedure with fugues is basically to intersperse sections of *exposition* (in which the main fugal subject is heard in all the individual voice parts) with sections of freer counterpoint, called *episodes.*

Fugues usually have just one main theme, though double and triple fugues do exist. Initially, the entire fugal theme or *subject* is heard alone in one voice, and then that melody line proceeds with free counterpoint. At no set interval of time, the composer devises a compatible point of entry for a second voice, which usually repeats the fugal theme transposed to the dominant. The third voice enters, typically in the tonic again; then the fourth, in the dominant; and so on until all the voices have entered. Six is about the usual maximum number; three or four voices are most common. After each statement of the theme, each voice in turn progresses in free counterpoint or a more clearly defined *countersubject,* until there is typically a cadence. The entrances then start up again, in another exposition, and the order of the voices need not be the same this time. A similar procedure with contrasting free episodes is followed, for as many sections as the composer chooses. Finally there is a big buildup called a *stretto,* when the fugal entries occur at closer time intervals than before, and this creates a climax for the end of the fugue.

Among the most exciting examples of fugues for students to investigate are the two volumes *The Well-Tempered Clavier* by J. S. Bach. Each includes sets of preludes and fugues for every key. Bach's organ fugues are also masterpieces, and because organists may choose different timbre settings, the entrances of the fugal themes may be particularly easy to follow.

Fugue as a formal procedure is alive and well. For example, jazz artist Stan Kenton titled one of his works simply "Fugue." In dance, choreographer Twyla Tharp employed analogous procedures for her dance work *The Fugue,* though it was performed in silence. Conceived originally for a cast of women, *The Fugue* was recast for men a decade later. Critic Marcia B. Siegel called it

> *Tharp's most rigorous surviving work, a last, pure indulgence in composition before she turned to the broader demands of theater dancing. An exercise in counterpoint, the dance is merely a series of variations on a movement theme, presented without music, in strict linear sequence, with no elaboration or artifice.*[6]

Freely Contrapuntal Pieces: Fuguing Tunes and Fantasias

Although choreographers have not taken much advantage of the fact, there does exist a body of contrapuntal musical literature that is distinctly American in flavor: fuguing tunes paired with homophonic hymns. The structures of the contrapuntal sections are imitative rather than fugal in the strictly formal sense just described. William Billings was among the composers in Colonial times who created vocal pieces in this style. In the twentieth century, Henry Cowell composed eighteen hymn and fuguing tunes, with various instrumentations, from duets all the way up to orchestra. The last, No. 18, for example, is a duet for the unusual pairing of a soprano saxophone and counterbass saxophone.

Other contrapuntal pieces that are freely imitative are *preludes* and *fantasies.* A good example of preludes are the ones paired by key in J. S. Bach's two volumes of *The Well-Tempered Clavier.* His Chromatic Fantasy and Fugue is also recommended listening for changing textures. One of Bach's sons, Carl Philip Emmanuel Bach, wrote many interesting fantasies.

Choreographers may also employ counterpoint and canonic imitation in their movement patterns even when these procedures are absent from the accompanying music. For an absolutely madcap potpourri of materials and procedures, Paul Taylor's *Ab Ovo Usque ad Mala (From Soup to Nuts)* is suggested, to music by "P. D. Q. Bach" (alias our contemporary Peter Schickele—humorist, musicologist, and quite a good composer).

Program and Character Music

In the literature of concert music, particularly the repertoire from the nineteenth century, the overall form of many pieces derives from the unfolding of specifically musical material. But the inspiration, or emotional suggestiveness, may be of a visual image, a character portrayal, or an attempt to tell a narrative story as a *tone poem.*

The piano literature includes thousands of pieces such as *Songs Without Words* by Felix Mendelssohn and the character portrayals by Robert Schumann in *Papillons, Davidsbündlertänze* and *Kinderscenen*. In the orchestra repertoire, Richard Strauss is best known for suggestive tone poems, including *Till Eulenspiegel,* which was used by Nijinsky for his last choreography. Other Strauss tone poems include *Don Juan* and *Ein Heldenleben.* Hector Berlioz's *Harold in Italy,* for solo viola and orchestra, is another favorite tone poem, along with Tchaikovsky's *Romeo and Juliet.* Symphonic colors were also used to suggest places in the real world, in pieces such as *The Planets* by Gustav Holst, or *The Pines of Rome,* by Ottorino Respighi. Mussorgsky's popular *Pictures At An Exhibition* has references to paintings; the musical sections retain the suggestive titles, and the work has been attractive to a number of regional dance companies. Among contemporary musical tone poems, David Del Tredici's *Alice, Part I: In Memory of a Summer Day* was choreographed by Glen Tetley for the National Ballet of Canada.

The symphonic tone poem perhaps best typifies the structure of many scores commissioned specifically for dramatic theatrical dance nowadays. The extensive repertoire commissioned by Martha Graham, of course, set a precedent of dramatic and psychological underpinnings: *Errand Into the Maze,* by Gian-Carlo Menotti; *Diversion of Angels,* by Norman Dello Joio; *Cave of the Heart,* by Samuel Barber; and *Night Journey,* by William Schuman.

Antony Tudor was among the many ballet choreographers in this century who have preferred to use extant music for their theatrical choreography. Tudor said that when he was searching for appropriate music, he would buy recordings and listen at great length. Because his ballets were essentially dramatic, with great attention to emotional nuance, it was important that the music add to the atmosphere in each case. Even for the sole score he ever commissioned, *Undertow,* Tudor gave composer William Schuman only generalized emotional suggestions. Schuman said he was surprised himself to see the specific events that were subsequently portrayed to his music.

For *Lilac Garden,* or *Jardin aux lilas,* Tudor chose the *Poème* for violin and orchestra by Ernest Chausson. When watching this and other Tudor works, students might pay particular attention to the way the choreographer fashioned the psychological underpinnings of his dance to relate to the unfolding of the music.

As with music that has more strictly formal structuring, choreographers and dancers can benefit from understanding how the music is put together, and then being aware of how a specific dance may take musical aspects into account.

Explorations and Assignments

1. Listen to the beginnings of ten pieces from the literature of ballet or modern dance. Using dot and dash shorthand or pictographs, indicate the general nature of the initial motif in each.

2. Using a fake book or collection of folk songs, examine the first few measures of a dozen tunes, and notice the main rhythmic patterns that serve as the seed of each melody. Tap out the rhythm, and demonstrate it in movement.

3. Devise a musical motif based on tone color alone, another based on dynamics alone, and another based on quality of attack or general flow. Mirror these in movement and suggest four different ways of extending each to make a complete form.

4. Using the rhythm of your or another's name, extend the rhythm and nuances into a series of variations, in both music and movement.

5. Create a rondo form in dance movement.

6. Choose one preclassic dance form for investigation. Look it up in an encyclopedia of music, and listen to three recorded examples. Write a one-paragraph summary of the structural common denominators.

7. Devise a brief movement pattern of five to ten counts and teach it to the class. Space the dancers however you wish, but have everyone in turn execute the initial movement pattern in a canonic way and improvise freely after each statement of the theme.

8. Analyze the structure of the musical score of a dance piece in which you are slated to perform. Chart the form on paper. How does the choreography relate to the musical form? Are there any important structural cues that help you as a dancer?

Long-Term Projects

1. Find a musical collaborator, either in the music department, or working with another dance student using percussion. Create a one- to two-minute piece together, either a solo for yourself or including other dancers in the choreography. The music can be scored for any feasible instrumental or vocal combination, but it should be performed live for the class showing. Describe how the collaboration developed and what you learned from it

in regard to relating music and dance. What would you do differently the next time?

2. Choreograph a brief dance that incorporates your own musical invention in an imitative way. Describe the musical form.

3. Devise some directions for a dance improvisation in which the dancers themselves must provide their own music, either vocally or with body percussion. Discuss the form in the context of such previously undetermined music.

4. Working with an instrumental soloist (other than piano or keyboards), choreograph a solo for yourself that includes the visual presence of the musician playing onstage. Discuss your feelings about the particular aesthetic relationships.

ONSTAGE WITH SOMETHING NEW!

W*e rehearsed and performed in silence because music communicates emotion and structure more easily to most people than movement, and it was movement we wanted to explore. Still, many of the questions in our investigation of movement came from lessons I had learned in music.*

—Twyla Tharp

Dance starts with a movement. All music, too, begins by something physically moving to produce sound waves. The preceding chapters have presented many aspects of music and musical collaboration for theatrical dance. These basics provide a never-ending source of materials for creativity in both music and dance.

Possibilities are all around us. One does not have to wait for more time or space or more money or anything else in order to find the beginnings of a new dance/music piece. A pen at hand can tap several timbres and rhythms on my mug of tea, while my other hand pats a firm counterpoint alternating between the tabletop and my chest. Or in silence, a single physical gesture can be varied, often in ways analogous to musical procedures, to suggest an emotion, a story, a character portrayal, a geometric design, the germ of an abstract dance.

Even the most polished theatrical dance and music works began with such limited ingredients, expanding in details of timing, dynamics, form, articulation, and texture. In both the creation and the rehearsal preparation of new dances, one can never give too much attention to the specifics of these ingredients. The materials listed in the bibliogra-

243

244 Part Two / Fundamentals of Music

phy, plus the lists of composers and organizations, should provide you with a blueprint for expanding your knowledge, understanding, and experience of music as a collaborative art.

Communicating with Musicians

Dancers' relationship to the art of music encompasses not only invisible sounds; it also involves musicians who often have less able bodies plus a different kind of training and different concerns in any collaborative venture. Counting has been identified as one area of confusion, and there may be others.

Particularly in an economic climate where musicians may be reluctant to work with dancers, it is an asset for dance teachers and choreographers, as well as for performing dancers, to cultivate effective methods of communicating what is needed in the music at any particular moment to help impel the dancers in their own efforts. Obviously this lays the major onus of knowledge upon dance artists, but in practice their jobs may also include the training of studio musicians who may lack both formal dance training and experience in working directly with dancers. In connection with the creation of collaborative works, it is almost always the choreographer who has ultimate responsibility for all components of any theatrical presentation, including the general style of the music and its specific use in relation to the dance itself.

Adding a touch of humor to the challenges of artistic communication during studio classwork is the following advice from one member of the International Guild of Musicians in Dance. The author is Larry Attaway (longtime West Coast music director for choreographer Bella Lewitzsky and also associate dean at the California Institute of the Arts).[1] This should provide some interesting topics for discussion:

THE TEN COMMANDMENTS FOR ALL TEACHERS OF DANCE

I. Thou shalt not use the word "accompanists" in reference to your dance musicians, but rather treat them as the true collaborative artists they are.

II. Thou shalt never say "four for nothing"; after all if it is for "nothing" then why bother; you, of course, really mean "four to prepare" or "four for tempo," etc.

III. Thou shalt demonstrate all movement sequences in "real" time, giving your musician a chance to see exactly how you want them performed.

IV. Thou shalt refrain from adding any unnecessary expressions of sound while the musician is playing.

V. Thou shalt *never* expect a musician to play more than two classes without a substantial period of rest and rejuvenation.

VI. Thou shalt avoid teaching an entire class in only one meter or tempo.

VII. Thou shalt at all times emphasize dancing with the music being played and encourage students to actually listen to the musician.

VIII. Thou shalt never allow any musical instrument to be used as a desk or ballet barre.

IX. Thou shalt make every effort to converse with your musicians as to your needs in matters of style, quality, timbre, etc.

X. Thou shalt at all times acknowledge the musicians and their efforts at the end of each and every class, and thou shalt pass along this point of etiquette to your students.

Balancing this wish list is an observation made by another guild musician, Gregory Presley of Florida State University: "Overall, dancers are fairly open-minded individuals, and generous with appreciation for musicians who are willing to try to bridge the gap."[2] And speaking of gaps, Bruce Marks, artistic director of the Boston Ballet, is among the many artists who like to envision preprofessional training in which dancers learn more about music and musicians learn more about dance. He comments: "Not enough choreographers are musically trained or know how to read a score. They don't know what it is they want, or how to express what it is they want. More time should be spent in getting musicians and dancers to learn about each others' art forms."[3] This implies, among other things, that most music students could benefit from knowing considerably more than they do about both ballet and modern dance.

The Search for Good Musical Collaborators

Among the most successful efforts to encourage dancers and musicians to exchange views and collaborate creatively has been the Young Composer/Choreographer Program of the American Dance Festival held at Duke University in Durham. Since 1985 the master composer has been codirector Carman Moore, who is apt to put in a plea that dancers use less "dead people's music."[4] He practices what he teaches, collaborating as a composer with choreographers such as Garth Fagan, Ruby Shang, Martha Clarke, Alvin Ailey, Elaine Summers, Anna Sokolow, Brenda Bufalino, and Donald Byrd. All that is in addition to teaching at Yale University and Carnegie Mellon Institute plus composing chamber music and conducting performances.

The qualities that Moore values in young composers might similarly serve dancers who are seeking their own musical collaborators. He suggests:

> The main thing we're listening for is a composer with an individual voice, a really special way with the notes. The composers chosen tend to be facile in their own style, but they do have a distinct style of their own. Some jazz composers will be very advanced and classically oriented. The bulk of the composers come from the new music world, both uptown and downtown. We have a fair number of "downtown-oriented" composers, of the school of Cage and Glass in style. There are some minimalists, but not strict ones.

> We usually reject composers whose pieces are tied by their forms. The thing that you sense is the form at work, as opposed to the music as an organism in itself. Of course the music can unfold through its form, but the important thing is that the music have a life of its own and maybe a little unpredictability about it.

> We've also had lots of electronic music people who have worked with us. However, they have to use the live ensemble. But we also have had people working with MIDIs (musical instrument digital interface equipment) to do sound collages. This has become a big thing in the dance world, partly because of economics: sampling, making pieces of sounds of doors, and so on. Some are very good. But basically, the people who write really nice chamber music end up coming to the American Dance Festival.

For their part, Moore points out, the emerging dance artists come to appreciate music more as a living form. "The choreographers learn that they can have some impact on the music. They can have what they want, as opposed to taking what is given." This is unusual, notes the composer, especially in academic milieus.

> Average musicians don't think about dance; they think of people just sort of cavorting around, and they don't really see the expressive end—until their consciousness is raised. Musicians must be taught dance, and they should have some classes in which they actually get up and move. That's the way music is taught in folk cultures. African musicians have to dance; Indonesian ones—many places. The idea that you can accom-

pany someone doing something when you haven't got the slightest idea of what's going on: that's a result of Western compartmentalization.

I think many musicians and composers see the expressive power of dance, but they don't see the formal wonders of it. You have to let your eyes show you what is there. In contrast, musicians are so trained to the teeth that the better they are, the more they know, then the more suspicious they are of other kinds of artists who may not have techniques with names like quarter notes and fugues.

In connection with initiating collaborations, there are also noticeable hesitations among dance artists. Partly these may stem from a lack of formal education in music as they were being trained. In regard to this situation, Moore is strident: "It is a dereliction of duty for people teaching choreography not to also teach music." In addition, he notices that choreographers often tend to apologize about their art form when they are in the company of musicians: "I think they are impressed by all the hardware that musicians have. Dancers just show up with leotards and shoes; musicians bring all these electronic wonders. The musicians have bodies, but the dancers don't have exterior instruments."

To help bridge such gaps, suggests Moore, "dance should definitely be a part of training for all composers. But it seems that everybody is wrapped up in what they are doing, and it is a big enough challenge just to learn how to compose—period. But I think most composers *can* be interested in the dance, if they were made more aware of it. When they do work with the dancers, then composers are usually very happy to be doing that."

Listening During Performances

We are surrounded by recordings and by the vast array of noises associated with fast-paced modern life to the extent that it has become common for people to tune out a great deal of the sounds that vie for human attention.

How is it with dancers' audiences? Do they listen more carefully when music is partnering barefooted, sneaker-footed, or pointe-shod soloists? Or is the visual impact of theatrical dance so strong that it causes people to blot out much of what they hear? How much attention can audience members appropriately give to the companionate music? If dancers can elicit excitement and other emotions through the sheer force of physical performances alone, then how much difference does it make what music is playing, or whether it is performed the same way each time by a tape or differently by live musicians? And since everything seems to pass by so quickly during theatrical performances, does anyone except a critic care whether the relation of dance movement is finely tuned with musical sounds or not?

Sometimes, without knowing exactly how or why, audiences do discern such relationships, and they are aware of varying degrees of musical sensitivity among dancers onstage. Consequently, despite our cultural habit of not paying close attention to what we hear, dancers (perhaps more than anyone else) need to listen attentively if they are to give their best efforts onstage. More than anything else related to music, dancers need simply to be aware of what it is they hear, moment by moment. If they want to gain artistic success as well as enthusiastic audiences, dancers need big ears.

What is it that successful dance artists most often listen for while they are performing? The following are some insights provided by the first American-born prima ballerina.

Maria Tallchief: Onstage for Balanchine

As a child growing up in Oklahoma, Maria Tallchief was propped on pillows so she could reach the piano keyboard.[5] "My mother thought I was Mozart," she laughs, recalling how she began music lessons a year before her early introduction to ballet at age four. Her piano studies focused on the classical repertoire, and she counted among her favorite compositions those by Mozart, Bach, and Chopin.

By her teenage years, Tallchief could play Chopin's E Minor piano concerto, yet her decisive performance of this work was as a dancer in the legendary Bronislava Nijinska's choreography before a huge audience in the Hollywood Bowl. Later her professional and marital partnership with George Balanchine included interludes of playing piano duets with the ballet master. In her distinguished career with New York City Ballet, many roles were choreographed for her by both Balanchine and Jerome Robbins, notably the repertoire with music composed by Igor Stravinsky. Subsequently, as founding artistic director of Chicago City Ballet, she experienced collaborative music from a different vantage point.

Despite her considerable training and knowledge of music, Tallchief stresses that she did not study the written scores to which she performed as a dancer. Instead, she learned everything she had to know about the music through careful listening during rehearsals. Furthermore, she never had to count, but would listen for cues of harmonic chord changes and other specific musical events, such as instrumental entrances.

"Dance is all about music," the former Balanchine ballerina observes. "The musicality is there in the choreography. You don't have to add anything to it because it has been done by the master musician. First and foremost, Balanchine was the ultimate musician. He was true to what was in the music."

In performing choreography that was so closely related to the scores, Tallchief frequently felt that it was the music that lifted and carried her. Yet her prime consideration was always tempo, the basic speed at which a musical piece is played. "A good beat or pulse was very important," she stresses.

Consequently, the role of the conductor was of tremendous concern. At New York City Ballet, for example, Robert Irving and Hugo Fiorato agreed with Balanchine that the music should be played as written. Tallchief maintains her disdain for conductors and dancers alike who insist upon distorting sections or entire pieces to accommodate the desires of a particular dancer or choreographer. Therefore, at least for the Balanchine repertoire, it is important for dancers to exert some knowledgeable taste about various classical styles of music.

But if the conductor rushes or drags the music during performance, what can the dance artist onstage do to have the tempo altered? If you are Maria Tallchief, "You can *look*," she asserts, simulating an impelling theatrical stare in the direction of an imaginary offending conductor. If you are a lesser light, you may have to learn to adjust your dancing, and give some thought to effective ways to communicate your general desires about tempo, during future rehearsals.

But keeping with the music is only the beginning of artistry. As Maria Tallchief notes, dancers can project a complementary sense of style even if they have not had formal music education. For example, the widely recognized musicality of Suzanne Farrell (another of Balanchine's ballerinas) may have created the impression that she never danced a role the same way twice. Instead, Farrell related to the specific way in which the musical performance was unfolding at any particular moment. This aspect of freshness for each performance is vital, emphasizes Tallchief. "Otherwise we could just have films."

Is such a sense of musicality innate, or is it something that young dancers of today could work on? Tallchief offers an optimistic viewpoint: "I think music studies would be very important if you didn't have very much of a natural musicality, because you can be made to look as if you did." She suggests that students make a conscious effort to keep to the musical beat as well as to listen carefully and be involved with the music. Above all, she cautions, "Don't *disregard* the music."

What Initiates a New Work:
Music or Movement?

Annabelle Gamson has earned an international reputation for her solo evocations of the modern dance pioneer Isadora Duncan. Gamson is also following the example of Duncan by forming her own troupe and choreographing new works, often using pieces from the repertoire of older European concert music. As an example of how such dance creation takes place, she discussed her *Tanzlieder,* set to chamber music and vocal quartets of Brahms.[6]

> *I usually start with some ideas and then listen to a lot of different pieces of music. I start playing around with movement material. But I also think what happens is that I buy a lot of music and put it on periodically and forget about it—but there is a residue that stays.*

> *So I came across an out-of-print recording that was made by the Gregg Smith singers. I love Brahms, but had never heard the vocal quartets. The thing that struck me about them is that they were not operatic, and they weren't really concert pieces. They seemed very intimate, as if people were standing around a piano enjoying music and singing at home. They seemed rather simple and leaned heavily on folk rhythms, folk material.*

> *I was looking for something for the first piece for my company, Dance Solos. I was especially looking for something sweet and gentle and civilized, because there was at the time a great influx of brutality on the stage. I had a reaction to all that and was very eager to do something that was calming and gentle and sweet, on a human scale.*

Touching upon the effect that live music had upon her dancers, Gamson observed: "They couldn't get into a warm bath of music where they know where every note is going to be and just step in and slide through it, because with each live performance, the tempos change, dynamics change, and they have to be very alert to these. I think it's a good lesson."

How are younger artists using music? "Generally speaking, most choreographers—especially ballet choreographers—lean heavily on music," Gamson said. "They depend on it as sort of an impetus." In contrast, Gamson said she is trying to encourage those she studies with at the Carlisle Project and elsewhere to try a different approach.

> *I now start workshops without music and want the dancers and choreographers to find the music within themselves. In the past, they sort of got trapped into having to fit something to a musical score. I am trying to*

work the other way around. Choreography is prime, and choreographers can use music without feeling awed by it.

It's not that I want silence particularly. I'm not against silence; I think silence is golden. But I think the way I would most like to work is to create a dance piece first and then have the music come afterwards, or else have the music created simultaneously with the movement. The main thing is that the piece is initiated from me, not from the music.

Simultaneous Arts, But Independent?

A further declaration of independence from musical structure was put into practice by choreographer Merce Cunningham in his many collaborations with composer John Cage. Speaking with Jacqueline Lesschaeve of his aesthetic viewpoint, Cunningham stated:

> *I think it is essential now to see all the elements of theater as both separate and interdependent. The idea of a single focus to which all adhere is no longer relevant. . . . In music, the advent of electronics also brought about a great change. The possibilities for both the sounds to be used in composing, as well as the methods of composition, were radically enlarged. Time didn't have to be measured in meter, but it could be measured in minutes and seconds, and in the case of magnetic tape in inches in space. The common denominator between music and dance is time. This brings up a new situation for dancers. If they are to involve themselves as dancers with a music measured not in beats but in actual time, how to work with it? Many choose to ignore it. I choose to see it as a necessary next step. A number of the contemporary composers were working in this not-metered way, whether they were using electronic sounds or conventional sounds. My work with John has convinced me that it was possible, even necessary for the dance to stand on its own legs rather than on the music, and also that the two arts could exist together using the same amount of time, each in its own way, one for the eye and the kinesthetic sense, the other for the ear.[7]*

Musical Choices for Contemporary Dance

Taking stock of musical collaboration for modern dance in the late 1950s, composer Lucia Dlugoszewski wrote some thoughts which are equally applicable to the current scene. She observed:

> *The dancer . . . and the composer, especially the composer involved in music for the dance, are confronted with two momentous trends that make more vivid than ever . . . this challenge of what it is to live in the present time of one's life.*

First we have as possible material at our disposal the unknown quantity of magnetic tape. And second, at an ever increasing speed, we have a constant barrage of every conceivable culture other than our own. . . .

The dialogue of existence for the artist is always between the extent of his material and what he will choose from it, and with our range of material widened to a veritable infinity, we have certainly a problem in reorganizing our attitude toward choice. Some musicians and dancers have chosen to pretend all this does not exist. Others in desperation have proclaimed that "everything is good." . . .

The modern dance did the bold unprecedented thing—composed complete movement structures in silence. So the new independent art of dance was born. And so, too, was born the still persisting problem of what music structure would be acceptable to this new dance.

The most imaginative composers working in this field today are still asking: why music for the dance, what music for the dance, and why even consider music and dance as entities that should exist together. . . . The modern history of dance in America certainly indicates that dancers can accept the challenge of any musical material to any degree of difficulty from tape sound to the most intricate "polyphonic" rhythmic events. . . .

It is interesting to review the various solutions that music has proposed in the recent history of new dance concerts. It is a richly varied list including western classical music, western romantic music, various "ethnic" music, jazz, music of the rhythmic structure, twelve tone, modal, and atonal music, involving mathematics, tape sound, structures of chance, ostinato structures, music of near silence, pure silence, and the structure of the heard pulse.[8]

Postmodern Collaboration—or Lack of It

A retrospective look at the way American postmodern choreographers related to music in the 1960s, 1970s, and 1980s is provided by Sally Banes in her definitive article titled "Dancing (with/to/before/on/in/over/after/against/away from/without) the Music: Vissitudes of Collaboration in American Postmodern Choreography," which appeared in the British journal *Choreography and Dance.*[9]

In her summation, Banes touched upon the reactionary discarding of Louis Horst's emphasis of musical structure in regard to choreography. Sometimes this led to presenting dances in total silence, or to depending on the dancers themselves to provide aural vocalizing, talking, or shrieking as deemed appropriate. And using the experiments of Cage and Cunningham as models, younger artists explored varying relationships between music and dance, even going to the extreme in the case of Simone Forti titling one dance *Accompaniment for La Monte's "2 sounds" and La Monte's "2 sounds,"* which ostensibly relegated the choreography to a secondary focus of attention.

As the century progressed, according to Banes, artists tended to concentrate on their own disciplines in a minimalist way. And so in the late sixties and into the seventies, the visual arts, music, and dancing all seemed to be looking inward, exploring the possibilities within their respective crafts.

It was also not a very happy period for musical collaboration. Indeed, as portrayed by Banes, those times could be characterized by some choreographers' outright hostility to music as well as toward musical collaborators in general. The choreographer Yvonne Rainer even went so far as to include her own taped voice for her *Performance Demonstration,* in which she declared that she was a music-hater and was jealous of any encroachment upon her own art of dance, refusing to share the limelight.

Another choreographer who eschewed music during those times was Trisha Brown. Yet after 1981, according to Banes,

> *Brown frankly stated that she was tired of seeing the larger audiences for which she was booked by the eighties walk out during her performances and wondered—in a reversal of the seventies principle in which it was claimed that the music obscured the dance—whether the absence of music created too much discomfort for them even to see the dancing.*

Indeed, as the postmodern choreographers expanded their experimentations, they began coming back to using music, but in vastly different ways than it had been used previously, and drawing upon popular styles that had not been incorporated into concert dance previously. Offering a summation of the 1980s, Banes wrote:

> *If in postmodernism anything can be used, why not old music, beautiful music, highbrow music—as well as the lowbrow, hackneyed, and despised? Why not canned music as well as commissioned? In other words, all the contradictory sides of the dance-music debates seem to coexist comfortably in late Eighties post-modern dance.*

Only a few years later, critic Sally Sommer could offer this analysis in *Dance Ink:*

> *The "Trisha Brown style" of dancing is so persuasive that it has shaped the way a good portion of the younger generation of dancers moves. Yet*

the musical elements—rhythm, harmony, and sound—and the powerful influence they have exerted on the evolution of her style barely get mention. . . . Moreover, Brown has the undeserved reputation of being a choreographer who doesn't use music. In truth, she has used every conceivable kind of music and sound: metronomes, motors, talking, whistling, everyday sounds, sounds of acoustic and electronic and newly invented musical instruments, formal compositions by everyone from Georges Bizet to Bob Dylan, and most often, contemporary works by new-music composers such as Robert Ashley, Laurie Anderson, Peter Zummo, Richard Landry, and Alvin Curran. So the issue isn't that she does not use music, but that she uses music in unconventional ways. . . .

Brown has said that "right now is a particularly interesting period for me because music is probably more central to the dancing than it ever has been before. But the way in which it works as an element goes beyond the fact that it is music. It is another ingredient in the collage.[10]

Dancers: Be Prepared!

The preceding aesthetic viewpoints are only a sampling of the various approaches to music that dancers may encounter when they work with different choreographers. As we approach a new millennium, there are hundreds of dance companies of various sizes and stylistic persuasions, thousands of composers with individual approaches and voices—and millions of dance students. Those dancers who are open to exploring many styles of music may well be the most likely to appear onstage professionally. For whether your interest is ballet or modern dance, it is likely that you will be called on to perform with both concert and popular music, both contemporary sounds and pieces composed in other times and places. For examples of such musical variety for choreographic purposes, one need look no further than the recent programs of the Joffrey Ballet, which has gained wider audiences from its commissioning of new choreography using music by the rock stylist Prince. Or, in contrast, the work that choreographer Mark Morris has done to both contemporary and older music has garnished such reviews as the following by Dale Harris in the *Wall Street Journal:*

Mr. Morris's musical sensitivity is a fundamental feature of his artistic personality. Not only is his taste eclectic, it is original: The programs at the Grand Ballroom encompassed Bach . . . Vivaldi, Haydn, Alexander Tcherepnin, Henry Cowell, Lou Harrison, Bob Wills and His Texas Playboys, the Louvin Brothers and the Violent Femmes. In every case, the choreography realizes the essential character of the music, both structurally and stylistically.[11]

Musicality and Garth Fagan

Another company that has won repeated praise, both for its musical component and the musicality of the dancers themselves, is Garth Fagan Dance. Complimenting his own company members, the choreographer/artistic director says: "They are dancers of great nuance and musical sensibilities. I love music, so I impress that on them daily in class."[12]

Where did Garth Fagan's own musicality come from? He reminisces a bit about his childhood in the Caribbean island of Jamaica:

> I started to learn the piano. But we got into problems over the fingering, and (arguing twerp that I was) I said "forget it." Anyway, I always heard good music in the home. They also had, in Jamaica, lunch-hour concerts at the art gallery. My parents used to trot me out there every week. I used to hate it, as a kid, because I had to sit still and be quiet. Fat ladies were singing and violins were squeaking, and it didn't mean anything to me. Anyhow, they wouldn't listen to my fussing, and I always got a malted milk afterwards. That was the bribe: they would take me to the soda fountain. I don't know exactly when I started enjoying the concerts so much that I would be punished by not being taken.

The sounds Fagan heard as a boy encompassed European classical music, traditional Jamaican forms, and American jazz—including that of Duke Ellington, whom the dancer came to consider one of his informal musical mentors. Fagan recalls their meeting in the early 1960s: "I was just a precocious young man. Ellington taught me a lot about jazz, about professionalism, a lot about going *further*, working harder." Did he teach the choreographer anything about specific jazz forms? "Just in conversation, and by example. Then I followed him around the country, wherever. To this day, I am a big Ellington fan, and I have done a dance in tribute to him, *Postscript Posthumous Ellington*, to his scores."

What is important to Fagan in setting dances with existing music?

> To respect the composer and the musician. To let the music live and breathe where it is full and rich in its own right. As in the Dvorak cello piece [for Oatka Trail], what are you going to do with that crescendo but just let it be? Why compete with it? Why not just let it pour over the body? Why not get in the underpinnings of the score, as opposed to just the surface things? I hate music visualization in choreography, where the choreography also just goes "plinky plunky plinky plunky."

No one would ever accuse this choreographer of doing that. But how does he get pertinent information in order to build a dance with whatever music he chooses? "From listening, but from listening seven million times before I even presume to use a score. I get a tape, and for months before I work on a piece, it's in my car, it's in my cassette player, it's in my house. So it's always going."

When it comes to performances, Fagan's preference is to dance to live music, and to have specially composed scores. "That is what we *all* prefer, and that is the way it ought to be. But because of costs, we can't always do it. But it is so much better for the audience and the dancers —and the composer too—if the music is played live, by competent musicians."

In the case of Garth Fagan Dance, "competent" is a decided understatement. He has had some of the world's outstanding musicians collaborate with him, including recently the trumpeter/composer Wynton Marsalis, who not only created the full-evening score for *Griot New York*, but also took his place in the pit and played the trumpet part while someone else conducted. Onstage, there were as many smiles as there were in the audience.

Such events are not easy to come by. Fagan acknowledges that "most of the time when you use live music, you have to compromise in the rehearsal time, because we can only afford so much. And then there are questions of tempi that may never get straightened out." Nevertheless, the advantage of working directly with a composer, he explains, is that everything can develop simultaneously and in a related way.

> When I am working on a choreographic piece—and the philosophical piece—I can only get "there" once. When I am into a particular piece, I work like hell to get my total being and consciousness there. I just can't stop it and say OK I'll pick it up next week. It doesn't happen like that: then I would be doing journey work, and at this stage of my career, I insist on doing truly inspired work.

That audiences feel and admire the results is suggested by this comment of Jamake Highwater:

> Oatka Trail *also underscores Fagan's exceptional musicality, which never allows him simply to supplement the emotional impact of the music or merely to articulate the obvious cadences. Garth Fagan's choreography is a response to the music, not an imitation of it.*"[13]

Carolyn Adams: Coaching Students for Auditions and Careers

Carolyn Adams, best known to theater audiences as a principal dancer with the Paul Taylor Company for seventeen years, has yet to stop moving. Carving out a second career for herself, she now wears multiple hats: as a teacher of modern dance at The Juilliard School and City College of New York, as director of education at Jacob's Pillow, and as artistic director of the School of Dance at the New York State Summer School of the Arts in Saratoga Springs. With a view to the youngest dancers of all, she is codirector of the Harlem Dance Studio with her sister, Julie A. Strandberg.

This dancer's own training was mainly with Bessie Schönberg at Sarah Lawrence College. In January of her senior year, she attended the auditions being held by Paul Taylor for his company. The session started at one o'clock. By six o'clock, Adams began to be worried—but not about the audition. She thanked Taylor but told him she had to leave to finish a term paper that was due. "Oh," replied the choreographer, "but you're the one I wanted!"[14]

Fortunately things were arranged so that the young dancer could finish her term paper, finish her college degree, and learn some of the Taylor repertoire. A few months after graduation, she joined the company, traveled around the world, and was on occasion partnered by guest artists including Mikhail Baryshnikov. Upon accepting her, Taylor told Adams: "You have nothing to prove here; you have only to dance." Nearly three decades later, Carolyn Adams herself says: "Our profession is all about show, tell, and remember. Dancers teach one another all the time."

Reflecting upon what onstage performance had felt like when she was the one centerstage, Adams says, "I think the music is what dancing is about for me. If I couldn't make sense out of the movement in relationship to the music, then nothing worked."

With Paul Taylor, sometimes the music used in rehearsal is not what audiences hear during performance. Carolyn Adams recalls:

> *Paul started more pieces to Vivaldi, and then changed the music. He set* Scudorama *to* The Rite of Spring—*did the whole piece, then called in another composer. He decided that was not going to be his* Sacre. *[He later set the Stravinsky score as* The Rehearsal.*] He choreographed my duet in* Public Domain *to the sound track from the movie* Barbarella. *[Later a score by Xenakis was substituted.] I held onto that* Barbarella *tune forever after. There was no discernible pulse in the Xenakis; there will be periods of silence and bleeps. So I hummed that movie tune for ten years and stayed with its beat.*

When Taylor would change from Vivaldi to Bach, that did not seem like such a difficult transition. Adams says:

> *What is much harder for a dancer—it's a dancer's nightmare—is to have the same piece of music played differently, rendered differently. It*

makes you realize that you in fact do build your dance interpretation on the structure and nuances you hear in the music, and that if that changes, the whole emphasis is changed also. I don't mind so much a change in the tempo, within a certain range: if it is much too fast, you can't do it; if it is much too slow, you can't stand on one leg. But within a certain range, tempo variation is not so critical as a change in the shading of the phrasing. Does a change in tempo really alter the quality of the dance? That is something dancers are really concerned about.

Turning her attention to her current role as mentor to a fresh generation of professional dancers, the dancer/educator suggests:

I don't think everybody hears music in the same way or listens with the same kind of intensity at the same point. Part of the goal is to let students know that at some point in the process there needs to be a contact with the sound. It's a very personal thing. How do they gain access to it?

I happen to hear the music first. The first thing that I hear or see or understand is the music. We talk about this in connection with auditions: What do you see first? What do you hear first? At an audition, very often the movement will be shown without the music. So most dancers express relief when the music comes on, because they have been shown a step, and the music is what tells them how to dance it. Especially in jazz combinations, music has that connotation of being the thing that completes the dance. We are trying to put the dancers in charge of the process of learning. But at what point do dancers need to listen most attentively: is it immediately, or after the movement has been learned? Do they build movement phrases and sound phrases together? There may not be a single way of doing this, but somehow we have to give students access to the process of listening.

It is difficult to generalize about the musical background of today's dance students, but Adams ventures some reservations.

They haven't had a lot of exposure to music, and so they come and don't know how to count. They can get their legs up and turn out, but they don't really know how to listen to music. They don't seem to have a very wide musical palette; they don't know about a lot of musical forms. They tend to listen to one kind of music, and even in school are not exposed to different styles.

Dancers need ongoing access to a variety of music. They also have to deal with somebody else's interpretation of that music, and match that against the way they themselves hear it. I realize that we are all editing all the time, and hearing different aspects of sound, making our own for-

mat of them. When somebody else (the choreographer) says, "This is the way I am going to organize movement in relationship to these sounds," you have to make an adjustment, though it may be an unconscious one.

For example, in Junction, *Paul was listening and seeing and visualizing the action of a bow [of a string player]. To understand that is to be able to approach that scribble movement very differently than if you were asking simply how is he counting. I think you become musical to the extent that you try to incorporate the way you are hearing sounds into the way you are being asked to move to them. These are not always the same thing. I think dancers learn to hear in the choreographic process, by trying to mesh what they hear with what somebody else is hearing. That's where the communication, the transfer, takes place.*

When Carolyn Adams teaches "her" part in *Aureole* to students, she says:

I don't talk about the music [Handel's Concerto Grosso in G *and excerpts from* Alexander's Feast*]. I talk about the timing. I start out by saying that* Aureole *was built on the notion of syncopation, which always surprises people. So I tell them it is the* unevenness *we are looking for. Then I immediately make the analogy between unevenness and weight shift. What is creating the rhythmic unevenness is the fact that Taylor has the dancer lingering longer on one foot than on another. The relationship is not "tick-tock, tick-tock." It's "down-UP—; down-UP—." There is a reason why the weight is shifting, and it relates to the syncopation. Even if students learned the part in silence or in counts, those musical ideas would have to be imparted, or dancers won't be able to reproduce the movement.*

What else does this dancer do when passing her art on to someone else? "I sing. Not all music is hummable. It is very hard to do *Runes;* it's pretty hard to hum that little tune," Adams says with a laugh. "But *Runes* is so drivingly rhythmic, you could almost teach it with a metronome. There, you would focus on the quality and the accents, the sharpness: what's soft and what isn't. But the movement in that dance is often running against the sounds. The music is sort of hammering out, and the dance has varying degrees of weight and texture."

Taylor sets his dances with counts. Adams qualifies that: "Except, there are places where we will go five-six-seven-eight—and then we wait for some kind of a bong, and nobody seems to agree upon whether it is seven counts until the bong, or seven and a half. In *Runes,* without those bongs you are totally lost."

Nowadays, when Adams watches other dancers during classes, auditions, and performances, she finds that she does notice when someone is particularly musical.

Who is this performer?

> *The dancer who instinctively knows how to find all the room for interpretation within a phrase. Without in any way distorting what is being asked, there is all that space for physical nuance to take place. To find that: to be inside the time and inside the sound; to find that movement range within the sound is really what it's about. When one sees that, it isn't something that you can verbalize. You are just absolutely—ZAP!—drawn to it. It is inescapable. It has nothing to do with being on the beat.*

Toward Artistry

Among contemporary troupes that balance ongoing presentations of modern classics with new dance works is the Limón Company. The company's current artistic director, Carla Maxwell, was also the last dancer trained personally by José Limón. She is particularly in touch with aspiring young dancers of today because the company gives many residency workshops in connection with performances at colleges and universities. What does she notice about the way dance students relate to music?

> *I've been bugging my classes like crazy because they don't listen and they don't phrase. I say to them, "You are not doing an exercise; you are making a physical statement. You want to communicate something. So where is the beginning, and where is the end? If you don't finish with the measure, maybe that's not the end. And if you want to go on, you won't be ready for what comes next. Make yourself finish at the end!"*[15]

Maxwell touches upon the musicality of the company's founder:

> *Every year José made a new piece, and he either had a new score commissioned or he found some incredible piece of music. More than almost any other choreographer I know, José was incredibly musical. That was the worst sin to him: if you didn't dance with the music. Music was not a background; there was a marriage between the dance and the music. The elements that created a dance work were the choreography and the music. Music was never merely accompaniment. José used it as a musician would; he never Mickey Moused it.*

Such observations are underscored by Carlos Orta, the principal dancer who now performs many of the roles Limón created for himself. He advises:

> *Anybody who wants to be a dancer should study music. In dance, there has to be a harmony. You may know nothing formally about music, but there is still a sense of harmony: you will see that something is happening, and be with it. You have a sense of being there. You are making poetry, almost painting—in space.*

In performance, Orta projects a strong impression, using his arms to carve out space and make it his own while portraying Limón's villainous Traitor, or the tragic but noble Moor, or when gifting the audience with an allegory of fresh life in *There Is a Time*. There is in his theatrical presence a commanding style, a sense of timing, and a beautiful expression that all serve to make his performances extraordinarily compelling—and musical.

Speaking of his personal experience of Limón's art, Orta says: "The basis of José's dance was so organic, in harmony with whatever he was doing. I found he used the space even when he was doing inner, introverted moods. There was an intensity, a countertension: one part of the body might be tense, another relaxing. He used this theme of the universe: tension and relaxation."

How does this dancer know where to be at any particular moment in a dance? "Somehow, it's like the birds in the ocean: they don't have counts; they *feel* each other," Orta says. It should be the same with music and dancers.

So highly did José Limón value the relationship of music and dance that he once entitled an address to Juilliard students, "Dancers Are Musicians Are Dancers."[16] Maxwell emphasizes the point:

> *He really believed that if you weren't a musician, you could not be a good dancer. What he meant by that was this: if you didn't know how to phrase, if you didn't know how to use dynamics and texture, if you didn't know how to relate to the music that you're dancing to.*
>
> *Music is a partner; it's not something that is just keeping a beat for you. The music is swelling: what do you do? Does that make your movements swell? It might. Or are you going to go in contrast to that? If it is an adagio, you might give something very fast against it. But how do you use the music so that it becomes an organic living thing, where the music and the dance come together to make one statement? If you take every-*

thing away from your dances—costumes, stage, lights, everything (and this has happened to us on tour when the tape machine has broken, or the lights), then you should still be able to have a sense of a musical *dance.*

I told the dancers this morning when we were rehearsing one of the sections of There Is a Time, *"The music is coming out of the soles of your feet, and it can't happen unless your rhythm is implicit. It must seem as if the music is coming out of your body."*

appendixes

appendix 1

Suggested Listening
and Viewing

This section provides listings of theatrical dance works, companies, and choreographers that are noteworthy for their musical scores, the ways in which choreographed movement relates to music, or the exceptional musicality of the dancers themselves. It is recommended that students see live performances whenever possible.

For current audiovisual materials, see the Dance Films Association's *Dance Film and Video Guide,* compiled by Deirdre Towers (Pennington, N.J.: Dance Horizons/Princeton Book Company, Publishers, 1991). In the near future, some of the considerable filmings from the television productions of *Dance in America* may soon be made available commercially; currently it is not legal to show any tapes of these programs in public settings. For current availability of sound recordings, consult the separate Schwann catalogues available in record stores for jazz, popular, and classical styles.

Ballets

Ballets are listed chronologically with composers of scores, choreographers, and performances of unusual interest listed where appropriate. Notice in connection with these scores the tempos, meters, dramatic episodes, character of melodies, textures, orchestration, use of accents and dynamics, and specific rhythms in relation to the choreographed dance movements, plus various sections that include national character dances. Depending upon library materials available to students, it is also recommended that recordings be heard in connection with score reading.

Classical Ballets

Giselle, Adolphe Adam. Dance Theatre of Harlem has an unusual American setting.

Coppélia, Léo Delibes. Boston Ballet does a nice version.

Sylvia, Delibes. Royal Ballet stagings.

Don Quixote, Ludwig Minkus. American Ballet Theatre video with Mikhail Baryshnikov.

La Bayadère, Minkus. Staging by Natalia Makarova for American Ballet Theatre.

Swan Lake, Pyotr Ilyich Tchaikovsky. Many stagings in traditional style. Nureyev's setting for Paris Opera Ballet was quite unusual.

Sleeping Beauty, Tchaikovsky. Live performances by the London Royal Ballet are apparently based quite closely on the original Petipa choreography. Also recommended is the Lar Lubovitch version for ice skaters, on video.

The Nutcracker, Tchaikovsky. Balanchine's setting for New York City Ballet.

Raymonda, Alexander Glazunov. Not often staged now, but listen to a recording of the music. Various companies do excerpts.

The Seasons, Glazunov. Again, listen to a recording, for the orchestration.

Twentieth-Century Ballet

TO SCORE BY CLAUDE DEBUSSY

L'après-midi d'un faune. Joffrey Ballet reconstruction of choreography by Vaslav Nijinsky. A totally different story was choreographed by Jerome Robbins for New York City Ballet, as a duet for two contemporary dancers in a studio.

TO EARLY SCORES BY IGOR STRAVINSKY

Petroushka. American Ballet Theatre staging.

Firebird. Dance Theatre of Harlem.

The Rite of Spring. Joffrey Ballet reconstruction of choreography by Nijinsky. Paul Taylor's choreography uses the two-piano version and is titled *The Rehearsal.*

Les Noces. Modern reconstructions of original choreography by Bronislava Nijinska.

BY SERGEI PROKOFIEV

The Prodigal Son. Choreography by George Balanchine.

Romeo and Juliet. The Bolshoi Ballet mounting.

Peter and the Wolf. Children's ballet for identifying instruments of the orchestra.

TO SCORES BY MAURICE RAVEL

Ma Mère l'Oyle (Mother Goose). Amusing resetting by Jerome Robbins.

La Valse. Originally set by Nijinska. Later setting by Balanchine incorporates the composer's *Valses Nobles et Sentimentales.*

Piano Concerto in G. Choreography by Jerome Robbins.

Daphnis and Chloe. Originally set by Michel Fokine.

Le Tombeau de Couperin. Choreography by Balanchine.

TO MUSIC BY JACQUES OFFENBACH

Gaité Parisienne. Choreography by Leonide Massine. A lighthearted ballet. Reconstruction by American Ballet Theatre is lavishly costumed.

CHOREOGRAPHY BY AGNES DE MILLE

Rodeo, score by Aaron Copland. American Ballet Theatre.

Fall River Legend, score by Morton Gould. Dance Theatre of Harlem.

The Informer, arrangement of Irish music. American Ballet Theatre.

ALL CHOREOGRAPHY BY JEROME ROBBINS
FOR NEW YORK CITY BALLET, INCLUDING:

Fancy Free and *Facsimile,* Leonard Bernstein.

Interplay, Morton Gould.

Dances at a Gathering, The Concert, and *Other Dances,* all three to piano music by Frederic Chopin.

Fanfare, to Benjamin Britten's music, *A Young Person's Guide to the Orchestra.*

Glass Pieces, Philip Glass.

Ives, Songs, Charles Ives.

ALL CHOREOGRAPHY BY GEORGE BALANCHINE
FOR NEW YORK CITY BALLET, INCLUDING:

Serenade, Pëtr Tchaikovsky.

Divertimento No. 15, Wolfgang Amadeus Mozart.

Concerto Barocco, J. S. Bach.

Jewels, Gabriel Fauré, Igor Stravinsky, Pëtr Tchaikovsky.

Symphony in C, Georges Bizet.

The Four Temperaments, Paul Hindemith.

Le Tombeau de Couperin, Maurice Ravel.
Variations pour une porte et un soupir, Pierre Henry.
Vienna Waltzes, Johann Strauss the Younger.

To music by Igor Stravinsky:

Agon
Apollo
Danses Concertantes
Duo Concertant
Movements for Piano and Orchestra
Violin Concerto

ALL CHOREOGRAPHY BY ELIOT FELD,
FOR HIS OWN COMPANY, INCLUDING:

El Salon Mexico, Copland.
Harbinger, Prokofiev.
Skara Brae, traditional Breton, Scottish, and Welsh music.
Endsong
Contra Pose, C. P. E. Bach.
Over the Pavements, Charles Ives.
Intermezzo, Johannes Brahms.

ALL CHOREOGRAPHY BY ANTONY TUDOR,
INCLUDING:

The Leaves Are Fading, Anton Dvořák.
Jardin aux lilas, Ernest Chausson.
Dark Elegies, Gustav Mahler.

Ballet Companies

American Ballet Theatre
Atlanta Ballet
Ballet West
Boston Ballet
Dance Theatre of Harlem
Feld Ballets/NY
Les Grands Ballets Canadiens
Houston Ballet
Joffrey Ballet
Louisville Ballet

Miami City Ballet
Milwaukee Ballet
Missouri State Ballet
National Ballet of Canada
New York City Ballet
Pacific Northwest Ballet
Paris Opera Ballet
Pennsylvania Ballet
Royal Ballet (London)
Royal Danish Ballet
Royal Winnipeg Ballet
San Francisco Ballet

Modern Dance

Following is a list of choreographers with their own companies:

Alvin Ailey American Dance Theater
Battery Dance Company (Johathan Hollander)
Merce Cunningham
Laura Dean Dancers and Musicians
Jean Erdman
Garth Fagan
Annabelle Gamson/Dance Solos
Martha Graham
Danny Grossman
Erick Hawkins
Bill T. Jones/Arnie Zane Company
Phyllis Lamhut
Rachel Lampert and Dancers
Bella Lewitzsky
José Limón
Lar Lubovitch
Meredith Monk/The House
Mark Morris Dance Group
Jennifer Muller/The Works
Alwin Nikolais/Murray Louis Dance
Pilobolus Dance Theatre
Ririe-Woodbury Dance Company
Kei Takei/Moving Earth
Paul Taylor Dance Company
Twyla Tharp
Urban Bush Women (Jawolle Willa Jo Zollar)

Wild Angels Unlimited (Meg Wolfe)
Sallie Wilson
Kevin Wynn Collection

Other Recommended Companies and Choreographers

American Tap Dance Orchestra
Ballet Hispanico
Chuck Davis African-American Dance Company
Katherine Dunham
George Faison
Donald McKayle
Michael Moschen
National Dance Institute (Jacques d'Amboise's organization
    for children)
New York Baroque Dance Company

Traditonal Styles

Audiences have to catch companies visiting from abroad as luck allows,
or through videotapes. The following are especially recommended.

annual Dance Africa weekend festivals at the Brooklyn Academy
    of Music
annual Scottish Games in Greenwich, Connecticut
gatherings of the Country Dance and Song Society
historical workshops at the University of Maryland in Towson,
    Maryland
dance programs at Williamsburg Restoration
American Indian Dance Theatre
Kodo Drummers of Japan
Flamenco Puro from Spain
Ballet Folklorico de Mexico
Moiseyev Dance Company
Hungarian State Dance Company
National Dance Company of Senegal
Javanese-style gamelan concerts at Wesleyan, Cornell, and San Jose State
    universities
Inbal Dance Company from Israel
Ladyship Black Mambazo singers

Jazz Dance

For proper attention to show styles, students are referred to titles in the bibliography. At the very least, however, films by Fred Astaire, the recent taping of the Broadway show *Black and Blue* for television, and all the work of Bob Fosse are recommended.

Lifetime Listening and Viewing

With the demands of their own training, young dancers understandably cannot study all the collaborative styles of the world. But particularly for those who work on their own choreography, it can be stimulating to experience and analyze at least a few examples of the following styles: medieval dance forms and Renaissance dances from Europe; national character dances from Europe; traditional West African drumming and dancing; preclassic court dances of Europe; Romantic ballet; classic ballet; ragtime; early twentieth-century ballroom forms; American square and contra dancing; jazz dance as seen in Broadway shows and Hollywood musicals; break dancing; disco styles; reconstructions of pioneer modern dance choreographers in the U.S.; Latin American popular styles; sacred and ritual dancing from Asia; rock video dancing; classic tap dancing; dance portrayals in operas and musical comedy.

Even brief sampling and analysis of the various kinetic-musical relationships found in these varied styles may serve as an antidote to the tunnel vision that dancers and musicians alike may experience in concentrating on their own particular brands of collaborative work.

In regard to purely musical works, it can be noted that the large existing treasure of American compositions and improvised jazz works have only begun to be used for modern dance choreography. Students are urged to explore the catalog of Composers Recordings, the Louisville recordings, and the Smithsonian collections of early jazz classics.

Unfortunately, the New Music Distribution Service, which used to provide mail order customers with a practical way of buying unusual contemporary music recorded on small labels, has ceased operation. No other vendor has stepped in to take its place. Consequently, university lending libraries are probably students' best source for listening explorations. One helpful volume is Ted Libbey's *The NPR Guide to Building a Classical CD Collection.*

appendix 2

Sources of Information on Contemporary Music

American Composers Alliance, 170 West 74th Street, New York, NY 10023

American Music Center, 30 West 26th Street, Suite 10001, New York, NY 10010-2011

American Orff-Schulwerk Association (for Music and Movement Education) P.O. Box 391089, Cleveland, OH 44139-8089.

American Society of Composers, Authors and Publishers (ASCAP), One Lincoln Center Plaza, New York, NY 10023

Broadcast Music, Inc. (BMI), 320 West 57th Street, New York, NY 10019

Canadian Music Centre, 20 St. Joseph St., Toronto ON M44, 1J9, Canada

Composers Recordings Inc. (CRI), 73 Spring Street, Room 506, New York, NY 10012

International Guild of Musicians in Dance, c/o Larry Attaway, 33105 Santiago Road, #23, Acton, CA 93510

International League of Women Composers, Box 670, Southshore Road, Point Peninsula, Three Mile Bay, NY 13693

Library of Congress, Music Division, Washington, D.C. 20036

Meet the Composer, 2112 Broadway, Suite 505, New York, NY 10023

The New York Public Library for the Performing Arts, Lincoln Center, New York, NY 10023

San Francisco Performing Arts Library and Museum, 399 Grove Street, San Francisco, CA 94102

Society of Composers, Inc., P.O. Box 296, Old Chelsea Station, New York, NY 10011-9998

Sonneck Society for American Music, P.O. Box 476, Canton, MA 02021

Volunteer Lawyers for the Arts, 1285 Avenue of the Americas, New York, NY 10019

World Music Institute, 49 West 27th Street, Suite 810, New York, NY 10001

appendix 3

Workshops in Choreographic Collaboration

American Dance Festival, P.O. Box 6098, College Station, Durham, NC 27708-6097

The Carlisle Project, 9 South Pitt Street, Carlisle, PA 17013

Jacob's Pillow Dance Festival, P.O. Box 287, Lee, MA 01238

Regional Dance Craft of Choreography Conferences. Held in different locations annually. Consult *Dance Magazine* or contact main office, 1570 S. Dairy Ashford, #200, Houston, TX 77077

appendix 4

Composers of Interest to Dancers

This is a select list, encompassing composers of many styles of music, mostly from North and South America, Europe, and Russia. Some are contemporary; some were born in the nineteenth century but died in this century. Particular care has been taken to include those whose music has been used for modern dance. The names, listed alphabetically by composer, are intended as an ongoing checklist for listening explorations, because many public and college libraries include lending collections of recordings. Those names indicated by an asterisk (*) are current members of the International Guild of Musicians in Dance.

Adams, John
Albeniz, Isaac
Amram, David
Anderson, Laurie
Anderson, Leroy
Antheil, George
*Attaway, Larry
Ballard, Louis
Ballou, Esther Williamson
Barber, Samuel
Bartók, Béla
Bauer, Marion
Beach, Amy
Beach, Louise
Becker, John
Beeson, Jack
*Benford, Robert

Bennett, Richard Rodney
Bennett, Robert Russell
Berg, Alban
Berio, Luciano
Berlin, Irving
Berners, Lord
Bernstein, Leonard
Blitzstein, Marc
Bloch, Ernest
Bolcom, William
Bolling, Claude
Bond, Victoria
Boulanger, Lili
Boulez, Pierre
Bowles, Paul
Brant, Henry
Britten, Benjamin

*Brooks, Ray
Browne, Earle
Burleigh, Henry Thacker
Busoni, Ferruccio
Cage, John
*Cameron-Wolfe, Richard
Canteloube de Malaret, Marie-
  Joseph
Carlos, Wendy
Carter, Elliott
Casella, Alfredo
Castelnuovo-Tedesco, Mario
Chaminade, Cécile
Chavez, Carlos
Chihara, Paul
*Childs, John
Chou Wen-chung
Claflin, Avery
*Colman, John
Copland, Aaron
Cowell, Henry
Crawford, Ruth
Creston, Paul
Crumb, George
Davidovsky, Mario
Davies, Peter Maxwell
Debussy, Claude
*DeLewis, Marjorie Landsmark
Dello Joio, Norman
Del Tredici, David
Dett, Nathaniel
Diamond, David
Dlugoszewski, Lucia
Dodge, Charles
Dohnanyi, Ernst von
Dowdell, Linda
Dukas, Paul
Dupré, Marcel
El-Dabh, Halim
Elgar, Edward
Falla, Manuel de
Fauré, Gabriel
Feldman, Morton

Fine, Irving
Fine, Vivian
Finney, Ross Lee
*Follett, Karen M.
Foss, Lucas
Françaix, Jean
Freestone, Norma Reynolds
Ge Gan-ru
*George, Ron
Gershwin, George
Gideon, Miriam
*Gilbert, Natalie
*Gilbert, Pia
Ginastera, Alberto
Glanville-Hicks, Peggy
Glass, Philip
Glazunov, Alexander
Glière, Reingold
Goldmark, Karl
Gould, Morton
Grainger, Percy
Granados, Enrique
Green, Ray
Harris, Roy
Harrison, Lou
Hazard, Ben
Herbert, Victor
Hindemith, Paul
Holst, Gustav
Honegger, Arthur
Hoover, Katherine
Horst, Louis
Hovhaness, Alan
Howe, Mary
Husa, Karel
Ibert, Jacques
Ince, Kamran
Ives, Charles
Ivey, Jean Eichelberger
Janáček, Leoš
Johnson, Hunter
Jolas, Betsy
Kabalevsky, Dmitri

*Kaplan, Robert
Kay, Ulysses
*Ketchum, Gregory
Khachaturian, Amram
Kodály, Zoltán
Kolb, Barbara
Křenek, Ernst
Kubik, Gail
Kupferman, Meyer
Laderman, Ezra
Lambert, Constant
Lanner, Josef
Larsen, Libby
Lecuona, Ernesto
Lehár, Franz
León, Tania
Lester, Eugene
Ligeti, Gyorgy
Lloyd, Norman
Lloyd Webber, Andrew
Luening, Otto
Lutyens, Elisabeth
Lyadov, Anatol
MacDowell, Edward
Mahler, Gustav
Mamlok, Ursula
Marsalis, Wynton
Martinu, Bohuslav
Massenet, Jules
Mayuzumi, Toshiro
McBride, Robert
McPhee, Colin
*Meeker, Jess
*Mehocic, Beth
Menotti, Gian Carlo
Messager, André
Messiaen, Olivier
Middleton, Robert
Milhaud, Darius
Mompou, Federico
Monk, Meredith
Moore, Carman
Moore, Douglas

Moszkowski, Moritz
*Moulton, William
Musgrave, Thea
Nabokov, Nicholas
Nazareth, Ernesto
Nielsen, Carl
Nin-Culmel, Joaquin
Nordoff, Paul
North, Alex
Nowak, Lionel
Nunlist, Juli
Oliveros, Pauline
Orff, Carl
*Otis, Mollye
Partch, Harry
Peeters, Flor
Perry, Julia
Piazzolla, Astor
Pinkham, Daniel
Pinto, Octavio
Piston, Walter
Porter, Quincy
Poulenc, Francis
*Presley, Gregory
Prokofiev, Sergei
Puccini, Giacomo
Rachmaninoff, Sergei
Ran, Shulamit
Ravel, Maurice
Reich, Steve
Reiser, Joseph
Respighi, Ottorino
Revueltas, Silvestre
Reynolds, Roger
Riegger, Wallingford
Rieti, Vittorio
Riley, Terry
Rittmann, Trude
Rodrigo, Joaquin
Rozsa, Miklos
Rudhyar, Dane
*Rush, Stephen
Saint-Saëns, Camille

Satie, Erik
Schafer, R. Murray
*Schenk, Richard
Schickele, Peter
Schlenck, John
Schnittke, Alfred
Schoenberg, Arnold
Schonthal, Ruth
Schuller, Gunther
Schuman, William
Schwantner, Joseph
Scoville, Jon
Scriabin, Alexander
Searle, Humphrey
Sessions, Roger
Shields, Alice
Shostakovitch, Dmitri
Sibelius, Jean
Siegmeister, Elie
Simons, Netty
Smith, Hale
Smith, William O.
Sousa, John Philip
*Spangenberg, Saul
Stevens, Halsey
Still, William Grant
Strauss, Richard
Stravinsky, Igor
Surinach, Carlos
Swados, Elizabeth
Szymanowski, Karol

Tailleferre, Germaine
Takemitsu, Toru
Talma, Louise
Tansman, Alexandre
Tcherepnin, Alexander
Thomson, Virgil
Torke, Michael
Tower, Joan
Tudor, David
Turina, Joaquin
Twining, Toby
Ussachevsky, Vladimir
Van Appledorn, Mary Jeanne
*VanDerBeek, Maximus
van Tieghem, David
Varèse, Edgard
Vaughan-Williams, Ralph
Villa-Lobos, Heitor
*Watson, Gwendolyn
Weber, Ben
Webern, Anton
Weill, Kurt
Westergaard, Peter
Wolpe, Stefan
Wuorinen, Charles
Xenakis, Iannis
*Yoken, David
*York, Donald
Zaimont, Judith Lang
Zwilich, Ellen Taaffe

American Ragtime, Swing, and Jazz Artists

This is a brief personal selection, again alphabetical. For details, consult Gunther Schuller's two-volume history of jazz, plus *The New Grove Dictionary of Jazz.* For a discography, consult Max Harrison, Charles Fox, and Eric Thacker, *The Essential Jazz Records* (New York: Da Capo, 1984) and the current Schwann catalogs available in record stores.

Armstrong, Louis
Art Ensemble of Chicago
Astaire, Fred

Aufderheide, May
Basie, William "Count"
Beiderbecke, Bix

Blake, Eubie
Brubeck, Dave
Carmichael, Judy
Chauvin, Louis
Coleman, Ornette
Coltrane, John
Corea, Chick
Davis, Miles
Dorsey, Jimmy
Eckstine, Billy
Eldridge, Roy
Ellington, Edward Kennedy
  "Duke"
Fitzgerald, Ella
Gillespie, John Birks "Dizzy"
Giuffre, Jimmy
Goodman, Benny
Gordon, Dexter
Hampton, Lionel
Hancock, Herbie
Handy, W. C.
Hawkins, Coleman
Hayden, Scott
Henderson, Fletcher
Hines, Earl "Fatha"
Holiday, Billie
Hunter, Charles H.
Jarrett, Keith
Johnson, James P.

Joplin, Scott
Kenton, Stan
Lamb, Joseph
Mangione, Chuck
Marsalis, Wynton
Marshall, Arthur
Mingus, Charlie
Modern Jazz Quartet
Monk, Thelonius
Morath, Max
Morton, Ferdinand "Jelly Roll"
Mulligan, Gerry
Niebergall, Julie
Oliver, Joe "King"
Page, Walter
Parker, Charlie "Bird"
Peterson, Oscar
Redman, Don
Scott, James
Smith, Bessie
Smith, Willie "The Lion"
Tatum, Art
Terry, Clark
Turpin, Tom
Waller, Fats (Thomas Wright)
Wenrich, Percy
Williams, Mary Lou
Young, Lester

European Composers of Concert Music, from Previous Centuries

These names are included as a selective and ongoing checklist for exploration. They are listed alphabetically as an indication that dance students can draw equally from the musical heritage of past centuries, and that one's listening need not progress in chronological order of composition. For biographical information and lists of works, consult the reference works listed in the bibliography. For information on scores used for theatrical dance, consult the catalog of the dance collection, the New York Public Library for the Performing Arts. As a general indication of style, composers of the Baroque era worked from roughly 1600 to 1750; the Classical era spans 1775–1824; and the Romantic era includes the rest of the nineteenth century.

Adam, Adolphe (1803–56)

Bach, Carl Philip Emmanuel (1714–88)

Bach, Johann Christian (1735–82)

Bach, Johann Sebastian (1685–1750)

Beethoven, Ludwig van (1770–1827)

Bizet, Georges (1838–75)

Borodin, Alexander (1833–87)

Boyce, William (1710–79)

Brahms, Johannes (1833–97)

Byrd, William (1543–1623)

Bull, John (1562–1628)

Chopin, Frédéric (1810–49)

Clementi, Muzio (1752–1832)

Corelli, Arcangelo (1653–1713)

Couperin, Francois (1668–1733)

Delibes, Léo (1836–91)

Dufay, Guillaume (1400–1474)

Dvořák, Anton (1841–1904)

Farnaby, Giles (1565–98)

Field, John (1782–1837)

Frescobaldi, Girolamo (1583–1643)

Gabrielli, Giovanni (1557–1612)

Gibbons, Orlando (1615–76)

Gluck, Christoph Willibald (1714–87)

Goldmark, Karl (1829–69)

Gottschalk, Louis Moreau (1829–69)

Greig, Edvard (1843–1907)

Handel, George Friderick (1685–1759)

Haydn, Franz Joseph (1732–1809)

Josquin des Prez (c. 1440–1521)

Liszt, Franz (1811–86)

Lully, Jean-Baptiste (1632–87)

Machaut, Guilláume de (c. 1300–1377)

Massenet, Jules (1842–1912)

Mendelssohn-Bartholdy, Felix (1809–1847)

Minkus, Ludwig (1826–91)

Monteverdi, Claudio (1567–1643)

Mozart, Wolfgang Amadeus (1756–91)

Mussorgsky, Modest (1839–81)

Offenbach, Jacques (1819–80)

Pachelbel, Johann (1653–1706)

Palestrina, Giovanni Pierluigi da (c. 1525–94)

Purcell, Henry (1658–95)

Rameau, Jean-Philippe (1683–1764)

Rossini, Giacchino (1792–1868)

Rimsky-Korsakov, Nicolai (1844–1908)

Rubinstein, Anton (1829–94)

Scarlatti, Domenico (1685–1757)

Schubert, Franz (1797–1828)

Schumann, Clara (1819–96)

Schumann, Robert (1810–56)

Smetana, Friedrich (1824–84)

Strauss, Johann the Younger (1825–99)

Tchaikovsky, Pëtr Ilyich (1840–93)

Telemann, Georg Philipp (1681–1767)

Verdi, Giuseppe (1813–1901)

Vivaldi, Antonio (1678–1741)

Wagner, Richard 1813–83)

Weber, Carl Maria von (1786–1826)

Wolf, Hugo (1860–1903)

GLOSSARY OF
MUSICAL TERMS

absolute pitch a sense (that only some people have) of the precise degree of high or low in regard to musical tones, in contrast to relative pitch.

accelerando getting faster little by little.

accent stress given to a particular sound, either through dynamics or by a change in instrumentation, texture, or sustaining.

accidentals sharps, flats, and natural signs used to indicate a semitone change in notated pitches that follow. Double sharps and double flats indicate a change of two semitones in pitch.

adagio quite slow.

additive procedure the musical process of creating rhythms by combining patterns of time segments based on a rather quick pulse or beat, as in much African and Indian music.

agogic accent stress on a particular note created by means other than dynamics, as in an elongated sustaining, etc.

allegro bright and lively tempo.

alto clef a sign to indicate that middle C is on the third (middle) line of the staff.

anacrusis unstressed note or group of notes before an important downbeat in metric music; an upbeat.

andante slow, but flowing.

antiphonal using choirs of voices or instruments either separated by distance, or sounding as if they were.

arpeggio a chord played harplike, one note after another in pitch succession, instead of simultaneously.

articulation as in speech, the manner in which sounds are initiated and released; for example, legato or staccato.

atonal   in the general sense, lacking a continuing sense of diatonic key center and related functional harmony; often in reference to serial music.

attack   in performance, the way in which a sound is initiated or a phrase begun.

augmentation   process of proportionately increasing time values of each note; for example, every eighth note becomes a quarter note.

augmented intervals   two pitches separated by a distance equal to a perfect or major interval plus a semitone.

augmented triad   a three-note chord consisting of two major thirds.

backbeat   strong offbeat, as in rock styles, especially in 4/4, stress on beats two and four.

bar   a metrical measure.

bar lines   vertical lines that visually separate metric measures in the Western system of notation.

Baroque period   roughly 1600 to 1750 in Europe, characterized by music that is basically contrapuntal.

bass   the lowest male voice; double bass instrument; the lowest part in keyboard or ensemble music.

bass clef   a written sign to indicate that F below middle C is on the fourth line of the staff.

basso continuo   in Baroque music, the part played by cello plus the left hand of the keyboardist, who would then elaborate on the numerical abbreviations for chords related to each notated pitch.

beat   the basic pulse unit of metric music. Can vary depending on tempo chosen.

binary form   musical structure in two sections, traditionally beginning in the tonic key, modulating to the dominant at the end of the first section, and then returning to the tonic at the conclusion of the second section.

bitonal   in two keys simultaneously.

blue note   lowered note of the major scale, generally third and seventh degrees, but also the fifth, characteristic of jazz melodies.

blues   slow African-American ballad style, in 4/4, with twelve-bar harmonic structure based on only tonic, dominant, and subdominant chords.

bowing   curved markings in string parts to denote upbow and downbow strokes.

break   in jazz, a solo interpolation between choruses (usually improvised).

bridge passage   material not as distinctive as major themes, used as connection, often modulating in order to get to a new section of more importance.

cadence   point of harmonic closing or pause, especially in functional tonal harmony.

cadenza unaccompanied instrumental solo passage, often virtuosic, within an orchestral concerto.

call and response vocal form in which soloist intones phrases of a chant and a group alternately responds.

canon contrapuntal procedure in which original theme is either imitated exactly by another voice or part, or with recognizable alterations such as pitch or rhythmic transposition, mirror, or retrograde.

chamber music pieces written for and performed by a small instrumental ensemble (sometimes with voices), with usually one performer on each part. Most numerous are string quartets.

chamber orchestra smaller than modern orchestra, a group of about twenty to thirty players, normally with only double winds as in the eighteenth century. Strings predominate.

chance music pieces that are not thoroughly composed before performance, with important variables left to performers; also, music created by such procedures as throwing dice, etc. Also called aleatory music.

character piece short, descriptive piano work that is essentially lyrical or programmatic in nature, a favorite especially in the nineteenth century.

chorale prelude organ piece based on church hymn, as in multiple settings by J. S. Bach.

chord simultaneously sounded or implied combination of three or more pitches.

chromatic based on the twelve semitones available in each octave of equal tempered tuning, but usually still retaining a sense of major or minor tonality.

chromaticism in diatonic music, the use of pitches requiring accidentals; denotes an extended harmonic vocabulary.

classical music in the general sense, music composed for formal concert performance.

Classical period roughly 1750 to 1830 in European concert music, characterized by tonal organization and homophonic textures (predominant melody plus accompaniment), plus certain expected forms such as the sonata.

clefs written symbols placed on the staff to indicate the pitch location of note heads.

closing theme in sonata form, the melodic material heard just before the end of the exposition.

coda "tail"; a brief section that concludes a movement or piece; also, in ballet repertoire, a light, fast section that concludes a pas de deux or ends an entire act.

common time metric 4/4, also indicated ₵.

compound meter any meter in which the basic beat is normally subdivided into three equal time segments or implied pulsations, in contrast to duple meter.

concerto orchestral work featuring a solo instrumentalist.

concerto grosso in Baroque music, a form emphasizing the contrast between the entire orchestra (tutti) and a smaller soloistic ensemble within the orchestra.

consonance the harmonic aspect of music in which intervals sound pleasing or at rest and stable, without an impetus to resolve to other intervals.

contrary motion in counterpoint, when one melodic line moves up and another down in pitch.

counterpoint procedure of composition in which several related but complete melodic lines are heard simultaneously.

crescendo gradually getting louder.

cross rhythm effect of the simultaneous playing of at least two different rhythms in different parts, producing resultant rhythms.

cut time **2/2** meter, indicated ₵.

cyclic form lengthy work in which several movements make use of the same thematic material.

dance suite any grouping of shorter dance-based musical movements into a larger whole;

examples include preclassic suites such as the keyboard works of J. S. Bach, or extractions from full-length ballets, such as *The Nutcracker Suite* of Tchaikovsky. Modern examples include Debussy's *Suite bergamesque* (consisting of Prelude, Menuet, Clair de lune, and Passepied); Ravel's *Tombeau de Couperin* (choreographed by Balanchine); Hindemith's *1922 Suite* of early jazz dances; and Milhaud's *Suadades do Brazil*.

decay in acoustics, the decline in intensity of any sound.

decrescendo getting softer little by little.

development in sonata form, the central section, in which original themes are extended and presented in various transpositons.

diatonic scale a scale of seven different pitches in the equal tempered tuning system, consisting of various arrangements of whole steps and half steps (semitones). Most familiar are the major and minor.

diminished seventh chord four-note chord, often with root on seventh degree of the scale, but in any case consisting of three conjunct minor thirds.

diminished triad three-note chord consisting of two minor thirds.

diminuendo gradually getting softer.

diminution process of proportionately decreasing the values of a musical theme or other material.

dissonance intervalic pitch relation that sounds as if it requires resolution.

dominant the fifth degree of the diatonic scale.

dominant seventh chord strongest active chord in the tonal system, based on the fifth degree of the scale and consisting of a major third and two minor thirds.

dotted note note head followed by one, two, or three dots to the right. One dot increases the total duration by 50 percent of the original value of the note head (totaling 150 percent the value of the note head). Less commonly, a second dot increases the value by another 25 percent of the original note, and a third dot, by an additional 12.5 percent of the note head's value. Not to be confused with staccato notes, where a dot over or beneath the note head implies detached articulation.

doubling duplication of a melody or part by other voices or instruments, either at the unison, octave, or other interval.

downbeat the strong first beat in each measure of metric music; also, the first strong beat of any piece.

drone continuous low pitch or several low pitches used as an unchanging bass for an entire piece or section.

duple time meter in which beats are usually expected to be subdivided into two equal parts or subdivisions of two.

dynamics the loud and soft aspects of music.

ear training instruction and practice in skills intended to improve musical perception of what is heard.

enharmonic tones identical sounding pitches notated differently to show harmonic function: for example, $G\sharp = A\flat$; $E\sharp = F$.

envelope the total acoustical profile of a tone, consisting of its attack, sustaining, and decay.

episode in fugue, a section following expository entrances of a main theme, more freely contrapuntal in nature.

equal temperament tuning system in which the octave is divided equally to result in twelve equally spaced semitones.

eurythmics a system of music education developed by Émile Jaques-Dalcroze, in which natural bodily movement patterns are employed for the purpose of teaching musical theory.

exposition in sonata form, the opening section, consisting of two main themes, bridge, and concluding material. In fugue, sections in which a main fugal subject is presented in different voices.

expression marks written directions concerning nuances in performance.

fermata hold or pause, indicated ⌢ .

figured bass see basso continuo.

flat notation to left of note head or in key signature indicating that pitch is to be one semitone lower than notated position on staff; a double flat indicates that the pitch is to be two semitones lower. Also, in performance, playing or singing out of tune, below correct pitch.

forte loud.

frequency the rate of occurrence of vibrations that produce sound waves, measured in hertz (Hz; cycles per second). Determines pitch.

fugue many-voiced contrapuntal composition consisting of alternating expositions (in which main theme or subject enters successively in each voice in contrasting intervals and/or keys), followed by a countersubject (often related to the main theme in some way), and episodes (connecting passages of more freely developed counterpoint).

fundamental the generating or lowest pitch of any series of harmonic overtones.

ground bass structural device of a melody in the lowest-pitched line that is repeated over and over while the higher parts are constantly changing.

harmonic rhythm the rhythmic pattern that evolves when the changes of harmony in a piece are analyzed according to their occurrence over proportional time.

harmony the relationship of simultaneously sounding pitches; the vertical aspect of notated music.

hemiola rhythmic device in which three notes of equal value occupy the time usually occupied by two—and vice versa.

heterophony texture in which the main melody is also simultaneously played with variants, in a sense providing its own accompaniment.

homophonic texture music in which there is a predominant melody accompanied by other, subordinate harmonic voices or parts.

imitation a main compositional device, especially important in contrapuntal music. Can be strict, as in fugue and canon, or free.

incidental music pieces written specifically for plays; for example, Mendelssohn's music for Shakespeare's *Midsummer Night's Dream,* subsequently used by a number of choreographers for separate ballets.

indeterminant music music in which many important compositional choices, such as pitch or rhythm, are left to the performer; for instance, in some of the music of John Cage.

interval   difference in pitch between two notes.

intonation   commonly, how accurately one is playing or singing in regard to tuned pitch.

inversion   a turning upside down, as with pitched intervals.

jazz rhythms   basically, characterized by uneven eighth notes and considerable syncopation, with a strong underlying sense of beat.

key   pitch center.

key signature   presence of sharps or flats at the beginning of a piece or section, to indicate key center. (If none is present, the piece may be in C major or A minor—or possibly in an atonal idiom.)

largo   extremely slow and broad.

leading tone   the seventh degree of the major or minor scale, so-called because of its felt tendency to progress melodically to the tonic above.

legato   smoothly connected, without gaps between sounds.

lento   very slow.

major scale   seven-tone scale consisting of two tetrachords, each of which consists of two whole steps followed by a semitone. The tetrachords themselves are separated by a whole step. The semitone steps,

therefore, fall between notes three and four and notes seven and eight.

major third   interval consisting of four semitones.

measure   main unit of grouping in metrical music.

mediant   third degree of the diatonic scale (halfway between tonic and dominant).

melodic contour   graphic shape of pitches in a melody.

melody   a succession of related pitched tones organized rhythmically so as to form a complete aesthetic statement with a recognizable shape.

meter   regular effect of grouping beats; most common are duple (in twos) and triple (in threes), with expectations of stronger and weaker beats.

microtone   any interval smaller than a semitone in equal tempered tuning.

minimalist   compositional procedure of using brief, condensed motif in ever-changing permutations.

minor scale   seven-tone scale in equal tempered tuning. Natural minor scale has semitones between notes two and three and notes five and six; harmonic minor, semitones between two and three, five and six, and seven and eight; melodic minor ascending semitones between notes two and three, seven and eight; melodic descending, six to five, four to three.

minor third interval consisting of three semitones.

mirror canon imitative procedure in which intervals of the initial theme are reversed; for example, if original theme progresses up a fourth, canonic part will go down a fourth.

mixed meter time signature of a piece in alternating meters, for example **2/4, 3/8**; or the metrical organization of a piece that changes often during its unfolding.

mode scale patterns used by ancient Greeks, in the Middle Ages in Europe, and in contemporary jazz. Using white notes of piano only as examples, they are, if played from one note to its octave: C, Ionian; D, Dorian; E, Phrygian; F, Lydian; G, Mixolydian; A, Aeolian; B, Locrian. Each mode is distinguished by a unique arrangement of whole tones and semitones.

modulation change of key center.

monophony style of music consisting mainly of a single melody, though there may also be percussion accompaniment.

motif germinal musical idea, consisting of a rhythmic pattern or patterns, with or without pitches.

movement in music, a self-contained section of a long work, such as a suite or symphony, that sometimes stands independently.

musique concrète music developed from recorded natural or everyday sounds that are subsequently manipulated electronically.

mutes mechanical devices used to alter the quality of sound and reduce the loudness of string and brass instruments.

natural accidental placed to the left of a note head or in a new key signature, canceling previous sharp or flat.

neoclassic twentieth-century style of composition that emphasizes clarity of form, as in some of Stravinsky's works.

notation system of writing music so that it can be performed. There have been many methods.

note in European notation, written symbol for a musical pitch and/or rhythm, consisting of a note head, or note head and stem, possibly with additional flags to indicate rhythmic subdivisions; also commonly, a simple synonym for any individual musical sound.

octave interval of eight notes in diatonic scale; notes of same letter names; acoustically, pitches in direct proportion so that frequency exactly doubles with each ascending octave.

offbeat the weak subdivision of a beat.

opus literally, a work; when followed by a number, an indication of the chronological catalog of the composer's output.

ornamentation decorative embellishments of a melody.

ostinato brief rhythmic pattern (either pitched or unpitched) that is persistently repeated.

overtones all the pitches of the natural harmonic series above each fundamental.

parallel motion in counterpoint, the relationship of two melodic parts that progress more or less at the same distance in terms of pitch interval.

pentatonic scales scales based on five pitches to the octave.

phasing in contemporary music, the practice of allowing one part to accelerate in speed until it is "out of synchronization" with the others, then continue accelerating until it shifts back into rhythmic synchronization.

phrase a melodic building block of musical form, equivalent to the complete statement of a sentence in language. In much European music, phrases are often four measures long, but they can comprise any number of measures or counts.

piano soft.

pickup commonly, an upbeat going into a strong downbeat, often for rehearsal cues.

pitch the high or low in music, determined by frequency of sound waves.

pizzicato plucked.

pointillism in music (similar to the painting technique of the same name), texture made by disjunct notes rather than connected melodies.

polymetric having several meters simultaneously.

polyphonic having several independent melodic parts simultaneously.

polyrhythmic having several rhythmic patterns simultaneously.

polytonal having several tonal key centers simultaneously.

prepared piano instrument altered by addition of objects on its strings, between the strings, or attached to hammers.

presto very fast.

program music compositions with specific narrative aspects, or that are suggestive of literal meanings.

progression in harmony, the way in which chord changes take place.

pulse the beat or basic unit of time in measured music.

quartal harmony using chords based on intervals of a fourth.

rāga from the Sanskrit word for "color," Indian scalar series and patterns, used as basis for classic styles of performance, associated with moods and occasions as well.

ragtime turn-of-the century piano style featuring regular beat and offbeat in left hand contrasted by strongly syncopated, lively melodies in right hand.

range   in pitch, the general compass of an instrument or human voice; the general pitch area of a melody or piece.

real time   actual clocked length, compared with relative time of tempo in measured music.

recapitulation   in sonata form, the final main section, in which initial themes are reintroduced in the tonic key.

reflection   in acoustics, the rerouting of sound waves as they encounter hard surfaces.

register   a segment of the total range of pitches available to an instrument or voice; for example, high register.

relative pitch   the sense that most people have about the definite level of high or low of a tone, compared with absolute pitch. People with a sense of relative pitch, for example, might recognize if an interval is a perfect fifth, but not necessarily whether the precise pitches are C–G or E–B.

repeat sign   indication that a section is to be played again immediately, sometimes with first and second endings.

resolutions   in tonal harmony, the progression of a dissonant interval or chord to a consonant one.

resonance   in acoustics, the phenomenon that occurs when the vibrations of an originating material cause something else to vibrate also, thus enlarging and enhancing the total sound heard.

rests   the notated silences in music.

retrograde   proceeding backward as in canons that use the same notes as an original theme but in reverse order.

rhythm   in this book, a proportional pattern of sounds and silences in measured music. In other, general usage, without the preceding article: everything in music having to do with duration.

ritardando   gradually getting slower.

roll   in percussion music, a rapid series of notes played by sticks.

Romantic period   in European music, mainly from 1830 to late nineteenth century, characterized by impact of emotional content and poetic references in regard to forms.

rondo form   musical structure in which repetitions of a main theme alternate with succeedingly new material.

root   lowest note of a chord; the note from which a chord gets its name.

rubato   literally "robbed" time; an elastic style of performance in which expressive phrasing results in slight deviations from a rigid tempo.

scale   from the Italian *scala*, ladder; a stepwise organization of all the pitches that comprise the basic material for a particular piece or section of music.

scat singing   a jazz style of vocalizing, originating in the 1920s, using nonsense syllables and often imitating sounds of instruments.

score   written composition for multiple instruments and/or voices, containing a collation of all the individual parts (in a full score) or a reduced arrangement, for either a conductor or for study purposes. Piano scores are even further reduced, generally for dance rehearsals.

semitone   pitch interval of a half step; in the chromatic scale on the piano, the distance from one note to the very next one (regardless of whether either is black or white); the basic pitch unit of diatonic music based on equal tempered tuning.

sequence   the repetition of brief melody or figure in successive transpositions either descending or ascending.

sequencer   in electronic music, equipment with which the user can produce automatic cycles of bass patterns, special effects, and so forth.

serial music   compositions in which the choice of pitched tones, dynamics, rhythms, and even timbres are closely ordered.

set form   in operas and ballets, sections that are self-contained and more likely to feature music that is abstract rather than closely linked to the drama for sound effects.

seventh chord   four-note chord formed using any note as a root, building by means of either major or minor thirds or a combination; chord consisting of root plus the following intervals above the root: third, fifth, and seventh.

sharp   accidental that raises the pitch of the note one semitone.

simple meter   meters such as 2/4 and 4/4, in which the basic beat is normally subdivided into two equal parts or multiples thereof.

slur   written curved line over note heads to indicate legato, smoothly connected performance.

sonata   in late Renaissance music, term used to denote an instrumental piece (as distinct from vocal music); from the Classical period onward, solo or chamber works with expected form in first movement.

sonata allegro form   musical structure consisting of exposition, development, recapitulation, and coda, with special attention to expected conventions of key relationships.

sound collage   particularly with electronic music, an accompanying sound track consisting of music that cannot be scored by traditional methods, and possibly incorporating many diverse noises, styles, and textures.

spacing   in harmony, the general layout of pitches in regard to register. For example, C-E could be a distance of a third, or of a tenth.

staccato   short and crisp articulation.

staff   design of five lines and four spaces used to indicate pitch in Western musical notation.

subdivisions   time segments of less than one beat in value.

subdominant   the fourth degree of the diatonic scale (a fifth below the tonic).

subject   in a fugue, the main theme that is introduced successively in each voice or instrumental part.

submediant   sixth degree of the diatonic scale (midway between the tonic and its subdominant).

suite   see dance suite.

supertonic   the second degree of the diatonic scale.

symphony   orchestral concert work usually consisting of several complete movements in contrasting tempos, meters, and keys.

syncopation   the rhythmic phenomenon in metric music that results when accents are introduced on offbeats usually expected to be weak, or by the injection of silences or sustained notes on beats normally felt to be strong.

tempo   chosen speed at which beats occur in measured music.

tenor clef   symbol used in Western notation to indicate that middle C is on the fourth line up on the staff.

ternary form   overall musical structure consisting of three main sections.

terraced dynamics   practice of maintaining a dynamic level for an entire section, with sometimes abrupt changes.

texture   the quality of density or sparseness in music.

theme   musical idea or melody.

tie   notated line from note head to note head of two identical pitches, indicating that the second note is not to be articulated, but rather that the first note should be sustained to include the timing of the second.

timbre   tone color, resulting from acoustical distribution of overtones.

time signature   numeric indication of meter, usually appearing at the beginning of a piece or section. The upper numeral tells how many beats are in a measure; the lower numeral shows what kind of note gets one beat.

tonality sense of key center or a home base in pitch.

tone clusters dense conglomerate sounds of neighboring notes played simultaneously, as when many piano keys are depressed with the forearm or fist, or when many closely pitched intervals are produced electronically.

tone poem music composed to follow poetic or expressive ideas rather than preset formal structures.

tone row an arrangement of pitches in any order chosen by a composer, subsequently used as basis of melodic and/or harmonic working out, as in serial composition.

transposition the process of playing similar-sounding material in another key or at another pitch level, moving everything by intervals of the same distance. (For example, ''up a major sixth.'')

treble clef the symbol in Western notation to indicate that G above middle C is on second line from the bottom on the staff.

triad a three-note chord composed of two intervals of a third each; the basis of common practice harmony in European music.

trill an ornamental, rapid alternation of two neighboring pitches.

triplet division of a beat or other time segment into three equal parts.

twelve-tone system *See* serial music.

uneven eighths in jazz performance, the practice of playing notated equal eighth notes generally in timing that more closely resembles a triplet comprised of a quarter note and eighth note, resulting in a swing rhythm.

upbeat the last subdivision of a measure going strongly into the following downbeat; often the beginning of a piece on an unstressed subdivision or beat.

variation process of working with thematic material. In aria and variation form, the complete theme is first played, followed by numerous renditions, in which harmony, mode, meter, instrumentation, dynamics, mood, accompaniment, textures, and rhythmic patterns may all be altered while still maintaining the recognizable substance of the main melody. The structure and number of counts is most likely to remain constant.

vibrato effect produced by a light, regular wavering in pitch, giving warmth and expression— for example in vocal, string, and wind performance.

vivace even faster and livelier than allegro.

vocalise   singing style in which syllables rather than words and sentences are used.

walking bass   particularly in Baroque and jazz music, a bass line that progresses evenly, usually with one note per metric beat—for example, in constant quarter notes.

whole-tone scale   in equal tempered tuning, a six-pitched scale consisting only of whole-step intervals.

NOTES

All tapes and transcripts of personal interviews remain in the possession of the author.

Part One. Motto is from George Balanchine and Francis Mason, *Balanchine's Complete Stories of Great Ballets,* rev. ed. (New York: Doubleday, 1977), p. 824.

Chapter 1. Epigraph is from the 1993 catalog of the School of American Ballet.

1. George Dorris, "On Being Musical," *Ballet Review,* Volume 3, No. 2, 1969, p. 50.

2. Doris Humphrey, *The Art of Making Dances.* rev. ed., Barabara Pollack. (Pennington, NJ: Dance Horizons/Princeton Book Company, Publishers, 1987) p. 142.

3. The author has observed Suki Schorer teaching upon a number of occasions, including March 24, 1993, at SAB, when Jeffrey Middleton was also interviewed. For a profile of Suki Schorer, see Marilyn Hunt, "Caring," *Dance Magazine,* February 1987, pp. 54–57.

4. The author has formulated the practical pointers in this chapter based on many years of observing both dance students and studio musicians at work. Appreciation is extended to presentations made at conferences of the International Guild of Musicians in Dance, especially those by Ben Hazard and Marjorie Landsmark DeLewis in Brockport, N.Y., 1992; John Childs in Miami, 1993; and Galina Begzuglaya in Salzburg, Austria, 1993. Similar topics were also discussed during several three-day seminars held by the late pianist Lynn Stanford at Lincoln Center, with demonstrations by dancer Todd Edson. The author also acknowledges conversations with dancer/musician Joel Mitchell about these points.

5. Underscoring the importance of musicality in the career of professional dancers, choreographer Robert North advised aspiring students at the Alvin Ailey American Dance Center concerning what he looks for during auditions: "I feel if they are not musical, they are not actually dancing. That is the most important thing for me."

Similarly, Herbert Saal reported dancer/director Edward Villella's opinion the *New York Times* of May 10, 1987, concerning the search for members of the newly formed Miami City Ballet: "The first thing that catches your eye is proportion, of head to neck, of length of thigh, of feet. I need all sorts, tall and short, lyric and dramatic. I look for people with interesting ways of moving. You can't teach that. And I must have a musical instrument. If musicality isn't there, it never will be."

Chapter 2. Epigraph is from Erick Hawkins, *The Body Is a Clear Place* (Pennington, NJ: Dance Horizons/Princeton Book Company, Publishers, 1992), p. 29.

1. Although this chapter was written according the author's experimentations, acknowledgement is made of the inspiration provided in the workshops led by Elina Lampinen at the January 1993 conference of the International Guild of Musicians in Dance, as well as the November 1993 conference of European dance musicians at the Orff Institute in Salzburg, Austria.

Chapter 3. The epigraph is from Mickey Hart with Jay Stevens, *Drumming on the Edge of Magic: A Journey into the Spirit of Percussion* (San Francisco: Harper Collins, 1990) p. 128.

1. Appreciation is extended to the following percussionists who work with dancers, for their inspiration and sharing: Lou Harrison, Robert Benford, Maximus VanDerBeek, Jon Scoville, Monti Louis Ellison, David Yoken, Khalid Saleem, and Ron George.

The author's own work as a musician for dance led to the construction of hundreds of percussion instruments, many displayed in a hands-on exhibit called *Hit It!* at the Hudson River Museum, Yonkers, N.Y., summer 1993.

2. Anna Kisselgoff, "Hawkins Troupe Paying Tribute," *New York Times*, February 2, 1992.

Chapter 4. The epigraph is from John Gruen, "Rosemary Dunleavy: A Teacher to the Corps," *Dance Magazine*, May 1993, p. 34. Underscoring Dunleavy's remark was Balanchine's own attitude, reported by Rona Kluger in the New York City Ballet *News* of 1986: "The music is always first. I cannot move, I can't even want to move, unless I hear the music first. I couldn't move without a reason, and the reason is music. . . . What I have really is that I see better than anyone else—and I hear better." The writer commented: "Balanchine's ballets still challenge us as audiences; they ask us to go deeper, be more aware, to listen more attentively."

1. Jennifer Muller was interviewed March 4, 1993 at the studios of The Works in New York.

Muller's dancing started at age three. She choreographed her first piece at age five and has since mounted over forty-five dances for The Works and for other companies that span both ballet and modern dance, including the Alvin Ailey American Dance Theater and the Lyon Opera Ballet. After entering the preparatory division of The Juilliard School at age ten, Jennifer Muller was dancing in Pearl Lang's company by fifteen. She completed the degree program in dance at Juilliard, with its required rigorous musical training, which she asserts has strongly influenced her approach to choreographic creation.

For nine years she was principal dancer with the José Limón Dance Company as well as associate artistic director of the Louis Falco Dance Company for seven years. Her company, The Works, has been in continuous existence since 1974. The troupe has served not only as a vehicle for Muller's choreographed dances, but also (in connection with its Emerging Artist's Program) as a showcase for creations by ten members and alumni. *Thesaurus* was premiered in 1992.

2. Twyla Tharp's remarks are drawn from her performances at New York's City Center, September 18, 1993, both matinee and evening.

3. Some of Shelley Washington's observations were made during the morning workshop preceding the Tharp performances. Part of the City Center Outreach projects, it was open to both young dancers and adults. The ballet mistress taught the group a section from the programmed work *In the Upper Room*. Further information was gathered in a taped phone interview with the author, September 27, 1993.

4. Robert Colton's remarks appeared in John Mueller and Don McDonagh, "Making Musical Dance: Robert Irving, Richard Colton, Kate Johnson, Karole Armitage," *Ballet Review*, Winter 1986, pp. 23–44.

Chapter 5. Epigraph is taken from remarks made by Shirley Ririe to the author during a personal interview in Salt Lake City, August 1991.

1. Martha Hill, "An Analysis of Accompaniment for the Dance," in Committee of Dance of the American Physical Education Association, *Dancing in the Schools* (New York: A. S. Barnes, 1933) p. 96.

2. Information about the Carlisle Project was gathered during the week of a workshop on music, June 1986. Barbara Weisberger subsequently edited a transcript of her taped interview, and Juli Nunlist provided further information in personal letters. See also Juli Nunlist, "Music: Your Silent Partner," *Dance Magazine,* August 1964; pp. 48, 49, 51.

3. The common denominators of dance and music were further investigated by Paul Hodgins in his book *Relationships Between Score and Choreography in Twentieth-Century Dance: Music, Movement, and Metaphor* (Lewiston, N.Y.: The Edwin Mellen Press, 1992), and in a summary article, "Making Sense of the Dance-Music Partnership: A Paradigm for Choreomusical Analysis," *International Guild of Musicians in Dance Journal,* Vol 1, 1991.

4. Doris Humphrey, *The Art of Making Dances,* Barbara Pollack, editor, (Pennington, NJ: Princeton Book Company, Publishers, 1987) p. 23.

5. Doris Hering was interviewed when she was executive director of Regional Dance America, on May 14, 1986. She subsequently edited the taped transcript and made many valuable suggestions and invitations to observe conferences, at the beginning of the author's research.

6. For an account of Louis Horst's career, see Janet Mansfield Soares, *Louis Horst: Musician in a Dancer's World* (Durham: Duke University Press, 1992.)

7. Norman Lloyd's description appeared in "American Composers Write for the Dance," *Dance Observer,* November 1951, pp. 101–104.

8. Bert Terborgh was interviewed after his formal presentation at the New York State Dance Festival on "Reconstructions," held at SUNY Purchase, April 19, 1986.

9. Students are referred to the annual *International Guild of Musicians in Dance Journal* for numerous first-hand accounts of contemporary collaborative projects. (1991-). In addition, see Katherine Teck, *Music for the Dance: Reflections on a Collaborative Art* (listed in Bibliography).

10. Barbara Greenfield, in a telephone interview, summer 1991.

11. For further details about Meet The Composer's special grants for collaborators, see the author's journal article listed in the Bibliography.

12. Ian Horvath's report is quoted here with permission from John Duffy, president of Meet The Composer.

13. John Duffy, in a personal interview, summer 1991.

14. Ella King Torrey, in a telephone interview, summer 1991.

15. Phillip Djwa's letter was published in *Dance Connection,* Feb/Mar 1993, p. 7. It is quoted here with his permission.

16. A vehement comment on "borrowing" music appears in Mary Clarke and Clement Crisp, *The Ballet Goer's Guide* (New York: Alfred A. Knopf, 1981) p. 61: "The doctoring of scores, which produces such vulgarities as the accompaniment to the Cranko *Carmen* and *Taming of the Shrew* and the Bolshoi's *Carmen Suite,* are to be deplored as a form of brutalism of defenceless music. In certain other cases it must seem that Baron Frankenstein has been entrusted with musical matters when scores are crassly compounded."

For further information on how copyright pertains to music in dance performances, see the author's journal article listed in the Bibliography.

Part Two. The opening motto is from Paul Draper, "Music and Dancing," *Dance Magazine,* August 1961, pp. 52–53. Born in 1909, this dancer created an almost unique international career for himself as a tap soloist who incorporated classical elements into his style. For a time, he toured with the composer/pianist John Colman as well as with the harmonica virtuoso Larry Adler. Still an ebullient personality in the 1980s, he offered eloquent advice to a new generation of young dancers when he accepted an award at a Dance Educators of America gala. For a charming recollection by Paul Draper concerning his career, see "Tapping Into the Classics," in Rusty E. Frank, *TAP! The Greatest Tap Dance Stars and Their Stories, 1900–1955* (New York: William Morrow, 1990) pp. 231–240.

Chapter 6. The epigraph is from Paul Taylor, *Private Domain* (New York: Alfred A. Knopf, 1987) p. 77–78, in connection with his 7 *New Dances*.

1. George Balanchine as quoted in Nancy Goldner, *The Stravinsky Festival of the New York City Ballet* (New York: The Eakins Press, 1973), p. 22.

Chapter 7. The epigraph is from Donald E. Hall, *Musical Acoustics* (Pacific Grove: Brooks/Cole Publishing Co., 2nd ed., 1991), p. 343. This text is eminently readable, and focuses on the art of music as well as scientific information on physics.

1. The dictionary definitions are drawn from *Webster's New International Dictionary,* unabridged (Springfield: Merriam-Webster, 1981), pp. 711, 2563.

2. Corroboration of the role of frequency in regard to loudness appears in Hall, *op. cit.* p. 104 as well as in Murray Campbell and Clive Greated, *The Musician's Guide to Acoustics* (New York: Schirmer Books, 1987), p. 100.

3. The Ann Arbor Dance Company program cited took place at the Cunningham Studios on May 30, 1992.

4. Igor Stravinsky's score to *Le Sacre du Printemps* (*The Rite of Spring*) is published by Edwin F. Kalmus, New York. The example cited is from page 11.

Chapter 8. The epigraph is from Gladys Andrews Fleming, *Creative Rhythmic Movement* (Englewood Cliffs: Prentice Hall, 1976) p. 30.

1. Alwin Nikolais explained his methods of timing and composing in a personal taped interview, May 20, 1986.

2. Steve Reich, *Writings about Music* (Halifax: Nova Scotia College of Art and Design; New York: New York University, 1974) p. 41.

3. For a succinct explanation of phasing in Steve Reich's *Piano Music,* see Judith Lang Zaimont, "Twentieth-Century Music: An Analysis and Appreciation," in Denes Agay, *Teaching Piano,* vol. 2 (New York: Yorktown Music Press, 1981) p. 503.

4. Ignacy Jan Paderewski, "Rhythm is Life," in Robert Cummings, ed. *They Talk About Music* (Rockville Centre, N.Y.: Belwin Mills, 1971) pp. 107–112.

5. For a brief discussion of various ways in which leading conductors have led irregular meters, see John Knight, "Conducting Irregular Meters," *The Instrumentalist,* June 1992, pp. 16–20.

For some suggestions about movement experiments in mixed meters, see Joyce Morganroth, *Dance Improvisation* (Pittsburg: University of Pittsburgh Press, 1987), section on "Sound Accompaniment."

6. W. A. Mathieu, *The Listening Book: Discovering Your Own Music* (Boston and London: Shambhala, 1991) pp. 85–87.

7. Martha Partridge made the concluding remark during the proceedings of the International Guild of Musicians in Dance conference in Miami, January 1993.

Chapter 9. Richard Cameron-Wolfe made the motto observation in writing to the author, February 1993.

1. The definition from *The Harvard Dictionary of Music* is from the 1958 edition edited by Willi Apel, p. 639.

The presentation of elements of music in all of Part Two is drawn from everything the author ever studied, starting with piano lessons at age nine. But particular mention must be made of the unique approaches and inspiration of Trude Rittmann, Norma Reynolds Freestone, and Lou Harrison in regard to rethinking the basics of all music with particular reference to dance.

2. Webster's, p. 1950.

3. Don Michael Randel, ed. *The New Harvard Dictionary of Music* (Cambridge: Harvard University Press, 1986) p. 704.

4. The graphing system is suggested in *Lou Harrison's Music Primer* (New York: C. F. Peters, 1971). Norma Reynolds Freestone explained her dash system to the author in January 1993.

Chapter 10. Epigraph is from Richard Kislan, *Hoofing on Broadway: A History of Show Dancing* (New York: Prentice Hall Press, 1987) p. 171.

1. Gwendolyn Watson's story appeared in the newsletter of the International Guild of Musicians in Dance, Vol. 1, No. 1, Spring 1991, p. 4.

2. George Balanchine as quoted in Nancy Goldner, *The Stravinsky Festival of New York City Ballet* (New York: Eakins Press, 1973) p. 25.

3. For an extensive description of scales and modes, see *The New Grove Dictionary of Music and Musicians*. For a compendium of scales, see the book by James Bastein, as well as the one by Don Schafer and Charles Colin, both listed in the bibliography.

4. The definition of melody in Webster's appears on page 1407.

Chapter 11. Epigraph is from Doris Humphrey, "What a Dancer Thinks About," in Jean Morrison Brown, editor, *The Vision of Modern Dance* (Pennington, NJ: Princeton Book Company, Publishers, 1979), p. 62.

1. This chapter is a fairly compact presentation of some six hundred years of harmonic practice in European and New World music. For dancers, the details are less important than an awareness of the fact that various progressions in the tonal system create their own tensions, impetus, and points of cadence or rest. The function of scales and tone rows in establishing an overall flavor is also important. Additionally, dancers and choreographers may find it helpful to become aware of underlying harmonic rhythm.

   For those who wish to explore tonal harmony in greater depth, an extensive keyboard harmony book that grew out of work with dance students (at Bennington College, Sarah Lawrence College, and The Juilliard School) is Ruth and Norman Lloyd, *Creative Keyboard Musicianship* (New York: Harper and Row, 1975). It is best used with an instructor.

2. Camille Saint-Saëns as quoted in Darius Milhaud, *Notes Without Music* (New York: Alfred A. Knopf, 1953) p. 107.

3. Judith Lang Zaimont, "Twentieth-Century Music: An Analysis and Appreciation," in Denes Agay, *Teaching Piano* vol. 2 (New York: Yorktown Music Press, 1981) p. 531.

4. Milan Kundera, *The Book of Laughter and Forgetting* (New York: Penguin, 1981) pp. 178–179.

5. *Ibid.*

6. Robert P. Morgan, *Twentieth Century Music* (New York: W. W. Norton, 1991) p. 308.

7. *Ibid.*, p. 312.

Chapter 12. Epigraph is from Roger Fiske, *Ballet Music* (London: George G. Harrap, 1958) p. 86.

1. Erick Hawkins, in a personal interview, November 17, 1986.

2. Sara Levi-Tanei, during a performance of the Inbal Dance Company in Yonkers, N.Y. in the late 1980s.

3. Mickey Hart with Jay Stevens, *Drumming on the Edge of Magic: A Journey Into the Spirit of Percussion* (New York: HarperCollins, 1990) p. 198.

4. Philip Glass as quoted in Robert T. Jones, "Pied Piper," *Ballet News*, October 1983, pp. 22–24, 42.

5. David Koblitz, "Minimalist Music for Maximum Choreography," *Dance Magazine*, February 1985, p. 52.

6. Anna Kisselgoff, "What is Repetition Doing to Choreography?" *New York Times*, October 19, 1986.

7. *Gamelan* uses Harrison's *Suite for Violin, Piano, and Small Orchestra*. For an introduction to traditional and new gamelan music, see Lou Harrison, "The Lasting Allures of Gamelan," *New York Times*, April 26, 1992, as well as Jody Diamond, "In the Beginning was the Melody: The Gamelan Music of Lou Harrison," in Peter Garland ed., *A Lou Harrison Reader* (Santa Fe: Soundings Press, 1987). For further information about Harrison's dance collaborations, see Katherine Teck, *Music for the Dance* (Westport, CT: Greenwood Press, 1989).

8. Anna Kisselgoff, review of *Beach Birds* in *New York Times*, March 19, 1991.

9. Malcolm Goldstein, *Dictionary of Contemporary Music* (New York: E. P. Dutton, 1974) p. 747.

Chapter 13. The opening quote is from Barbara Mettler, "New Directions in Dance and Music," *Journal of the American Association for Health, Physical Education, and Recreation*, Feb. 1952: 7, 34.

1. Martha Graham, *Blood Memory* (New York: Doubleday, 1991) p. 231.

2. Jon Scoville was interviewed by phone in August 1989. This quote also appeared in Katherine Teck, *Music for the Dance,* pp. 107–108.

Chapter 14. The quote from Martha Hill is drawn from her article "An Analysis of Accompaniment for Dance," in Committee of Dance of the American Physical Education Association, *Dancing in the Elementary Schools* (New York: A.S. Barnes, 1933) p. 95.

Percy Scholes' remark appears on page 331 of the 8th edition of the *Oxford Companion to Music.*

1. Joseph Machlis with Kristine Forney, *The Enjoyment of Music: An Introduction to Perceptive Listening* (New York: W. W. Norton, 6th ed., 1990) p. 315.

2. For translations of Marius Petipa's scenarios to *Sleeping Beauty* and *Nutcracker,* see the monumental study by Roland John Wiley, *Tchaikovsky's Ballets* (Oxford: Clarendon Press, 1985), pp. 355–386. Of particular interest in regard to formal structure are the choreographer's requests for both specific meters and numbers of bars, in addition to tempo indications. Also noteworthy are the distinctions between sections of essentially dramatic intent and variations and so forth that constitute more abstract set dance forms.

3. Leonard Bernstein's *Jubilee Games* was premiered in Avery Fisher Hall, September 13, 1986, with the composer conducting the Israel Philharmonic Orchestra.

4. Program notes of a concert by Ustad Vilayat Khan on sitar and Ustad Zamir Ahmad Khan on tabla, presented by the World Music Institute at Alice Tully Hall, New York, January 15, 1994.

5. Quotes are from a personal interview with Jean Erdman, in New York City, April 14, 1986. For another account of Louis Horst's teaching methods, see Janet Soares' book listed in the Bibliography. In his later years, Horst's approach to structure was not necessarily accepted by younger choreographers, and it is sometimes said that the postmodern dancers' insistence upon silence was precisely in reaction to Horst's emphasis on preclassic musical forms. Nevertheless, it can still be useful to students of today to become familiar with Horst's own book *Pre-Classic Dance Forms,* also listed in the Bibliography.

6. Marcia Siegel, review of Tharp's *Fugue,* reprinted in the critic's collected writings, *The Tail of the Dragon: New Dance, 1976–1982* (Durham: Duke University Press, 1991) p. 104.

Conclusion. Motto is from Twyla Tharp, *Push Comes to Shove: An Autobiography* (New York: Linda Grey Bantam Books, 1992), p. 99.

1. The Ten Commandments are reproduced here with the permission of Larry Attaway. They orginally appeared in the Spring 1991 *Journal-Update* of the International Guild of Musicians in Dance.

2. Gregory Presley's comment was made to the author in writing, January 1993.

3. Bruce Marks extended to the author both an interview and a guided tour of the new facilities of the Boston Center for Ballet, August 6, 1992. During the conversation, he enthusiastically set forth his vision for related preparatory conservatories of music and dance, with collaboration a requirement in both. Marks and the Boston Ballet II company have become an important component of the new program to nurture collaboration, initiated by Barbara Weisberger and the Carlisle Project and including musicians from Tanglewood. The author attended the first showcase of this effort, which included the following: *Quartet for Five,* music by Carl Voss, choreography by Michael Kane; *Maile's Dream,* music by Dalit Warshaw, choreography by Rebecca Kelly; *La Journee,* music by Adam Ben-David, choreography by Bonnie Scheibman; *Untitled,* music by Courtney Evans, choreography by Donald Byrd.

4. Carman Moore was interviewed in New York on May 13, 1991. His own compositions for dancers are both intriguing in style and effective as collaborations.

5. Maria Tallchief was interviewed by the author as part of the public proceedings of the January 1993 conference of the International Guild of Musicians in Dance, held at the New World School of the Arts in Miami. A videotape is part of the guild's archives, now at SUNY Brockport. Special thanks to Michael Lazzaro for arranging this interview, and for contributing questions and comments of his own. For a profile of Maria Tallchief, see Robert Tracy with Sharon DeLano, *Balanchine's Ballerinas: Conversations with the Muses* (New York: Linden Press/Simon & Schuster, 1983), pp. 102–109.

6. Annabelle Gamson was interviewed in her Westchester studio, in May 1991. Her *Tanzlieder* was premiered by her own company, Dance Solos, and later presented by the Limón Company.

A lovely new book is *Life into Art: Isadora and Her World* (New York: W. W. Norton, 1993), ed. Dorée Duncan, Carol Pratl, and Cynthia Splatt; with a foreword by Agnes de Mille.

7. Merce Cunningham's statement is drawn from the book based on interviews with Jacqueline Lesschaeve, *The Dancer and the Dance* (New York: Marion Boyars, 1985 and 1991), pp. 140–41.

8. Lucia Dlugoszewski, "Notes on New Music," *Dance Observer,* Nov. 1957, pp. 133–34. She herself is best known in the dance world as a long-time collaborator with Erick Hawkins.

9. The article by Sally Banes is a major piece of research, titled "[with/to/before/on/in/over/after/against/away/from/without] the music: Vissitudes of Collaboration in American Postmodern Choreography," *Choreography and Dance,* April 1974, pp. 49–51.

10. Sally Sommer, "The Sound of Movement," *Dance Ink,* Vol. 4, No. 1, Spring 1993, pp. 4–8.

11. Dale Harris, review in *The Wall Street Journal,* May 27, 1992.

12. Garth Fagan, personal, taped interview with the author, July 25, 1991, at Jacob's Pillow in Massachussetts.

13. Jamake Highwater, *Dance: Rituals of Experience* (Pennington, NJ: Princeton Book Company, Publishers, 3rd ed., 1992) p. 204. Particularly recommended is Fagan's recent collaboration with trumpeter/composer Wynton Marsalis, for a full-evening's work entitled *Griot New York.* The musician not only composed the score; he also played in the pit during performances with his seven-piece band (which included piano, tenor saxophone, alto saxophone, bass, drums, trombone, and trumpet). The dance was commissioned in 1991 for the Next Wave Festival at the Brooklyn Academy of Music.

14. Remarks by Carolyn Adams are drawn from interviews: by phone on May 18, 1993, and in person at Lincoln Center on April 8, 1993. See also her own article, "Lifeline to Taylor," *Ballet Review,* Winter 1986: 18–20. For a description of touring life with the Paul Taylor Dance Company, see the choreographer's autobiography, *Private Domain* (New York: Alfred A. Knopf, 1987).

15. Carla Maxwell was interviewed on July 10, 1991; Carlos Orta on July 19, 1991, both in Purchase, N.Y. Special thanks to The Limón Company for allowing the author to observe classes in addition to attending public lectures and performances at their summer residencies at SUNY Purchase.

16. José Limón delivered his address "Dancers Are Musicians Are Dancers" on October 5, 1955. It was published in the *Juilliard Annual Review* (1966–67) pp. 4–10.

For further information about this dance artist whose legacy continues to be so influential, see Barbara Pollack and Charles Humphrey Woodford, *Dance Is a Moment: A Portrait of José Limón in Words and Pictures* (Pennington, NJ: Princeton Book Company, Publishers, 1993).

BIBLIOGRAPHY

Dictionaries and Encyclopedias

Goldstein, Malcolm, ed. *Dictionary of Contemporary Music.* New York: E. P. Dutton, 1974.

Griffiths, Paul. *The Thames and Hudson Encyclopedia of 20th-Century Music.* New York: Thames and Hudson, 1986.

Hitchcock, H. Wiley, and Stanley Sadie, eds. *The New Grove Dictionary of American Music.* 4 vols. London: Macmillan, 1986.

Kennedy, Michael. *The Concise Oxford Dictionary of Music.* rev. ed. New York: Oxford University Press, 1980.

Kernfeld, Barry, ed. *The New Grove Dictionary of Jazz.* 2 vols. London: Macmillan, 1988.

Koegler, Horst. *The Concise Oxford Dictionary of Ballet.* London: Oxford University Press, 1982.

New York Public Library. *Dictionary Catalog of the Dance Collection* and annual vols. of updates. Also on computer disks. Boston: G. K. Hall, 1974–.

Randal, Don, ed. *The New Harvard Dictionary of Music.* Cambridge, MA: Belknap/Harvard University Press, 1986.

Sadie, Stanley, ed. *The New Grove Dictionary of Music and Musicians,* 20 vols. London: Macmillan, 1980.

———. *The New Grove Dictionary of Musical Instruments.* 3 vols. London: Macmillan, 1984.

Slonimsky, Nicolas. *Baker's Biographical Dictionary of Musicians.* 8th ed. New York: Schirmer Books, 1990.

Webster's Third New International Dictionary of the English Language. Springfield, MA.: Merriam-Webster, 1981.

Periodicals

American Music
American Record Guide
Annual Review of Jazz Studies
Attitude: The Dancer's Magazine
Ballet and Tanz International
Ballet Review
Choreography and Dance
Dance Connection
Dance Ink
Dance Magazine
Dance Pages
Dance Research Journal
Dance Teacher Now
Journal of the International Guild of Musicians in Dance

Annual Directories

Musical America
Music Directory Canada
Opus (Schwann Guide to Recorded Classical Music)
The Penguin Guide to Compact Discs and Cassettes
Stern's Performing Arts Directory

Books and Articles

Acocella, Joan. *Mark Morris*. New York: Farrar, Straus & Giroux, 1993.

Ammer, Christine. Unsung: A History of Women in American Music. Westport, CT: Greenwood, 1980.

Anderson, Jack. *The American Dance Festival*. Durham: Duke University Press, 1987.

Arvey, Verna. *Choreographic Music*. New York: E. P. Dutton, 1941.

Ashton, Geoffrey. *Giselle*. Woodbury, NY: Barrons, 1985.

———. *Petrushka*. Woodbury, NY: Barrons, 1985.

Attaway, Larry. "A Collaborative Process." *International Guild of Musicians in Dance Journal*, vol. 1, 1991, 17–23.

Balanchine, George, and Francis Mason. *Balanchine's Complete Stories of the Great Ballets*. Garden City: Doubleday and Co., 1977.

Banes, Sally. *Terpsichore in Sneakers: Post-Modern Dance*. Boston: Houghton Mifflin, Co., 1980.

———. "Vicissitudes of Collaboration in American Postmodern Choreography," *Choreography and Dance*, vol. 1, part 4, 1992, 3–22.

Bastien, James. *Intermediate Theory*. 3 vols. San Diego: Kjos Music Co., 1982.

———. *Scales, Chords & Arpeggios*. San Diego: Kjos Music Co., 1988.

Bastien, Jane Smisor, and James Bastien. *The Older Beginner Piano Course* (various volumes), especially *Musicianship for the Older Beginner*. San Diego: Kjos West, 1977.

Behague, Gerard, *Music in Latin America: An Introduction*. Englewood Cliffs, NJ: Prentice-Hall, 1979.

Benford, Robert. "Improving Music In Modern Dance Technique Classes," *International Guild of Musicians in Dance Journal*, vol. 1, 1991.

Berkson, Robert. *Musical Theater Choreography: A Practical Method for Preparing and Staging Dance in a Musical Show*. New York: Back Stage Books, 1990.

Berlin, Edward A. *Ragtime: A Musical and Cultural History*. Berkeley: University of California Press, 1980.

Bernstein, Leonard. "Music and the Dance." *Dance Magazine*, June 1946, 28, 32.

Bernstein, Seymour. *20 Lessons in Keyboard Choreography*. Milwaukee: Hal Leonard Publishing Co., 1991.

Blesh, Rudi, and Harriet Janis. *They All Played Ragtime*. 4th ed. New York: Oak Publications, 1971.

Blom, Lynne Anne, and L. Tarin Chaplin. *The Intimate Act of Choreography*. Pittsburgh: University of Pittsburgh Press, 1982.

Boas, Franziska. "Notes on Percussion Accompaniment for the Dance." *Dance Observer*, May 1938, 71.

Brimhall, John. *Exercises in Rhythm*. Miami Beach: Hansen House, 1968.

Buckle, Richard. *Diaghilev*. New York: Atheneum, 1979.

Bultman, Mary, with Jim Cliff, Lois Geiger, Gerry Landers, and Keith Mardak. *Ultimate Fake Book* (more than 1,200 songs). Milwaukee: Hal Leonard Publishing Co., 1981.

Cage, John. *Silence*. 5th printing. Middleton, CT: Wesleyan University Press, 1983.

Carner, Mosco. *The Waltz*. New York: Chanticleer Press, 1948.

Carse, Adam. *A History of Orchestration*. rpt. of 1925 ed. New York: Dover, 1964.

Chase, Mildred Portney. *Improvisation: Music from the Inside Out*. Berkeley: Creative Arts Book Co., 1988.

Cheney, Gay. *Basic Concepts in Modern Dance*. 3rd ed. Princeton, NJ: Dance Horizons/Princeton Book Company, Publishers, 1989.

Choksy, Lois, with Robert M. Abramson, Avon E. Gillespie, and David Woods. *Teaching Music in the Twentieth Century*. Englewood Cliffs, NJ: Prentice-Hall, 1986.

Choreography and Dance. Marilyn Cristofori, ed. Issue devoted to Hanya Holm, including a memoir by Alwin Nikolais. vol. 2, part 2, 1992.

Clarke, Mary, and Clement Crisp. *The Ballet Goer's Guide*. New York: Alfred A. Knopf, 1981.

———. *Making a Ballet*. New York: Macmillan, 1974.

Coe, Robert. *Dance in America*. New York: E. P. Dutton, 1985.

Cohen, Selma Jeanne. *Doris Humphrey: An Artist First*. Middletown, CT: Wesleyan University Press, 1972.

Cook, Gary D. *Teaching Percussion*. New York: Schirmer Books, 1988.

Cooper, Grosvenor, and Leonard B. Meyer. *The Rhythmic Structure of Music*. Chicago: University of Chicago Press, 1960.

Cooper, Helen. *How to Read Music.* New York: Amsco, 1983.

Cope, David. *New Music Composition.* New York: Schirmer Books. 1977.

———. *New Directions in Music.* 5th ed. Dubuque, IA: William C. Brown, 1989.

Copland, Aaron. *What to Listen for in Music.* rev. ed. New York: Mentor, 1963.

Copland, Aaron, and Vivian Perlis. *Copland: 1900 Through 1942.* New York: St. Martin's Press, 1984.

———. *Copland Since 1943.* New York: St. Martin's Press, 1989.

Cowell, Henry. "Relating Music and Concert Dance." *Dance Observer,* January 1937, 1, 7–9.

Cowell, Henry, and Sidney Cowell. *Charles Ives and His Music.* New York: Oxford University Press, 1955.

Crombie, David: *The Complete Synthesizer.* London: Omnibus Press, 1982.

Cunningham, Merce. *The Dance and the Dancer.* New York: Marion Boyars, 1991.

———. *Dancing in Space and Time.* Edited by Richard Kostelanetz. Pennington, NJ: a capella, 1992.

Dance Observer, six-part series on "Percussion Music and Its Relation to the Modern Dance," as follows: John Cage, "Introduction," and William Russell, "Hot Jazz and Percussion Music," October 1939, 166, 274; Henry Cowell, "East Indian Tala Music," and John Cage, "Goal: New Music, New Dance," December 1939, 296–97; Franziska Boas, "Fundamental Concepts," January 1940, 6–7; and Lou Harrison, "Statement," March 1940, 32.

Dance Perspectives. *Composer/Choreographer.* Includes articles on collaboration by William Schuman, Martha Graham, Louis Horst, Vivian Fine, Robert Starer, Norman Dello Joio, Lucia Dlugoszewski, Carlos Surinach, Alwin Nikolais, Gunther Schuller, John Cage, Halim El-Dabh, and Norman Lloyd. *Dance Perspectives.* Special Issue 16, 1963.

Darter, Tom, comp. Greg Armbruster, ed. *The Art of Electronic Music.* New York: Quill, 1984.

de Mille, Agnes. *America Dances.* New York: Macmillan, 1980.

———. *The Book of the Dance.* New York: Golden Press, 1963.

———. *Lizzie Borden: A Dance of Death.* Boston: Atlantic Monthly Press, 1968.

———. *Martha.* New York: Random House, 1991.

Denby, Edwin. "A Note to Composers," *Modern Music,* October 1939, reprinted in Denby's *Dance Writings,* 62–63. New York: Alfred A. Knopf, 1986.

Diagram Group. *Musical Instruments of the World: An Illustrated Encyclopedia.* New York: Facts on File, 1976.

Donato, Anthony. *Preparing Musical Manuscript.* Englewood Cliffs, NJ: Prentice-Hall, 1963.

Duncan, Isadora. *My Life.* New York: Liveright, 1927.

Eagle/Walking Turtle. *Indian America: A Traveler's Companion,* Santa Fe: John Muir Publications, 1991.

Eakins Press Foundation. *Choreography by George Balanchine: A Catalog of Works.* New York: Viking, 1984.

Emery, Lynne Fauley. *Black Dance in the United States from 1619 to Today.* Princeton, NJ: Princeton Book Co., Publishers, 1988.

Erickson, J. Gunnar, Edward R. Hearn, and Mark E. Halleran. *Musician's Guide to Copyright*. rev. ed. San Francisco Bay Area Lawyers for the Arts. New York: Charles Scribner's Sons, 1983.

Feldstein, Sandy. *Drum-Set Club Date Dictionary*. New York: Alfred Publishing Co., 1978.

———. *Practical Theory, Complete: A Self-Instruction Music Theory Course*. Also available on computer disk. New York: Alfred Publishing Co., 1982.

Fiske, Roger. *Ballet Music*. London: George C. Harrap, 1958.

———. *Score Reading Book 1, Orchestration*. Oxford: Oxford University Press, 1991.

Flatischler, Reinhard. *The Forgotten Power of Rhythm*. Mendocino, CA: LifeRhythm, 1992.

Frank, Rusty E. *Tap! The Greatest Tap Dance Stars and Their Stories, 1900–1955*. New York: William Morrow, 1990.

Fujioka, Sharon. "Musicality in Dance." *Ballet Review*, vol. 8, no. 1, 1980, 78–83.

Garafola, Lynn. *Diaghilev's Ballets Russes*. New York: Oxford University Press, 1989.

Garland, Peter, ed. *A Lou Harrison Reader*. Santa Fe: Soundings Press, 1987.

Gerard, Charley, and Marty Sheller. *Salsa: The Rhythm of Latin Music*. Crown Point, IN: White Cliffs, 1989.

Gilbert, Pia, and Aileene Lockhart. *Music for the Modern Dance*. Dubuque, IA: William C. Brown, 1961.

Goldner, Nancy. *The Stravinsky Festival of the New York City Ballet*. New York: Eakins Press, 1973.

Gottlieb, Jack. "Let There Be Music: A Composer Analyzes His Craft to Aid the Choreographer." *Dance Magazine*, April 1959, 52, 53, 78–80, and May 1959, 84–88.

Graham, Martha. *Blood Memory*. New York: Doubleday, 1991.

Green, Barry with W. Timothy Gallwey. *The Inner Game of Music*. New York: Doubleday, 1986.

Hall, Donald E. *Musical Acoustics*. rev. ed. Pacific Grove, CA: Brooks/Cole Publishing Co., 1991.

Harrison, Lou. *Music Primer*. New York: C. F. Peters, 1971.

Harrison, Max, Charles Fox, and Eric Thacker. *The Essential Jazz Records*. New York: Da Capo, 1984.

Hart, Mickey, with Jay Stevens. *Drumming on the Edge of Magic*. New York: Harper Collins, 1990.

Hasse, John Edward, ed. *Ragtime: Its History, Composers, and Music*. New York: Schirmer Books, 1985.

Hastings, Baird. *Choreographer and Composer: Theatrical Dance and Music in Western Culture*. Boston: Twayne, 1983.

Hawkins, Erick. *The Body Is a Clear Place and Other Writings*. Princeton, NJ: Dance Horizons/Princeton Book Company, Publishers, 1992.

Hindemith, Paul. *Elementary Training of Musicians*. New York: Associated Music Publishers, 1946.

Hodgins, Paul. "Making Sense of the Dance-Music Partnership: A Paradigm for Choreomusical Analysis." *Journal of the International Guild of Musicians in Dance*, vol. 1, 1991, 38–41.

————. *Relationships Between Score and Choreography in Twentieth-Century Dance: Music, Movement, and Metaphor.* Lewiston, NY: The Edwin Mellen Press, 1992.

Hofstetter, Fred T. *Computer Literacy for Musicians.* Englewood Cliffs, NJ: Prentice-Hall, 1988.

Holmes, Thomas B. *Electronic and Experimental Music.* New York: Charles Scribner's Sons, 1985.

Horst, Louis. *Pre-Classic Dance Forms.* rpt. of 1937 and 1940 ed. New York: Dance Horizons, 1968.

Horst, Louis, and Carroll Russell. *Modern Dance Forms in Relation to the Other Modern Arts.* New York: Dance Horizons, 1961.

Howard, John Tasker. *Our American Music.* 4th ed. New York: Crowell, 1965.

Humphrey, Doris. *The Art of Making Dances.* rev. ed. Princeton, NJ: Dance Horizons/Princeton Book Company, Publishers, 1987.

Jacob, Gordon. *How to Read a Score.* London: Boosey & Hawkes, 1944.

Jamison, Judith. *Dancing Spirit.* New York: Doubleday, 1993.

Jaques-Dalcroze, Emile. *Rhythm, Music and Education.* rev. ed. London: The Dalcroze Society, 1980.

Johnson, Monica Dale. "Dancers, Musicians, and Jaques-Dalcroze Eurhythmics." *International Guild of Musicians in Dance Journal,* vol. 2 1992, 11–18.

Johnson, Tom. *Imaginary Music.* New York: Schirmer Books, 1974.

Jones, George Thaddeus. *Music Theory.* New York: Harper & Row, 1974.

Karagianis, David. "An Approach To Effective Use of Music for Choreography." *International Guild of Musicians in Dance Journal,* Vol. 3, 1994, 12–16.

Kaufmann, Walter. *The Ragas of South India: A Catalogue of Scalar Material.* Bloomington: Indiana University Press, 1976.

Kaye, Deena, and James Lebrecht. *Sound and Music for the Theatre.* New York: Back Stage Books, 1992.

Kingman, Daniel. *American Music: A Panorama.* New York: Schirmer Books, 1979.

Kriegsman, Sali Ann. *Modern Dance in America: The Bennington Years.* Boston: G. K. Hall, 1981.

Kreemer, Connie. *Further Steps: 15 Choreographers on Modern Dance.* New York: Harper and Row, 1987.

Kuklin, Susan. *Reaching for Dreams: A Ballet from Rehearsal to Opening Night.* (Chronicles Alvin Ailey Company's production of Jennifer Muller's *Speeds.*) New York: Lothrop, Lee and Shepard, 1987.

Kundera, Milan. *The Book of Laughter and Forgetting.* New York: Penguin, 1981.

Laderman, Ezra. "An Experiment in Cooperation." *Dance Magazine,* March 1957, 37, 88.

Lawrence, Robert. *The Victor Book of Ballets and Ballet Music.* New York: Simon and Schuster, 1950.

Lederman, Minna. *Stravinsky in the Theatre.* New York: Da Capo, 1975.

Leonard, Hal. *Master Scale and Chord Guide for Piano.* Milwaukee: Hal Leonard Publishing Co., 1982.

Libbey, Ted. *The NPR Guide to Building a Classical CD Collection.* New York: Workman Publishing, 1994.

Limón, José. "Dancers Are Musicians Are Dancers." *Juilliard Annual Review,* 1966–67, 4–10.

Little, Meredith and Natalie Jenne. *Dance and the Music of J. S. Bach.* Bloomington: Indiana University Press, 1991.

Lloyd, Norman. "Composing for the Dance." *Juilliard Review,* Spring 1961.

Lloyd, Ruth and Norman. *Creative Keyboard Musicianship.* New York: Harper and Row, 1975.

Lomax, Alan. *The Folk Songs of North America.* Garden City, Doubleday, 1960.

Long, Richard A. *The Black Tradition in American Dance.* New York: Rizzoli, 1989.

Luening, Otto. *The Odyssey of An American Composer.* New York: Charles Scribner's Sons, 1980.

Machlis, Joseph. *Introduction to Contemporary Music.* 2d ed. New York: W. W. Norton, 1979.

Machlis, Joseph, with Kristine Forney. *The Enjoyment of Music: An Introduction to Perceptive Listening.* 6th standard ed. New York: W. W. Norton, 1990.

Maiorano, Robert, and Valerie Brooks. *Balanchine's Mozartiana: The Making of a Masterpiece.* New York: Freundlich Books, 1985.

Manuel, Peter. *Popular Musics of the Non-Western World.* New York: Oxford University Press, 1988.

Mather, Betty Bang. *Dance Rhythms of the French Baroque.* Bloomington: Indiana University Press, 1987.

Mathieu, W. A. *The Listening Book: Discovering Your Own Music.* Boston: Shambhala, 1991.

———. *The Musical Life: Reflections on What It Is and How to Live It.* Boston: Shambhala, 1994.

Mazo, Joseph H. *Prime Movers: The Makers of Modern Dance.* Princeton, NJ: Princeton Book Company, Publishers, 1977.

McElheran, Brock. *Conducting Technique.* rev. ed. New York: Oxford University Press, 1989.

Meisner, Gary. *Instant Keyboard.* Milwaukee: Hal Leonard Publishing Co., 1987.

———. *Instant Scale and Chord Guide for Keyboards.* Milwaukee: Hal Leonard Publishing Co., 1990.

Morgan, Robert P. *Twentieth-Century Music.* New York: W. W. Norton, 1991.

Moulton, William. "Craft and Inspiration—Opening Intuitive Channels in Improvisation," *International Guild of Musicians in Dance Journal,* vol. 2, 1992.

———. "Musicians in Dance: The Struggle for Legitimacy in Academia," *International Guild of Musicians in Dance Journal,* vol. 1, 1991.

Mueller, John, and Don McDonagh. "Making Musical Dance: Robert Irving, Richard Colton, Kate Johnson, Karole Armitage." *Ballet Review,* Winter 1986, 23–44.

Nettl, Bruno, and Charles Capwell, Philip V. Bohlman, Isabel K. F. Wong, and Thomas Turino. *Excursions in World Music.* Englewood Cliffs, NJ: Prentice-Hall, 1992.

Newman, Barbara. *The Nutcracker.* Woodbury, NY: Barron's, 1985.

Newquist, H. P. *Music & Technology.* New York: Billboard Books, 1989.

Nijinska, Bronislava. *Early Memoirs.* New York: Holt, Rinehart and Winston, 1981.

Nisbett, Alec. *The Technique of the Sound Studio.* rev. ed. London and Boston: Focal Press, 1987.

Nketia, J. H. Kwabena. *The Music of Africa.* New York: Norton, 1974.

Nugent, Ann. *Swan Lake.* Woodbury, NY: Barron's, 1985.

Oringer, Judith. *Passion for the Piano.* Los Angeles: Jeremy P. Tarcher, 1983.

Pace, Robert. *Music for Piano for the Older Beginner.* several vols. New York: Lee Roberts Music Publishers.

Partch, Harry. *Genesis of a Music.* 2d ed. New York: Da Capo, 1974.

Piston, Walter. *Orchestration.* New York: W. W. Norton, 1955.

Pollack, Barbara, and Charles Humphrey Woodford. *Dance is a Moment: A Portrait of José Limón in Words and Pictures.* Princeton, NJ: Princeton Book Company, Publishers, 1993.

Reck, David. *Music of the Whole Earth.* New York: Charles Scribner's Sons, 1977.

Reich, Steve. *Writings About Music.* Halifax and New York: Nova Scotia College of Art and Design and New York University, 1974.

Reid, Cornelius L. *A Dictionary of Vocal Terminology.* New York: Joseph Patelson Music House, 1983.

Reynolds, Nancy, and Susan Reimer-Torn. *Dance Classics: A Viewer's Guide to the Best-Loved Ballets and Modern Dances.* Pennington, NJ: a capella, 1991.

Richards, Emil. *World of Percussion.* with cassette. New York: Alfred Publishing Co., 1972.

Rockwell, John. *All American Music: Composition in the Late Twentieth Century.* New York: Vintage Books, 1984.

Rosencrans, Glen. *Music Notation Primer.* New York: Amsco Publications, 1979.

Rudhyar, Dane. "The Companionate Marriage of Music and Dancing." *Dance Observer,* March 1938, 37–38.

St. Denis, Ruth. "Music Visualization." Reprinted from *The Denishawn Magazine,* Spring 1925, in Selma Jeanne Cohen, *Dance as a Theatre Art.* New York: Harper, 1974.

Salzman, Eric. *Twentieth-Century Music: An Introduction.* 2d ed. Englewood Cliffs, NJ: Prentice Hall, 1974.

Schaefer, John. *New Sounds: A Listener's Guide to New Music.* New York: Harper and Row, 1987.

Schafer, Don, and Charles Colin. *Encyclopedia of Scales.* New York: Charles Colin, 1965.

Schafer, R. Murray. *Creative Music Education.* New York: Schirmer, 1976.

Schuller, Gunther. *Early Jazz: Its Roots and Musical Development.* New York: Oxford University Press, 1968.

———. *The Swing Era: The Development of Jazz, 1930–1945.* New York: Oxford University Press, 1989.

Searle, Humphrey. *Ballet Music.* 2d rev. ed. New York: Dover Publications, 1973.

Shanet, Howard. *Learn to Read Music.* New York: Fireside/Simon and Schuster, 1956.

Sherman, Jane. *The Drama of Denishawn Dance.* Middleton, CT: Wesleyan University Press, 1979.

Shook, Karel. *Elements of Classical Ballet Technique as Practiced in the School of the Dance Theatre of Harlem*. New York: Dance Horizons, 1977.

Siegel, Marcia B. *The Tail of the Dragon: New Dance, 1976–1982*. Durham: Duke University Press, 1991.

Sloboda, John A. *The Musical Mind: The Cognitive Psychology of Music*. corrected ed. Oxford: Clarendon Press, 1991.

Soares, Janet Mansfield. *Louis Horst: Musician in a Dancer's World*. Durham: Duke University Press, 1992.

Sorrell, Walter. *Hanya Holm*. Middleton, CT: Wesleyan University Press, 1969.

Southern, Eileen. *The Music of Black Americans*. New York: W. W. Norton, 1983.

Starer, Robert. *Rhythmic Training*. Milwaukee: MCA Music, 1969.

Stearns, Marshall and Jean. *Jazz Dance*. New York: Schirmer, 1968.

Stone, Kurt. *Music Notation in the Twentieth Century*. New York: Norton, 1980.

Swados, Elizabeth. *Listening Out Loud: Becoming a Composer*. New York: Harper & Row, 1988.

Taper, Bernard. *Balanchine: A Biography*. New York: Times Books, 1984.

Taylor, Paul. *Private Domain*. New York: Alfred A. Knopf, 1987.

Teck, Katherine. *Music for the Dance: Reflections on a Collaborative Art*. Westport, CT: Greenwood Press, 1989.

———. *Movement to Music: Musicians in the Dance Studio*. Westport, CT: Greenwood Press, 1990.

———. "First Conference for Dance Musicians." *Choreography and Dance*, vol. 1, part 4, 1992, 91–94.

———. "First Conference of European Musicians in Dance," *Dance Research Journal*, 26/1, spring 1994.

———. "How Copyright Law Affects Musicians for Dance." *Journal of the International Guild of Musicians in Dance*, vol. 2, 1992, 33–42.

———. "International Guild of Musicians in Dance," *Dance Teacher Now*, February 1994.

———. "International Guild of Musicians in Dance Conference." *Dance Research Journal*, Spring 1992.

———. "International Guild of Musicians in Dance: Second Annual Conference." *Dance Connection*, November 1993, 50–51.

———. "Meet the Composer's Composer/Choreographer Project: A Bold Vision with Far-Reaching Results." *Journal of the International Guild of Musicians in Dance*, vol. 1, 1991, 2–16.

———. "Music for Dance: A Conference Explores Many Traditions." *Attitude*, Spring 1994, 10–12.

———. "Musicians in Dance Explore Collaborative Skills and Art." *Attitude: The Dancer's Magazine*, Spring/Summer 1992, 37–39.

———. "Rosenella, or The Princess Musician." *Attitude*, Spring 1993, 68–70.

———. "A Sound Investment: New Music for New Dance," *Dance/USA Journal*, Summer 1991, 16–20. Also reprinted by the Dance Bay Area newsletter *In Dance*, December 1991, 1–2, 6.

———. "The Way Things Used to Be: Maurine Dewsnup, First Accompanist for

Dance at the University of Utah." *International Guild of Musicians in Dance Journal,* 1994, 18–23.

Terry, Clark, and Phil Rizzo. *The Interpretation of the Jazz Language.* Cleveland: M.A.S. Publishing Co., 1977.

Terry, Walter. *The Ballet Companion.* New York: Dodd, Mead, 1968.

———. *Isadora Duncan: Her Life, Her Art, Her Legacy.* New York: Dodd, Mead, 1963.

Tharp, Twyla. *Push Comes to Shove.* New York: Bantam Books, 1992.

Titon, Jeff Todd, ed., with James T. Koetting, David P. McAllester, David Reck, and Mark Slobin. *Worlds of Music: An Introduction to the Music of the World's Peoples.* New York: Schirmer, 1984.

Toenjes, John. "The Evolution of Martha Graham's Collaborations with Composers of Music for the Modern Dance." *Journal of the International Guild of Musicians in Dance,* vol. 2, 1992, 1–10.

Ulano, Sam. *Practical Guide for the Working Drummer.* New York: Lane Publishing Co., 1957.

Volkov, Solomen. *Balanchine's Tchaikovsky: Interviews with George Balanchine.* New York: Simon and Schuster, 1985.

Wiley, Roland John. *Tchaikovsky's Ballets.* Oxford: Clarendon Press, 1985.

Wolfe, Richard. *Legit Professional Fake Book.* New York: The Big Three Music Corp. (n.d.)

Wynne, Ron, ed. *All Music Guide to Jazz: The Best CDs, Albums & Tapes.* San Francisco: Miller Freeman, 1994.

Zaimont, Judith Lang. "Twentieth Century Composing: An Analysis and Appreciation." In Denes Agay, *Teaching Piano,* vol. 2. 489–548. New York: Yorktown Music, 1981.

INDEX

Tape recordings, 197-98, 216-17
Technique classes, 6-10
Tempo, 6, 84, 99-104, 249
Tempo: terms for, 101-2
Ternary forms, 229-30
Terraced dynamics, 83
Tetrachord, 160
Texture, 72, 76-77, 182-96
Timbre, 74, 77, 127-29, 197-218
Time elements in music, 97-149
Time signature, 110-11, 113-15
Timing, 44-45, 72, 97-149
Timpani, 36
Tonality, 173-75, 177-78
Tone clusters. *See* Clusters
Tone color. *See* Timbre
Tone poem, 239-40
Tone row. *See* Serial music
Tonic, 173
Transposition, 155, 174, 176
Triads, 170-72
Triple meter, 112-13
Triplets, 7, 16, 105-6
Trombone, 205-6
Trumpet, 205
Tuba, 205-6

Tuning, 152, 154-56
Twelve-tone music. *See* Serial music

Unaccompanied melody. *See* Monophony
Uneven rhythms, 13, 106
Unpulsed timing, 98-99

Variation techniques, 19, 233-36
Vibrations, 73
Viola, 207-8
Violin, 184, 207-8
Vocal music: for dance, 21-22, 185, 188-90, 199-200
Vocalization: techniques of, 19-22, 199-200

Walking bass, 187
Waltz, 112
Whistles, 203-4
Whole step, 152, 160-63
Whole-tone scale, 159
Woodwind instruments, 202-5

Xylophone, 34-35